Kids Out Wild

A Family's Tale of Love and Struggle on Four National Scenic Trails

ISBN: 9798857488676

Cover and Map by Christine Poyner (cpoyner@gmail.com)

Editing and Typesetting by Susanna Bergeson Dimig

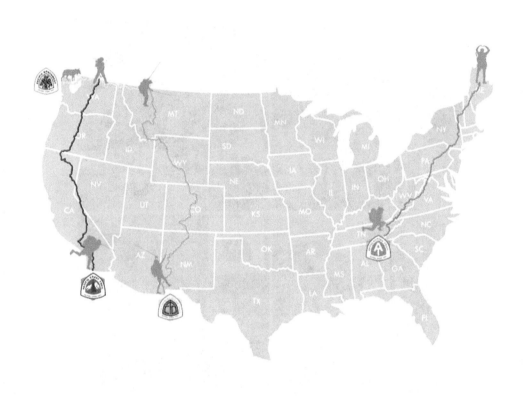

I dedicate this book to my husband, Adam, who came up with the idea of hiking the Triple Crown with his family as a young father and made it happen.

2:22 I love you!

"It is only after we get home that we really get over the mountain." —Henry David Thoreau

Open this book
Open to new inspiration for adventure
Open to help from trail angels, and a desire to be one
Open your eyes to the forests
Open heart, open mind, open soul

Be free to departing into the wilderness for longer than
civilization says you can
Be free for quality time and conversations with family,
tramily (trail family), and strangers
Be free to be healed by walking far

My heart thanks all who lift my family
My heart feels joy despite suffering
My heart yearns to support others as they set out to create
a beautiful journey

—Mindi "Wildflower" Bennett

Table of Contents

Prologue

It is a rare event in life when you get to spend a significant amount of time with people who are truly "living the dream"—not just tossing that phrase out sarcastically but actually doing what they've planned and sacrificed for, maybe for the better part of their lives. Setting a goal to thru-hike one of America's National Scenic Trails (or any long-distance trail for that matter) is a statistical nightmare. It's highly likely you'll face an overuse injury, or worse. You are going to want to trade out gear that doesn't suit you (which isn't easy when you are hundreds of miles from the nearest store, without a car), you might get sick or hate the food you pre-packed for yourself, and there will be obstacles like 200% snowpack in the Sierras or one of the East's hottest and most humid summers on record standing in your way. According to Appalachiantrail.org, "Approximately three million people visit the trail every year. More than 3,000 people attempt a thru-hike of the entire A.T. each year, with about a quarter of those completing the trail." Yet we are here to tell you that it is possible and 110% worth giving it a go.

In 2012, when our children were eight, six, four, and two, my husband presented the idea of hiking the Triple Crown as a family. I didn't know what the Triple Crown was, but I was enamored with the idea of our children getting to spend six months at a time with their dad and I without modern distractions. In case you were like I once was, unaware of what the term Triple Crown means in the backpacking world, it is hiking the Pacific Crest Trail (2,650 miles), the Continental Divide Trail (3,100 miles), and the Appalachian Trail (2,200 miles).

These are three out of the eleven National Scenic Trails in the United States, and combined, the Triple Crown totals nearly 8,000 miles.

Once we set our goal, we went into action implementing a budget and gathering gear. REI garage sales provided us with great deals, and my husband is an expert shopper. We spent seven years introducing the idea, gifting backpacking gear every Christmas, and going on prep hikes. We timed it so that the last three summers that our oldest would be with us could be spent together on the trail. Since we can't do these trails in three months, our plan wouldn't fit into the public school schedule. Homeschooling has been a big learning experience for us all, but in 2018–19, we got nine months of school done in about five months. We are so proud of our kids. From then on, the best form of education became "trail school."

When the time arrived to drive to California to start the PCT (March of 2019), our second oldest daughter begged her cousin to hit her with her car, hoping to break a leg and get out of hiking. However, that daughter is now our most enthusiastic about backpacking and is planning her future adventures. What seemed to change her mind was the people we met on the trail. Other hikers from all over the world, from all backgrounds and walks of life, instantly became our best friends because of our common goal. Most of all, the acts of kindness provided by trail angels to our family and other hikers was a great paradigm shift for us. The positive ripple effect of trail magic is impossible to measure, but without a doubt, the magnitude of the impact of their service led to the success and joy we felt in this experience.

In this tale, you will find trail notes written down by a tired mother each night after making sure everyone was settled. It pained me to not include the thousands of pictures that I took on these hikes, which tell the story so much better than my words. If you want to see all of our photos, please check out our website, Patreon, and/or our social media sites (all listed in the back of this book). I also added some quotes that were inspirational to us from books we were listening to on the trail, poems, or just awesome things people have said. Our names are Mindi, Adam, Sierra, Kaia, Tristan, Ruby, and Muir the trail dog. This is our story:

Part 1: Pacific Crest Trail

March–September 2019

Picture this: you are near the Mojave Desert in California with no car and everything you hope you need to survive on your back, and one of your four children has an injury. You need to get food in the nearest town, but you're still several miles away from Highway 58, and from there it is 12 miles to Tehachapi. A list has been created on Facebook under a group called Tehachapi Pass PCT Trail Angels of people in this area who are willing to help hikers. Seeing as you are not the "normal" single hiker, rather a family/circus of six plus a dog, you hesitate who you should call. Reaching out to the one who seems to be in charge, you are greeted with an enthusiastic response, as if he just lives for this kind of challenge! Soon, your whole family is loading into an RV and headed off to a stranger's house. If you want to read the end of this cliffhanger before you begin, flip to PCT Day #55.

PCT Day #1

"A journey of [2,650 miles] begins with a single step." —Lao Tzu (Might I add, it also takes a multitudinous amount of logistics!)

One of the things I was most looking forward to about thru-hiking is the people we would meet. I had read that the hiker community is phenomenal and that there are those called trail angels that help hikers in a variety of ways. Carl, a trail angel we found through a couple named Scout and Frodo, picked us up from our hotel in San Diego and let us store our car in his driveway. He and his wife, Ellen, took two cars to drive us to the monument at the Mexico border so we would be more comfortable (there are seven of us and our dog!) and gave us lots of helpful tips and encouragement. Plus, he is picking up my father-in-law from the airport in two weeks so that he can drive our car and my mother-in-law, Le Anne, back to Washington. Le Anne helped me drive from Washington to California. She is a problem solver, a cheerleader, a hard-core backpacker, and someone who makes cool stuff happen. She is hiking the first 110 miles with us, and it might be the most wonderful gift she could have given us to help make this journey a success.

As we caravanned past Campo, California, to the southern PCT monument, we picked up a hitchhiker named Evan (we later gave him the trail name Ninja). He is from Detroit, and this is his second PCT thru-hike attempt (last year he had to pull off the trail because of plantar fasciitis and kidney stones). We joined him at the monument and took several of the mandatory photos. I also wanted a group photo by the wall. I was chatting with Carl and looking up at the razor wire on top of the wall between us and Mexico when suddenly I was on the ground in a terrible amount of pain—it was so bad that I almost passed out. I had stepped in a rut in the dirt road and rolled my ankle. It is an old injury from my junior high softball glory days, and it haunts me occasionally. Why didn't I just keep an eye on where I was stepping! We weren't even on the official trail yet. Luckily it stopped hurting so badly, and I could just walk it off (and would probably be fine if I didn't continue to roll it on rocks and roots).

We met another hiker named Traveler. He is an older gentleman, is very nice, and is fun to chat with. He found us after we set up camp, and we invited him to join us. Turns out he is also a member of The Church of Jesus Christ of Latter-day Saints, and he had kids at BYU the same years I was there. He was a little too nice to our dog, Muir, though. He kept feeding him from his MREs (meals ready to eat, not known for benefiting digestion in humans or dogs).

My favorite memories from family events like these are when we are all laughing together. I'm encouraging the kids to all keep daily journals and record things they are grateful for, positive things that happen to them, and things that made them laugh. We had a few funny things yesterday, but of course as I type this I can't remember. I'll check with my kids and see if any of them listened to me and wrote them down. (P.S. They didn't.)

Stats for day #1: 7.4 miles; only 2,642.6 more to get to Canada. No trail names have been awarded to us yet, something that is eagerly anticipated. (Mostly by Tristan. Okay, okay, by me too.)

PCT Day #2

"If you want to go fast, go alone. If you want to go far, go together." —African proverb

We all survived our first night on the trail! It rained on us off and on through the night and continued through breakfast. That was fun. Then we broke camp, and I got Tristan, Ruby, Muir, and I lost—well, not really. We were following an old road from where we camped back to the trail, and I was convinced they would intersect at some point. I was wrong. We heard Adam calling to us from way up on the hill (our road had gone downhill, away from the trail), and we had to bushwhack to get back to him. It was a long slog uphill, and I was grumpy for making that dumb mistake and adding extra "non-trail" miles. Ruby was grumpy because her pack was not quite sitting right, and something inside was stabbing her in the back. I quickly learned that Ruby's sensory issues were going to be an extra fun challenge while backpacking. We stopped and adjusted her pack, and I asked her to tell me three things she was grateful for. That made us both feel better, and we quickly caught up to the others. The hike today was so beautiful. I had expected to see more cactus and more typical desert views. Most of the YouTube videos I'd watched of hikers on the trail were done in April of last year; what a difference a month makes, especially since this area has been getting so much moisture lately. The seasonal streams are flowing (which is awesome because we don't have to carry more than two liters each), and the desert is in bloom! We made it almost nine miles today in less time than it took us to do seven yesterday. Improvement!

Adam rigged everything for hanging food bags, then got settled in the tent he and I share. Le Anne, Ruby, and I got the last of the trash and food together and started trying to hang the six bags. Somehow Ruby pulled on the rope just wrong, and it all came down from the tree. We laughed so hard as we tried to come up with our own system to hang the bags. They are so heavy! I was in charge of food, and I need to mention now that my biggest fear in life is starving to death or even being slightly hungry. I weighed our three-day supply before we left Washington, and it was at 31.5 pounds. Somehow, on day two, when it should be nearly gone, it seems to weigh 50 pounds (I may or may not have added extra, unnecessary food at the last minute). Adam thinks "hiker hunger" is a myth, but I sure don't want to find out the hard way.

We are camped by Hauser Creek tonight, with a big switchback climb in the morning into Lake Morena. A hiker named Down Under is sharing our camp with us. He did 15+ miles today and was beat by the time he rolled in. He is from Australia and hiked the Appalachian

Trail a few years ago. He has an Appalachian Trail belt and jacket and mentioned that his story has been published in a hiker magazine. I told him we aren't famous, and we still don't have trail names. He's a super nice guy. I overheard him chatting with Le Anne, and he said (in an awesome, thick Australian accent), "I can tell you are a knowledgeable outdoors woman—er, I mean girl."

I twisted my ankle again today. I have the following (radio edited) lyrics from Ani DiFranco stuck in my head while I walk: "Cuz when I look down I miss all the good stuff. When I look up I just trip over things . . ."

Don't think that a tiny size toothpaste is going to be all you need for a family of six in the wild. Even if you use very small amounts, it won't last more than three days. However, if you get the 2.5 oz size, it will last a month. I can't explain why, other than I suspect the tiniest size is mostly filled with air.

Adam discovered that if he cut a Fiji water bottle in half, he can store his Smart water bottle inside of it. When he gets to a water source that is too awkward and small to fill a Smart water bottle directly, he can use the shorter Fiji (with square corners for easy pouring) as a scoop, then pour into the Smart bottle. It's a great discovery; I'm going to start using that stratagem too. We are using two different sizes of Sawyer squeeze filters and loving them.

PCT Day #3

"Most people don't do great things because most great things don't feel great while you are doing them." —Author unknown, heard on the Homemade Wanderlust YouTube Channel

Another rainy night and breakfast. We had a great campsite, though, and Adam rigged the tarp high enough so we could stand under it while we ate our oatmeal. We knew we had a big climb, but it was only five miles to get into Lake Morena.

Ruby has been leaving smiley faces carved into the path with her trekking pole. Once when we stopped for lunch, she drew a big elaborate one and wrote her name too. This morning as we left camp, we met a couple who said to Ruby, "You were the one drawing all the smiley faces? We loved them! We tried to imagine what this Ruby looked like, but we definitely didn't picture you!" Then they asked to take a selfie with her. She loved it. There have been three other times we've been asked for photos. Everyone is so positive out here about our hiking family. I really like how we have seen people of all abilities with the same goal to get to Canada. We've met grandmas and grandpas, ladies hiking alone, a guy with a prosthetic leg, and a guy with a dog the size of a large mouse—people of all ages and sizes.

When we reached the highest point of the day, 3,496 feet, we had just enough time to get our umbrellas up before we got pelted with hail, then sleet, then rain, then sunshine, then wind—lots of piercing wind! During lunch we finished off the last of our delicious Costco beef jerky and did a food assessment. I packed too much food! We laughed at one another as we stood up from lunch and did our own versions of the "hiker hobble." About two hundred yards from where we took a lunch break on some rocks were some very comfortable-looking picnic benches. Oh well. Being the cheapskates that we are, we wandered around trying to find the best deal for a campsite. In the end, we were able to avoid the $5 per person charge for the PCT camp area and just paid $20 for our big group (the price of a regular tent spot). It was nice to have a faucet, even though you still must filter the water due to E. coli reports.

There is no cell coverage in this little town, but there is a malt shop/grocery/restaurant that freely shares its WiFi. Their pizza special includes a big salad, and it is delicious. The resupply was surprisingly good, and we hear it is much less expensive here than at Mt. Laguna, our next resupply. Our friend, Traveler, was staying at the campground, too, but in a $50 per night cabin. His friend had left a car for him here, and he is going to take a "zero day" in San Diego tomorrow. (A zero day is when no PCT miles are accomplished, as opposed to a "nero," where only a few miles are logged.) We were all jealous. But he is a nice guy and gave half of us a ride back to camp from the malt shop. (Temps had dropped suddenly and the .4 miles back to camp felt much longer!) Even though we only did about five miles of the trail today (technically a nero), we added at least three more to our legs (according to Adam's watch) by searching for a tent site, paying the ranger, and getting food.

PCT Day #4

"When you don't know what you are doing, be sure to do it with confidence."
—*Warren Miller*

I woke up and said, "Oh, there is ice all over the tent!" Adam replied, "Good, that means it'll just shake off." Last night at the malt shop, Le Anne started chatting with a fellow hiker. This lady was all alone, had her water filtration system and stove fail on her the first day, lost her phone, and had struggled to get to Lake Morena. From there she took the bus into San Diego to get a new Sawyer squeeze, stove, and phone. Sierra told her that her trail name should be "Lucky Charm" because surely her luck is about to change! She teared up, gave Sierra a big hug, and told us all the reasons why she has been lucky and why she loves that trail name. Her puffy jacket even looks like a big marshmallow, so it's the perfect name! Then she told us all about her grandkids and dogs. She's a sweet lady.

We decided to take the morning slow because our gear needed to dry out (shaking off all the ice didn't magically make all the moisture disappear). Plus, poor Kaia has been struggling with sinus infection symptoms and didn't get a good night's sleep. She is sleeping now while the rest of us shower and journal. My ankle is doing much, much better. (After the lecture I got from Adam about paying more attention to where I step or I'll have to get off the trail, I'm trying so hard to be careful and aware!)

Today is Le Anne's birthday! We celebrated with a stack of smashed Little Debbie's that we bought before we started and a candle that wouldn't stay lit in the wind.

PCT Day #5

"Only those who will risk going too far can possibly find out how far one can go."
—*T. S. Eliot*

Lucky Charm and I are both carrying a cloth heart with us on the trail called "Debbie's heart." Debbie is a nice lady I found on Instagram who isn't physically able to hike the trail, so she has asked hikers to take her "heart" along and keep her updated with photos.

Today was a day of "firsts." First thing in the morning, we met a thru-hiking couple. He's wearing a kilt, has a big white beard, and is hilarious to boot. He has hiked the Appalachian Trail two times. She's in a long skirt, has hiked the Appalachian Trail once, and looks like a younger version of Grandma Gatewood. (Have you read that story yet? You should!) They were getting off trail to avoid what they heard was a foot of snow and 60 mph winds. That wasn't what my weather app was saying, so I thought it was our first encounter with fear mongering. But we've got a kid fighting sinus infection symptoms, and we didn't want to risk their weather predictions being right. So, we headed off down Highway 80 with our new friend Lucky Charm.

A few miles later, we experienced our first trail magic when Bo (trail name: No Man, as in the opposite of his friend, Yes Man) drove up with a dozen donuts, fresh fruit, and a big bag of chips. It was so fun to chat with him about his PCT thru-hike last year and hear all his words of encouragement. He just decided he was going to head out and pay it forward for all the trail magic he received. I'm so grateful we were the first hikers he found because we descended like locusts and took out (almost) all that food.

We took off again with more pep in our step and walked through a border patrol checkpoint for the first time. The officer there was very nice, told us he had seen our friend in a kilt a few hours earlier, and told us to have a good walk.

We stopped for lunch at a fire station and were so happy to have a picnic table to sit at. Road walking isn't our favorite; it's much harder on the body than the soft, sandy trail we've gotten used to. As we entered the thriving metropolis of Pine Valley, Adam surprised us and said he thought we should get a hotel for the night. There was much rejoicing (internally; we were too tired to jump for joy).

It was my first time doing all our laundry and wearing only rain gear! Luckily for us, the grocery store is only a few steps away from the motel (we've already been there three times tonight). Now we are trying to figure out how to avoid this storm and get ourselves back on the trail.

PCT Day #6

"Nature is full of genius, full of divinity; so that not a snowflake escapes its fashioning hand." —Henry David Thoreau

We had a zero day today because we are waiting out a snowstorm at this hotel. Zero days are really boring. Highlights included watching movies with grandma, organizing our food supply, and finding a playground to burn off some energy. The hype for the pizza at the Pine Valley store was on point.

PCT Day #7

"Voiceless it cries, Wingless flutters, Toothless bites, Mouthless mutters." —J.R.R. *Tolkien*

Early yesterday morning, I posted on a Facebook page for the PCT Trail Angels. I was just looking for a way for us to avoid the snowstorm and keep moving in the general direction of Canada. I got a plethora of responses, including one guy accusing us of leaving a campfire burning back at Boulder Oaks Campground. Someone else stood up for us to prove that we weren't even there on that date, and Adam had me write, "We don't do campfires; we like our gear too much." The accuser later sent me a message apologizing. But aside from the drama, something great came from that Facebook post: an awesome trail angel volunteered to give us all a ride up to Mount Laguna! It took two trips to get the eight of us and Muir up there (Lucky Charm is with us too). We learned that her trail angel name is Fruitbowl. She has been helping PCT hikers for 19 years and hopes to thru-hike next year! She's a super great lady. She dropped us off at the Pine House Cafe. I met a young hiker from Finland who was thru-hiking with his three friends. They had braved the snowstorm last night, and they looked cold.

As we were about to leave, the manager of the cafe came out with a plate of chili cheese fries. She said one of her customers just ordered them, but it wasn't what he expected (I wonder if it was the Finnish kid?), so he ordered something else. She was about to throw those out, but she figured we would eat them. We did, quickly and gratefully!

Then what had been bright sunshine before turned into rolling fog and snow. Our first mile and a half was a cold slog through mud (once we found the trail). This area was supposed to have grand views, but we were socked in. Bummer. The sun did finally come out, and we stopped for lunch with a grand vista. With about five miles left to our day, we met a hiker named Dana. He chatted with Le Anne and Adam all the way to camp (while I sang "The Ants Go Marching" to try to keep Ruby's morale up). When we finally got to the Pioneer Mail Picnic Area, the kids were cold and spent. Dana came over to introduce himself to them and raved about how impressed he was with their hiking that day. Kind words at just the right moment do wonders to lift spirits. (P.S. This was hands down the coldest, windiest night of our backpacking career!)

PCT Day #8

"If you will go with me to the mountains,
And sleep on the leaf carpeted floors
And enjoy the bigness of nature
And the beauty of all out-of doors.
You'll find your troubles all fading,
And feel the Creator was not man
That made lovely mountains and forests
Which only a Supreme Power can.
When we trust in the power above
And with the realm of nature hold fast
We will have a jewel of great price
To brighten our lives until the last.
For the love of Nature is healing
If we will only give it a try
And the reward will be forthcoming
If we go deeper than what meets the eye." —Emma "Grandma" Gatewood, "The Rewards of Nature"

It was a rough night—super windy. It was the kind of wind that carries a mist into your tent to soak your sleeping bag and get between you and your air mat. But I don't want to write about that.

I asked the kids for a positive experience from the first week on the trail. Kaia: "Um, we got to stay in a hotel." Sierra: "We got a donut from Noman." Ruby: "The beautiful views." (But really, I prodded her to say that.) Tristan: "Listening to my audio book."

Today was all sunshine and awesome vistas. We got about 11 miles in, mostly downhill. At one point, the trail cut close to the Sunshine

Highway. I saw a road biker pushing hard up a big hill. He looked down at us and waved, and I waved back. It was as if he was saying, "You are doing something hard, and I'm doing something hard. That makes us friends." Then I thought, "Everyone in the world is doing hard things; we should all just be friends." Then I started quoting *Three Amigos*, and I changed my favorite line: "In a way, all of us has an El Guapo to face. For some, shyness might be their El Guapo. For others, a lack of education might be their El Guapo. For us, El Guapo is a [2,650-mile footpath]."

Currently, California is experiencing a "super bloom" and a butterfly migration. We've seen a few flowers, but I hear more are coming up soon. We did hike with thousands of butterflies today, though. (A group of butterflies is officially called a kaleidoscope. So fun!) They're very tricky to catch on video because they are so small and fast, but I tried. I was worried that the section Le Anne is joining us for wouldn't be so pretty. I mean, she's used to backpacking the most beautiful sections of Washington state, which most PCT thru-hikers claim is their favorite part of the entire trail. But we all agree this area is lovely, a different beauty than we are accustomed to. I should write a book titled "How to Move Your Family to California with Different Million Dollar Views Each Day for Less than $3,000 a Month."

We are still hiking with our friend, Lucky Charm. She likes to take a little slower pace, so we forge ahead and usually see her when we stop for lunch and then at camp. Tonight, she found us about an hour after we had set up our tents. We all cheered when we saw her. She gave Adam and me high fives and then hugs. She is such a joy to have around! She turns 60 in September, and her goal is to make it to Canada by her birthday!

PCT Day #9
"You can't fight the desert. You have to ride with it." —*Louis L'Amour*

We made it 13.4 miles today. Almost everything in the desert looks like it wants to hurt us! A little joke I made up while hiking: Why did the PCT hikers cross the road? To get to the "Scissors Crossing" water cache!" Last time we had access to water was over eight miles behind us, so we were so grateful for the trail angels who supply water here!

PCT Day #10

"I believe that appreciation is a holy thing—that when we look for what's best in a person we happen to be with at the moment, we're doing what God does all the time. So in loving and appreciating our neighbor, we're participating in something sacred." —Fred Rogers

It was a trail-magical kind of day! We had planned to take a nero, but all this magic happened: First, we were trying to figure out how to get our big group to Julian, a hiker-friendly town seven miles from where we camped. I needed to do an emergency load of laundry (including a sleeping bag that cannot be put in a washing machine). Adam was tossing around the idea of hitchhiking or ordering a Lyft ride. (Funny, but they are available in the area where we are!) I walked over to the water cache and started chatting with a man there. Turns out he is a trail angel named Ghost, and he was just looking for thru-hikers to help today! I explained our situation and he immediately came up with a plan. He drove me to the Stage Coach RV park so I could do laundry. He drove the rest of the family to Julian so they could get free pie and lemonade at Mom's Pies and do our resupply. (Ghost also took them to Julian Cider Mill for free cider samples and PCT hiker treat bags!) Then he brought us all back to Scissors Crossing, where he knew three other trail angels (Carmen, Ice, and Mama Bear) were setting up trail magic. They fed us hot dogs, chips, fresh fruit (like grapefruit-off-a-neighbor's-tree fresh!), homemade brownies, and cold drinks. Plus, they had these awesome "buffs" that have the PCT logo, pictures of milestones, and their trail angel names, and they gave one to each of us! It was so fun to sit around and visit with them for hours! We dropped the idea of making forward progress and just enjoyed the love. I thought the interactions we had with other people on the trail would be my favorite part of the journey, and I think I'm right! Ice gave Sierra her trail name, "Amazon" (because she was helping carry down the trail magic supplies, including a super heavy cooler). We also visited with a hiker named AJ, who said he was from Folsom, California. We were joking about him being a member of the gated community there, so Tristan said his trail name should be Inmate. He liked it! And thus shall it be. We have a big day tomorrow; I'm so glad we had such a magical zero to help us get ready!

Tips for washing clothes on the trail: We paid $3 for a washer and $3 for a dryer (and one of the washers didn't have a great spin cycle, so we had to dry the load twice!) at the Pine Valley Inn Motel. At the Stage Coach RV park, it was only $4 for wash and dry! If someone gives you the extra time on their dryer because their clothes are dry before the 45 min cycle, add a quarter before the time runs out so that you can add 15 min and avoid the $1.75 start charge (I learned this too late). Anyway, be prepared to spend more than you'd like on laundry (but RV parks tend to be a better deal than hotels)!

PCT Day #11

"We shall not cease from exploration/And the end of all our exploring/Will be to arrive where we started/And know the place for the first time." —T. S. Eliot, "Little Gidding"

Long distance backpacking is hard. Parenting is hard. In a counter-intuitive way, combining two hard things sometimes makes them easier. Now, I'm not wearing rose colored Smith sunglasses out here; we all still have our grumpy moments, but I'd say our parenting/backpacking combo is going surprisingly well (and not just in a "the prisoners are easier to manage while marching" kind of way). I really like watching how my kids interact with other hikers and trail angels. They are developing better conversation skills with adults.

Today we met a group of six day-hikers, all retired couples. They were so interested in chatting with all of us about our journey that we probably stood there with them for thirty minutes. They took pictures of us and gave us all sorts of pointers for what lies ahead. One lady showed us a picture on her phone of some tracks in the sand about ten miles back (in the direction we were going) and explained why she believed they were mountain lion tracks. Later, Kaia spotted the exact same tracks.

This couple we were talking with asked all about the kids homeschooling, saying so many positive things about what we are doing. As we were about to walk away the husband said, "When you get up in the Sierras and have to use a bear can, it'll most likely be the one I invented. We just sold that company, and now we do section hikes." They were really awesome people.

Today was a 15-mile day with lots of elevation gain, our biggest mileage day yet. We had to carry lots of water because there was none on this stretch; plus, we were loaded down with a fresh three-day supply of food.

We've been making lunches our biggest meal of the day; breakfasts and dinners seem to always be rushed. A trail angel told us to get a Pringle's can, eat all the yummy chips as fast as we could, then stuff the can with spinach. She said it'll stay good for three days in there! So, lunch was wraps with cheese, salmon, spinach, and Fritos smashed inside. Then we had seven leftover brownies from yesterday's trail magic. Gourmet! It was so awesome to see all the beautiful wildflowers as we hiked (and a pleasant juxtaposition to all the other pokey desert plants).

PCT Day #12

"Keep away from people who belittle your ambitions. Small people always do that, but the really great make you feel that you, too, can become great." —Mark Twain

After we broke camp this morning, we went to the water cache to fill up. There were five trucks and about fifteen volunteers there, all busily unloading cases of water. A few stopped to chat with us and take our picture. They gave us all Twix candy bars and handfuls of sour apple candy. We thanked them profusely. If they didn't stock water here, it would be a 24-mile dry stretch! The oldest looking gentlemen, probably in his 80s, came up and asked Ruby if he could shake her hand. He told her he was proud of her for getting out here and hiking this trail. A thru-hiker in his 20s asked the trail angels if he could offer them a suggestion. I remember thinking, "Just say thank you, man!" But then he told them how difficult it is for hikers to add cash to their donation jar, and they should set up a Venmo account instead. He had to explain what Venmo was, and then a trail angel shouted, "The future!" Hopefully they will take him up on the idea.

It was another clear sky day, and we had a lovely ten-mile hike into camp. We passed the 100-mile mark! There is a running faucet here for a water source; it was so cold and refreshing. A fun group of people are camped here with us, and we had a great time visiting with everyone. I especially love Rick and Deb from Pensacola, Florida. We've run into them several times the past few days, and they are full of great stories and tips. Deb is 66, Rick is 68, and this is their third PCT thru-hike attempt! Last year Deb blew out her knee at mile 750 and had to be life flighted off the mountain. She's had two hips replaced, one knee replaced, her spine fused, and she's down to one windpipe, so uphills are a real struggle. But here they are again, giving it their best shot. I mentioned to her that Adam had bad blisters, and she jumped up and said, "Let me grab my blister kit!" Rick then said, "Oh, Deb is a real miracle worker with blisters." She used needles, dental floss, alcohol, antibiotic cream, and special medical tape and fixed him right up. We've used her blister system many times since, and we have a YouTube video showing the process. It saved our hike! Then she showed us how to retie our shoes with special "hiker knots." She was so helpful! She wouldn't let us reimburse her for all the materials she used. "Just pay it forward and help someone else on the trail," she said. Evan, another hiker here tonight, has a California fire permit, so the kids helped him gather firewood, and we sat around the fire and visited until "hiker midnight" (about 9 p.m.). One hiker brought his ukulele and entertained us with songs he wrote. Another magical day on the trail!

PCT Days #13–15

"Two roads diverged in a wood, and I... I took the one less traveled by, and that has made all the difference." —Robert Frost

Around mid-day, we encountered trail angels Scott and Lara in a parking lot with an awesome set up! We had the best sandwiches here and loved visiting with them! They had signs leading to their trail magic which said, "You walked 100 miles and wouldn't it be tragic if in 100 yards there wasn't trail magic." Turns out, it was Scott's birthday and he wanted to celebrate by feeding a bunch of hikers!

Eagle Rock was a landmark I was really looking forward to in this section. It is a phenomenal rock formation (which looks just like an eagle spreading its wings). It was fun to sit in the shade here and meet up with our friends, Lucky Charm and Inmate.

We hiked into Warner Springs and had two zero days there. The community center in Warner Springs has a great set-up to take care of hikers. I'm so glad we got to meet 2 Foot Adventures! We've been following them on Instagram and reading their blog long before this adventure started. Their store catering to hikers is amazing and so helpful! We got to chat with our friend Ghost again too! Ruby loved the bucket laundry and showers they have at the community center. She offered to do everyone's laundry for them! She and Tristan helped the volunteers load laundry soap into cups and clean up and were rewarded with ice cream, donuts, and all sorts of goodies. Le Anne helped Sierra with the washing and rebraiding of her hair. I met one of my cousin's Navy buddies, Shane, there too! Twice we got trail magic, and we were richly rewarded for scavenging through the "hiker boxes." Pa just picked us up, and we get to spend a night in a cabin with them (perfect timing because it just started to pour rain).

PCT Day #16

"It was one of those March days when the sun shines hot and the wind blows cold, when it is summer in the light and winter in the shade." —Charles Dickens

After two zero days, it was great to get our feet back on the trail, although it was super difficult to wave "see you later" to Le Anne and Ellery. We knew rain was in the forecast, and we also knew we didn't leave as early as we planned (11 a.m. instead of 9 a.m.). But we got a lot accomplished, including Le Anne operating on Adam's blisters under blisters, which was gruesome. Once we were on the trail, it felt like we were in an Irish countryside with rolling green hills and cows. Then we started to climb, and before I knew it, we were in a Costa Rica cloud forest look-alike. It was amazing and very wet. It probably rained on us for eight out of ten miles. Plus, we had to cross the same stream no less than six times as the trail snaked along! Poor Ruby had her leg slip into the water, but she's tough and is now tucked in her sleeping bag with warm, dry sleeping socks on. In fact, right after we set up camp, ate dinner, and cleaned up, everyone got in their sleeping bags for the night (even while it was still light out). I think it was a bedtime speed record. I've finally found the solution to my kids staying up later than I think they should. We did get to watch the sunset, though, and it was the best yet!

My tip on backpacking toothbrushes: sometimes when you break the handle of your toothbrush to save weight, it breaks off way too short. Then when you brush your teeth, it gets slippery and impossible to hold. Don't bother breaking the handle; the extra weight is worth it, friends!

PCT Day #17

If we all had to pick theme songs/lyrics for ourselves at this point on the trail it would look like this:

Adam: "Every silver lining has a touch of gray..." —Grateful Dead

Mindi: "Even if things get heavy, we'll all float on..." —Modest Mouse

Sierra: "She's a brick house, she's mighty mighty... built like an Amazon" —Commodores

Kaia: "Wake me up when September ends..." —Green Day (although we just found out that Kaia told Le Anne that she was glad we were doing this hike. Just saying what grandma wants to hear? Nope, I believe she was being sincere.)

Tristan: "Ooooooooooo that smell, can't you smell that smell..." —Lynyrd Skynyrd (Tristan thinks his song should be "Born for This" by The Score, but I think that should be Muir's song, and I get final say.)

Ruby: The only one I've come up with is the drum beat for the Energizer Bunny because she just keeps going and going and going!

Tonight, we had a near-fatal culinary disaster (not my first). We had heard that "hiker hunger" kicks in at about the third week of backpacking. It hit hard today. We easily could have consumed twice the couscous I had cooked for lunch (but I wouldn't let them, or we wouldn't have any tomorrow). Instead, everyone finished off twelve servings of trail mix Adam's dad brought us that should have lasted at least two days. We were a little late rolling into camp, and everyone was so hungry. I had decided to experiment with cold soaking, so at lunch I filled two empty peanut butter jars (specially cleaned for this purpose) with dehydrated veggies and Knorr's chicken flavored rice and let those soak for six hours. Trying to use those dehydrated veggies was my mistake. They weren't quite done when the rice was done, and they were overpowering. (It wasn't truly "cold soaking" because I did use the propane stove to cook it.) Fortunately, we also had individual packets of chicken salad to go with it. Everyone ate it, but no one (except Muir) liked it. I quickly wrote down exactly what Kaia told me so I would have it recorded word for word: "I know you did your best. But it was bad. It was horrible. Cole (the cousin we hope will join us on the trail eventually) would starve if he had to eat with us." And when Sierra came over and started with chicken salad, saying how much she loved the crunchy peppers in there, Kaia sarcastically said, "Oh good, then you're in for a real treat when you get to the rice!"

The good news is we've decided that hot breakfasts of oatmeal just aren't going to work for us and have switched to protein bars. We have extra bars with us so if we eat all our other food before our resupply on Monday, we can at least survive on those! And today was a bright, beautiful day (made even more lovely because of our gratitude that it wasn't pouring rain on us again).

PCT Day #18

"People who don't take risks generally make about two big mistakes a year. People who do take risks generally make about two big mistakes a year." —Peter F. Drucker

I rolled my ankle again on a camouflaged rut in the trail. I'm so mad at myself. While I was doing rest/ice/compression/elevation (minus the ice because we have none), our sweet dog came over and laid down just perfectly to be a pillow. It was while I was resting that I realized I left our six long-handled spoons where we had stopped for lunch, 2.5 miles back. Kaia jumped up and volunteered to run back to get them. She didn't take her pack or any water and just took off. Looking back now I think I should have thought that through better, but she returned a few hours later with the spoons and a funny story about a hiker very surprised to see a 14-year-old girl just on her own in the middle of nowhere.

I love being outside. I love being with my husband and my kids every day, and I love the freedom of the trail! I'm so grateful after a good rest I was able to walk a few more miles to camp.

PCT Day #19

"Once we believe in ourselves, we can risk curiosity, wonder, spontaneous delight, or any experience that reveals the human spirit." —e. e. cummings

Today we met trail angel Mary. Her property backs up to the PCT at mile 145. She has a 50-gallon water barrel that she hand fills for the hikers. Yesterday she was putting the finishing touches on an outhouse/shower she was building (all by herself!) for hikers to use. She has two giant picnic tables at this "oasis" (it feels so good to sit down!), and she lets hikers camp here too. She has a tiny library and cool life-sized photos of Whitman, Muir, and Thoreau. The tiny library has tiny print paper copies of some of the best works of literature out there and postcards Mary made that you can send off to your family and friends. She doesn't want you to just sign the registry; she wants you to do some deep philosophical thinking and answer the question she has on the first page, like Whitman would. She was so supportive when I talked with her about bringing our kids and dog on the trail. "This is the opportunity of a lifetime for them," she said. Her oasis will always be special to us!

150 miles! We made it to the famous Paradise Valley Cafe! Did I mention how hungry we were these last two days? We ate every bit of food we had (minus six power bars no one wanted) and have been looking forward to the food here for too long. The best part was that Le Anne and Ellery met us here with a big resupply. We whimpered enough that they stopped by Costco, Walmart, and the Dollar Store for us (even though they are supposed to be on vacation in San Diego).

PCT Day #20

"I know not all that may be coming, but be it what it will, I'll go to it laughing." —Herman Melville, "Moby Dick"

Zero day in Idyllwild! It was a super fun day just relaxing and laughing—lots of laughing. We love this town! It reminds us of

Estes Park, Colorado. The mayor of the town is actually a dog. We had high hopes of getting our picture taken with the mayor, but we had no such luck. We did get to chat with Jon King, who runs the sanjacjon.com website. This guy is amazing. He climbs Mt. San Jacinto and the surrounding trails five or six days a week and updates all the trail conditions. He cleared up some rumors we had heard in town and wholeheartedly approved of our plan to take the lower elevation alternate with our family. Most of the hikers we chatted with today attempted the trail but turned around at about mile 169. I'd say the most popular YouTube channel involving the PCT this season is Second Chance Hiker. He is genuine, laughs a lot, and is open about why he is out here on the trail. I stayed up way after hiker midnight tonight to catch up on his videos. It is so fun to see all the places we've been, even though he started over a month before us. He just got some self-arrest ice ax lessons from Jon but also ended up going the alternate route.

We spent the morning in our rain clothes (laundry day). Adam got a different rain kilt and passed his kilt down to Tristan. In town, we watched the filming of a Hallmark movie! It was so cool to see all the equipment and "behind the scenes" action. It is a Christmas movie, so there was fake snow all over.

There is a hiker named Ben that we ran into a few days ago on the trail who stood on a big rock above where we were eating lunch and said, "Happy first day of spring! More light, less dark! More wag, less bark!" (Muir was barking at him, maybe because he doesn't have a tail to wag?) Muir still barks at almost everyone, even our friends.

I overheard Adam telling another hiker friend today, "Being on the trail is like starting kindergarten. You feel like you have twenty-five new best friends." We ran into a few people in town who asked, "Are you the Bennetts?!" or "Are you that big hiking family?" We even got called the Von Trapp family (that is not our trail name).

PCT Day #21

"The world is a colossal university, and no matter how far removed you may be from great institutions of learning, if you are alert and eager to learn you can always

absorb something from your environment. We are all in God's great kindergarten, where everything is trying to teach us its lesson." —Orison Swett Marden

We got out of Idyllwild later than we wanted to (12:45 p.m.) and did some road walking that our mothers would never approve of, but all's well that ends well. On February 14th this year, the Idyllwild area was hit with a huge storm that resulted in major flooding and roads being washed out. Dump trucks are bringing up tons of dirt, and road repair is underway. We had heard from some hikers that road crews wouldn't let hikers pass, but Jon King told us they were friendly to hikers, and we wouldn't have any trouble. He was right. One construction worker stopped to visit with us, pet Muir, and ask for tips on how to hike the PCT with his dog. There is a bit of snow up here, but it's no worse than we expected. We gained over 3,000 feet today; it was just as hard as it sounds. We are 2.3 miles from the PCT. We did about 13 miles today, plan on doing 12-ish tomorrow, and will hike maybe 8 to get into town on Thursday night or Friday morning. (The goal of being able to eat In-N-Out on Friday is going to get us through!) Also, I had a goal to get a picture of every sunrise and sunset on the trail. That didn't last past the first day, but tonight's sunset was amazing.

Favorite part of the day: overhearing Sierra and Adam talk together as they walked. For several hours I heard her firing questions at him, like "How did you afford to go to Europe when you were in college?" and "How am I going to afford college?" etc. Adam told her about his different jobs and the business he started. He pointed out different trees to all of us, including the biggest cedar trees I've ever seen! My grandma, Gram, recently told me about the gift Dr. Phil asked his son to give him (one hour of his time per week for a year) and the different topics they covered. What a gift it is for us to have this trail time with all our children!

PCT Day #22

"Everyone has a 'risk muscle.' You keep it in shape by trying new things. If you don't, it atrophies. Make a point of using it at least once a day." —Roger von Oech

I would never want to be on this trail without the Guthook app (now called FarOut). Even when we don't have cell coverage, we can use the app and know exactly where we are. It shows us where we can camp, where to get water, what hikers ahead of us are saying about trail conditions, and which towns have hiker-friendly amenities. I carry paper maps too, just in case something goes wrong with our phones. I absolutely loved the area we were hiking on Black Mountain Road. It was so unbelievably beautiful! The kids had a blast sliding on the snow. (Of course, it helped that the temps were warm and the sun was shining!) We hit the PCT at mile 190.7. It was slippery for about two miles, then, much to the children's disappointment, the snow faded away with our descent.

Sierra's notes: "This morning Ruby made a sliding ramp using a snow hill. She told me to come up and try. I went up, and before I went down, Ruby was going to tell me how to stop. I told her, 'I don't stop! I just go!' As I was going down my feet came out from under me, and I went down the rest of the way on my back. There was a lot of snow for us to walk on today (and for me to fall on). We reached 200 miles!"

PCT Day #23

Our campsite last night was one of my very favorites. Hikers ahead of us warned us that it could get windy, and boy was it ever (from about 2 a.m. until 5 a.m.). We had an 8.6 mile walk down to the underpass below I-10. We passed a work crew repairing the trail from what they called "the Valentine's Day massacre" (the storm on February 14th). The trail crew said they left a cooler with some trail magic under their truck: Gatorade!

There was also trail magic under the bridge near Cabazon! We were so grateful! The strong wind blowing sand into our eyes for the last several miles almost did us in. Adam got on the Lyft app and ordered us a ride to a hotel. When the driver picked us up on the side of the frontage road, she asked Adam (in a very confused voice), "Were you guys out hiking or something?" Ha! Now we are getting our resupply in order. We're so very thankful that Adam's parents left it (four boxes worth!) at this hotel along with some much-needed new clothes.

PCT Day #24

Nero Day! In-N-Out Day! Super Challenging Transportation Day! We enjoyed staying at the hotel in Banning; showering is always nice. The staff was super kind. When they found out we were PCT hikers, they left three times the normal amount of shampoo, conditioner, and soap. There were no laundry facilities there, so we just washed a few of the dirtiest items in the sink and hung them to dry. (Those that didn't dry overnight were safety-pinned to the outside of our packs and were dry in no time in the hot SoCal sun!) We walked from our hotel 1.2 miles to the post office carrying three heavy boxes.

Two boxes were filled with food we were sending up to Big Bear, and one was gear going back to Adam's parent's house. Deciding we didn't need certain items was a big deal. By now we know that we want our packs as light as possible (of course, Adam has been telling us this all along), and it is tempting to ship off even the essentials because they are too heavy. Which reminds me of this quote from *The Hobbit:* "You will have to manage without pocket-handkerchiefs, and a good many other things, before you get to the journey's end." —Dwalin (I did send back my favorite bandanna). The postal worker asked, "Are you PCT hikers?!" with admiration in his voice. Turns out that he section hikes El Camino de Santiago and other trails in Europe. He had a lot of interesting stories, and we left feeling like best friends.

From there it took us about an hour and some scrambling to catch the city bus (we lucked out, and it was a free day), which took us to the big casino, which had a free shuttle to the In-N-Out. We savored every bite of our double-doubles, fries, and shakes. Then a Lyft driver came to pick us up and drop us off at the side of the highway, where we slipped under the overpass and rejoined the trail. He, too, was surprised to hear what we were doing but assured us several times that he thought it was an awesome thing to do.

We camped that night near a giant windmill farm. Signs warned us that flying debris was a hazard in that area. Several of the windmills were broken, an ominous sight. (Where had those blades flown off to?) We met a hiker from Germany who has worked with windmills, and she shared all sorts of interesting facts (if the blades come off while in motion, they can fly over 1,000 feet; a high percentage of people who work with windmills suffer concussions or other problems from the constant motion of the blades, the sounds they make, or seeing the repetition from the shadow they cast, etc.).

PCT Day #25

"A crude meal, no doubt, but the best of all sauces is hunger." —*Edward Abby*

Today was our first 15-mile day, and it was a tough one! We left camp early and had to battle 1,000 feet elevation gain right off the bat. Ruby was angry, but we got her a second power bar, and she got better. We've got a new system of one protein bar as we leave camp and a second protein bar and some sort of snack in an easy-to-reach pocket, and that hopefully gets us through to lunch. Today we entered the San Gorgonio wilderness, and the wildflowers are astonishing!

I know I've mentioned Second Chance Hiker and his YouTube channel before, but today we got to meet him! We walked up to a small stream, and he and a guy named Justin were there getting water. He laughed when he saw us and said he wanted to hear our story. He was so kind and complimentary to all of us and so fun to chat with. He has two sons, ten and eight years old. Turns out Justin has five kids; he and his wife homeschooled them and lived in a converted school bus for two years (and starred in a "wife-swap" reality TV show). It was super interesting to chat with him too! Second Chance was concerned about the river crossing that day and asked if we could all cross together. The Whitewater River is supposed to be the deepest water crossing in the Southern California section of the PCT. It wasn't bad at all. After the crossing, we all took a break and had lunch. I noticed Second Chance was eating his Mountain House meal without a spoon. He said he had lost his long handled plastic spoon and had just been pouring the meal into his mouth or cutting the bag and eating with his knife. I loaned him one of our six spoons, with the agreement to meet up and get it back from him in Big Bear.

PCT Day #26

"No misfortune is so bad that whining about it won't make it worse." —*Jeffrey R. Holland*

This was definitely a hard day. We had about four miles of exhausting bushwhacking and navigating through Mission Creek (which took us four hours, two hours longer than we had anticipated). The water we were drinking (filtered of course) tasted nasty and made me feel nauseous (Adam said there was a petroleum taste to it). Muir would turn up his nose at some water but eagerly drink in other places. We started to only filter where he would drink— another benefit of having a trail dog! We met a hiker at about 4 p.m. who had gotten a ride from where the PCT connects with I-10 to Big Bear and was hiking back down. She has a prosthetic leg from about the mid-thigh down on her left leg. Her trail name, Sochi, was given to her because she competed in the Sochi Paralympic Winter Games in 2014. She warned us that mile 243 had some very steep, icy sections that were very scary. We took her advice seriously and wished her luck on the bushwhacking battle ahead of her. At about 5 p.m. Adam very wisely said we'd had enough for the day, and we set up camp. It was so nice to have a leisurely dinner, sitting together and laughing, without having to rush because it was getting dark and cold.

PCT Day #27

We started out the day at 6,637.5 feet and jumped off the trail to head into Big Bear at about 8,200 feet! It was about four miles of trail and washed-out dirt roads to get from the PCT to the main highway. I had cell coverage, so I called our trail friend, Deb from Pensacola. Her description of what the trail was like after mile 242 was horrific. She said, "I was in Bosnia during the night of the conflict, and it wasn't nearly as scary as crossing those slopes covered in ice." We were so grateful that we jumped off the trail when we did after hearing all she had to say!

The first thing we did when we got to Highway 38 was to hitch a ride. Kaia asked Adam if it was illegal to hitchhike in California. He told her he didn't really know. After about an hour of trying different tactics (first, all of us stood there with our thumbs up, then three of us and Muir went off to "hide," aka nap), I went to tell Adam we needed a new plan. Über would have cost us about $40. Just then a highway patrol officer pulls up and started questioning Kaia and Ruby. Kaia, still confused as to the legality of her situation, tried to dodge the officer's questions. I ran up there, and the officer said, "We've been getting calls that there are kids on the side of the road hitchhiking. Is that true?" I said, "Yes, we are trying to get a ride into Big Bear. Is it illegal to hitchhike?" The officer said, "Well, no, but are you hitchhiking?" When I said we were, she pointed at Kaia and said, "Well she just told me you weren't!" Kaia had a deer-in-the-headlights look!

Everything turned out fine. The officer stayed parked near us for about ten minutes, but it turned out she was just trying to get the phone numbers for some trail angels for us. She did empathize several times about the many calls they got about us and said that if we didn't get a ride by dark, she might be able to help (it was about 4 p.m.). Luckily, we found a trail angel who could fit four of us and Muir. Adam and Ruby were able to find another hitch almost instantly. Finding a place to stay that night quickly turned into a fiasco. Originally, we thought we could camp in a trail angel's yard. They feed thousands of hikers each season, let them shower and do laundry at their place, etc. On the way there, though, we were told that they have a new puppy who hasn't had all his shots, so they didn't want him around Muir, which is totally understandable. Adam thought he found us a campground for $35 a night, but when the trail angel got us there (which was tricky to find), we discovered it was closed. We knew some other hikers who were staying in the Motel 6, so the trail angel got us all there (in two trips) and would only accept a $10 gas donation. Our friend, No ID, and her boyfriend, Grant, who has the funniest trail name of Grant-My-Wish (because he is here to support No ID and her trail family) came to our hotel room and visited and laughed with us for a long time. They're such good people!

PCT Days #28–29

"The parent who wonders if the stress and strain of raising children—going against the flow of the culture, teaching them biblical values, spending the necessary time and money to give them the best opportunities—is really worth it need only remember the law of deposit and return. That which is sown today will bear fruit in the years to come." —Daily Bible Study Book

I had some very lofty goals of how we would spend down time on the trail: memorizing poetry, scriptures, writing in journals daily, keeping Ruby up on her multiplication tables, etc. The first three weeks went by so quickly, we struggled for a routine and were just doing the essentials. But now that we've officially been on the trail for a month, I think we are getting the hang of things (and I'm usually able to remember to read a poem or two to them while they eat). They've all listened to a plethora of books already, and not just silly fluff books.

Town days are complicated—not so much for the kids, I suppose. They enjoy wall outlets for their devices, TV, flush toilets, showers, etc. First thing in the morning, Adam and I walked across the street from the Motel 6 to the first farmers market of the season for Big Bear. It was great to see and sample all the fresh fruit, treats, jerky, etc. We ended up getting six breakfast burritos from a nearby Mexican restaurant (where the man taking Adam's order was from an area in Mexico near where his amigo Miguel is from, which led Adam to change into his "Spanglish voice"). Then he and I walked 1.2 miles to the post office to pick up our resupply. There was a PCT logbook with a few names we recognized of other hikers who were there just before us. Our boxes were heavy to carry, and the road back was narrow, so we were so grateful when a guy in a Sprinter van stopped to pick us up. He has four kids too, ages sixteen, eleven, eight, and three. His oldest daughter is a high school competitive mountain biker, and his real estate company had a clever mountain bike theme (that was all over the outside of his van). He's a super nice guy. He had great stories about his brother who hiked the PCT last year. He was super impressed we had our kids with us.

It was a scramble to organize the food bags, clean laundry, find Tristan's lost pair of shorts (under the bed), and check out in time. In fact, we were an hour and a half late getting out of there. Housekeeping was super nice about it! Then we went back to the highway to try for another hitch. Miraculously, a carpenter pulling a trailer pulled over and had room for all of us in his Durango, with a few packs in the trailer. He took us to the trailhead closest to town, about eight miles away. We had decided to just go .4 miles back on the trail (to mile 266) and camp for the night, instead of blowing the budget on another night in a hotel. We are waiting for six sets of micro spikes and a new pair of shoes for Tristan to arrive, hopefully by Thursday. So, we are just killing time. As we started walking south on the trail, we met up with five hikers we had been hiking with near the Mission Creek stretch, including Magellan (who shouted "I can't believe it! I've been trying so hard to get ahead of you guys!"). We assured him he was ahead of us and listened to their stories of crossing the snow and ice (much different from Deb from Pensacola's account, but I guess a lot depends on the time of day you are on the ice). Today I read on Instagram that our friend with the prosthetic leg and her father had to be rescued from that section by helicopter last week!

PCT Day #30

This was our third zero day in Big Bear. Adam and Sierra caught a hitch into town in the morning to pick up a package and charge devices. They ended up walking to a church one mile from the post office to charge devices on the outside electrical outlets. About an hour before the post office closed, Adam got a text that our second package arrived. He walked to the post office again, and Sierra stayed at the church to guard the chargers. As she was sitting there, eating an apple, the missionaries showed up. She was very embarrassed to shake all their hands (which she realized afterwards were sticky from apple juice) and explain her situation.

Meanwhile, back at the camp, I was trying to keep Kaia, Ruby, and Tristan from dying of boredom! We tried playing cards, I taught Kaia a little German, we did our best to finish off our non-trail-friendly foods, etc. Mostly we just listened to books and used up too much precious battery power. I must admit I enjoyed the rest, but I'm so grateful that both packages arrived so that we didn't have to wait one more day!

PCT Day #31

We only made it 10.9 miles today; we had hoped to make it at least 15. But with a full five-day resupply and lots of water (big stretches between water sources in this section, about eight to ten miles), we were really feeling it. So, when the fog rolled in and everyone got cold and our feet were screaming, this cozy tent site came along, and we took it. We were set up before 4 p.m. That's a record!

PCT Day #32

I know you are worried about us only making it 9 miles today when we had hoped to make it 15.5 miles. It's okay. It feels a little bit like credit card debt, though. "Oh, we'll just pay this off in August…" It's a bad plan. Plus, we have the Mojave desert ahead of us, and we really want to get there before it gets too hot! We celebrated the arrival of the Easter bunny, let our tents dry, and didn't get out of camp until 10 a.m. [P.S. Later, I checked the calendar on my phone and noticed that Easter isn't until the 21st of this month! We really thought it was the first weekend in April, so that's when we celebrated it.]

We are setting a two-ish mph pace these days, unless we are on snow, fording streams, or bushwhacking. Today we were on snow. After only making it about one mile per hour for a few miles, we came into the Little Bear camp. A solar composting toilet, a giant picnic bench, and a stream all signaled to us this was a great place to call home for the night.

As we were hiking, Sierra said, "We've been on the trail for over a month, and the only tree I can recognize is a pine tree!" This nearly set me into a panic! We've definitely been talking about more than just pine trees! Luckily, we were in an area with a large variety of trees, so we started pointing out cedars, manzanitas, willows, several types of pine, and the fact that she saw the very memorable Joshua trees near Big Bear! So now we annoy the kids as much as possible with tree identification.

P.S. I thought none of the kids would ever know that we had celebrated Easter on the wrong day on trail, but I was wrong. Here are Sierra's notes from this day: "The Easter bunny arrived, and it left snickers and Airheads in the shape of a heart. Usually, Easter is in the beginning of April, but this year it's on the 21st or something. The bunny came early, though, and we celebrated Easter, not knowing until later that it wasn't actually Easter. We walked through a lot of snow today. Around lunch we came across a car that was high centered. We helped push them out of the snow. There was a camp that someone apparently abandoned. My parents called the police; it was creepy. That night there was a solar composting toilet, and Tristan set up in a horse corral."

PCT Day #33

"The sky broke like an egg into sunrise, and set the water on fire." —*Pamela Hansford Johnson*

It was a "fire in the sky" kind of sunrise this morning! We hiked through miles and miles of sandy trail and set up camp near the Deep Creek Bridge. I failed to log the mileage or take any other notes. Sierra's notes: "Most of the day was downhill. We got up early so that we could get to Splinter's Cabin before it got too hot. We were able to stay out of the sun until the last three miles. After 15 miles we made it, but dad's feet were killing him. When we got to the cabin there weren't many people there, so we could make our camp anywhere. We talked to some people that were really impressed our family was out here together. The grandma asked if we were going to be in the Guinness Book of World Records. It was a good day."

PCT Day #34

We hit the 300-mile marker today and took what possibly could be the best family photo of the whole hike thus far (because Muir is smiling!). Adam has really honed in his skills in making his favorite lunch: Hiker Pad Thai (and today he made it for the whole family in our little Talenti's cups). Deep Creek/Mojave River is so very beautiful! We walked along it for 14.6 miles today. We never did find the secret hot springs location that another hiker told us about (not the Deep Creek hot spring; we'd heard too many warnings about that one). But we did take an extra-long lunch break at a side stream to let the kids swim (it was a hot day). We pushed our mileage and walked until sunset to get out of the canyon to set up camp. We were rewarded with some incredible views of the Mojave Dam and beyond into Mt. Baden-Powell.

PCT Day #35

Zero day today. We found a campground with showers (not operated by coins or tokens!) and electricity. Adam and Kaia hitched into town for our resupply and returned with ice cream sandwiches! They got a Lyft ride on the way home because they had so many groceries (and didn't want the ice cream to melt). Resupply days are joyful days indeed! We have 24 miles until we hit I-15/Cajon Pass, which should take us two days, but we didn't quite have enough food to make that stretch. Now we have too much food—just the way I like it.

Trail angels Jamie and Andrew (aka the Homeboys of the PCT) found us tonight and brought us trail magic! We were also obviously starved for fun people to talk with because we talked their ears off for hours! I'm so grateful for these awesome trail angels who bring so much happiness to weary hikers.

PCT Day #36

We may not be in tune enough with the real world to know when to celebrate holidays, but we are thriving in our unscheduled lifestyle. Yesterday our kids did "hiker laundry" (which is washing your clothes while you shower; it's super efficient). Adam noticed hours after Tristan hung his clothes on the tree to dry that he only had three socks. He told him to go find his sock and lectured him about always making sure his socks were in pairs (he only has two pairs!). Admitting that he knew he had only hung three socks, he reluctantly went back to the bathroom and found it, but only after he stepped on it. It reminds me of that book called "It Was on Fire When I Laid Down On It!" by Robert Fulghum. Someday, something will trigger in my brilliant boy's brain that when he hangs up three socks, he should immediately go look for the lost fourth (hopefully).

There was a huge variety of terrain today. We started at mile 317 with a beautiful view of Mt. Baden-Powell and some ponds. We crossed some concrete bridges, walked really close to a huge dam, and passed a power plant. Then we popped over a ridge to see the lovely view of Silverwood Lake (a very welcome sight on a toasty day!). We found the campground; unfortunately, the bathrooms and showers we were looking forward to are locked. Oh well—there are lots of picnic tables, running water that we don't have to filter (at least we hope we are right about that! Sierra did filter her water, just so she can be the healthy one to help all of us if we get sick), and electricity. We spent a lot of time after dinner discussing the obstacles ahead and how we are going to maneuver the next 100 miles or so.

PCT Day #37

"After a good dinner one can forgive anybody, including one's own relations."
—*Oscar Wilde*

Today was a day we had looked forward to for a long time: the day when a McDonald's would be right next to the trail. Tristan talked almost the whole way about all the food he wanted to order. I have to admit, it all tasted delicious, especially those hot fudge sundaes! We mostly stayed outside because we knew we didn't smell so fresh. A guy asked Ruby and Tristan if they were on a hike and how far they were going. When they said they were going to Canada, the guy didn't believe them. Sierra walked up and had to convince him it was true. She said his jaw dropped, and it looked like his mind was blown. Unfortunately, our outdoor seating was right next to the windows, and we had lots of stares as we stuffed 12 extra cheeseburgers into our empty peanut butter jars for breakfast the next morning (it worked really well). A lady in the parking lot stopped us and asked, "Are you all one big family?! Hiking the PCT together the whole way?!" She asked for our Instagram account and followed us immediately. She was super nice.

We knew we wanted to camp as far from I-15 as we could get. It was quite the adventure getting away from civilization: under the highway, under the train track, through a galvanized pipe, and over the train track.

At the end of the day, Ruby had me climbing all over the place, following her instructions on how to get the perfect sunset photo. 14.1 PCT miles today, plus an extra .5 to get to McDonalds and a gas station for a resupply.

PCT Day #38

"The sea is dangerous and its storms terrible, but these obstacles have never been sufficient reason to remain ashore . . . Unlike the mediocre, intrepid spirits seek victory over those things that seem impossible . . . It is with an iron will that they embark on the most daring of all endeavors . . . to meet the shadowy future without fear and conquer the unknown." —Ferdinand Magellan

It was a rough night, maybe the second worst thus far (the first being that crazy windy night at Pioneer Mail Picnic Area). It was windy, and poor Tristan's tent collapsed and Adam got up at 2 a.m. to help him fix it. But that wasn't the worst part. The train was the worst! I guess a plethora of trains run in this area, especially between 2 a.m. and 6 a.m. And they must blow their horns twice as often at night as during the day, or something.

But we were all excited for our breakfast of champions: cheeseburgers (until we walked uphill for several miles and Ruby said, "That McDonalds doesn't feel so good in my stomach." And I wholeheartedly agreed with her).

This is a very dry stretch into Wrightwood. We are so grateful to the trail angels who stock this water cache with 40+ gallons of water. Yesterday and today, we ran into five hikers that were fun to visit with. Atlantis is from Germany, Lauren just got back from climbing Mt. Kilimanjaro, Herc (like Hercules) and Two Packs are from Israel (they got their trail names from starting with really heavy packs), and Kermit is from Poland.

We also experimented with a new lunch: a few packages of mashed potatoes, a few Knorr creamy pestos, too many mayonnaise packets, and three McDonalds ranch dips. Kaia assured me hiker hunger is real and that we needed to eat this. It was quite flavorful but didn't sit well after another five miles and 2,100 feet of elevation gain. Don't try this at home! It was fun to sign the register and see our friends who are ahead of us. Magellan put a fun fact about the actual Magellan: it was 500 years ago exactly that he sailed around the tip of South America, found the Strait of Magellan, and made some bad choices of friends in the Philippines (who killed him during an uprising on the way home, I'm guessing). We only did about nine miles and called it a day. We have another 9.5 miles to get into Wrightwood tomorrow, where we will spend a few zeros waiting for two packages to arrive. We're really looking forward to some showers and laundry!

PCT Day #39

"Ruby Bennett (age 9) pack weight: 14 lbs with food and water" (written on the chalkboard at the Wrightwood hardware store where other hikers were posting their pack weight…Ruby's was the lightest by 6.5 lbs. Later on, we did meet other hikers with lighter packs).

Wrightwood is the greatest trail town we've yet encountered! As we first walked into town, a man sweeping his driveway stopped us and asked, "Are you PCT hikers? Congratulations! Welcome to Wrightwood!" Then he ran into his house (well, he didn't run because he must be in his 70s or so) and got six cold water bottles for us. That cold water tasted so good; we were all thirsty! We visited with him for at least ten minutes. He said we were the first hikers to pass by his house this season. He moved from Tacoma, Washington, to Wrightwood in 1971 and said the area has grown like crazy since. It is such a great town! We had to walk for several miles through the town to get to the hardware store (where we heard PCT hikers were supposed to check in). The houses here are all so adorable! When we got to Mountain Hardware, they gave us a special PCT pin to put on our packs and let us weigh our packs, go through the hiker boxes, use their bathrooms, sit in their shade, and leave our packs in a safe spot so we could wander the town pack-free. One employee drew us a map of all the best places to eat and was so helpful. We ended up getting two giant pizzas at Mile High Pizza. They gave us the hiker discount: buy one, get one half off. Those two pizzas cost half of what our McDonalds run cost us the other day, and they were enough to feed us for two meals! While in the hardware store, one of the employees tried to give Adam the trail name of Buttercup, but he refused it. The kids and I are so disappointed. A lady who works at the grocery store, Angella, has been following us on Kids Out Wild and was eagerly anticipating our arrival. She got water for Muir, showed the kids where free bins of stuff were at the front of the grocery store (stuff like lip balm and dry shampoo that are priceless treasures to the teenagers), and visited with us for a long time. Everyone is so positive about us having our kids out here with us; it's so great! We found this sweet trail angel named Dottie who is housing us in her basement apartment for the next two nights, just out of the kindness of her heart! We even get to do laundry for free!

PCT Day #40

"Welcome hikers! It is nice to have you!" —sign in Wrightwood, CA

We have enjoyed our time in Wrightwood so much! This morning we walked from our trail angel's home to The Church of Jesus Christ of Latter-day Saints. We were warmly welcomed, despite being embarrassed at only having our hiking clothes to wear! In fact, they announced from the pulpit, "We have hikers from the PCT visiting with us today! They are all sitting on the back row!" As most of the congregation turned to look at us, we all went bright red (except for Adam who is sunburnt and already red). But so many people stopped to visit with us, compliment us on our adventure, and offer to help. If the two packages we are waiting for arrive in the morning, a lady from the congregation volunteered to drive us to the trailhead! This brought tears to my eyes because it would be so hard for all of us to hitchhike in that direction!

After church we wandered around town visiting with hiker friends. Grant-My-Wish saw us walking and pulled over to chat with us. We also met up with Gumby, who is staying with a couple who makes the PCT 2019 patches that are given away for free at the coffee shop. He told us all about their home (a huge embroidery business set up in their basement, along with arcade games and memorabilia from bands like Led Zeppelin and Metallica—including signed guitars and drumsticks). Then we ran into this same couple later today (they said they wished they would have found us before we called Dottie so that we could have stayed with them!) and visited with them and other hikers for hours. The younger kids needed to burn off energy at the park, so we spent a lot of time there too!

PCT Day #41

There have been a lot of recent helicopter rescues in the Mt. Baden-Powell/PCT area. We don't want to be one of them, so we took the low road. We encountered several road workers driving past in trucks and backhoes to clear the road. All of them gave us a friendly wave, as though saying, "We'll allow it." We walked right into the clouds and wind—a lot of wind. I wish I would have taken a video of the girls' struggle to get their tent up. They are pros by now, but the wind was intense and thwarted all their know-how. But we are all tucked in, safe and warm! Goodnight!

PCT Day #42

We have friends who summited Mt. Baden-Powell and did the icy section by Mt. Williamson. When they caught up to us, they were so relieved that we took the low road. One guy said he was trying to kick in nice, wide footprints in the snow just in case the Bennett kids were behind him! We've had several people say when they were in different areas they were concerned for our safety if we were following behind. Adam said it is like we have extra grandparents, aunts, uncles, and cousins out here on the trail looking out for us! It's so nice having a trail family! We passed the 400-mile marker; only 22.5 of those one-hundred-mile markers to go! We camped at Camp Glenwood tonight. There's no running water or electricity, but we have flat tent spots, picnic tables, and pit toilets.

PCT Day #43

We left camp at 8:10 a.m., which is pretty good for us! There was a sled left at this camp area and a steep gravel hill. All Ruby wanted to do was sled, and all Muir wanted to do was bite said sled and protect Ruby from sliding to her perceived death (and bark a lot). We are such a circus juxtaposed with the calm, tranquil forest.

We met up with some day hikers, a husband and wife and their friend, all retired. The wife said, "Are you that family, Kids Gone Wild? I watch your YouTube videos!" Adam quickly corrected her that we are Kids Out Wild (not to be confused with that R-rated page, Girls Gone Wild. We are G-rated and family friendly!). I gave her one of our stickers, hoping it would prevent her from ever getting our name wrong again.

At 11 a.m. (our favorite time to stop for our elevenses snack), we hit a water source and met up with our friends Stork and Bye Bye Stick. We bartered some "trail gold" (Juanita's tortilla chips) for four oranges (cutie size). Stork is trying to come up with a trail name for Kaia, but so far nothing is sticking. I mentioned to them that Juanita's should sponsor us, and it turns out that Bye Bye Stick is from Hood River, Oregon (where the Juanita's factory is, which we toured as a family about five years ago). He knows one of Juanita's sons!

We have officially left any part of the trail that is higher in elevation than 6,700 feet in the SoCal section. It is so sad to me to be leaving these mountains behind. I loved them! Our 3 p.m. Little Debbie's Cosmic Brownies break has become a regular this stretch. It is the kids' favorite trail fuel. Unfortunately, we just ate the last of them. Today was our first 18-mile day!

PCT Day #44

Last night was a horrible, very bad, no good night's sleep! We had avoided two different potential camp spots yesterday because our Guthook app had comments warning us that they were notorious for high winds. We pushed on to the fire station. I could hear the wind rushing down the canyon like a freight train, and then it hit us almost as hard. I'm sure it would have been worse up on the ridges. It wasn't a cold night, about 50 degrees, but the wind carried tiny specks of sand with it—so tiny they infiltrated our tents through the bug nets. There was sand on our mats, in our sleeping bags, and in our eyes, teeth, noses, and hair! The kids said they slept pretty well, but I sure didn't! Another part of my problem was one of the Guthook comments said that the fire chief doesn't like hikers and will come over to yell at you and kick you out of the day use area. I really don't like getting yelled at and was so worried that would happen! Another comment noted that we had every right to camp in that area and gave a list of three numbers of those superior to the fire captain to call and complain if you do get chewed out. (This same comment also gave the number of a pizza place that delivers to this parking lot. I wish we would have called for pizza!) Anyway, all my worrying was for naught. We never got yelled at, thank goodness (it probably helps that we had the kids up and rolling before 6 a.m. to get out of Dodge). We walked through the area burned by a two-month long fire in 2009. There were so many giant trees gone! Yet there is much new growth filling in for that which was lost. Tonight's destination, after 17.5 miles, was a ranger station known for selling pop to hikers for $1. Sierra and Kaia were so excited, forging ahead of us to make sure they didn't miss out. On the way, Sierra heard the eerie sound of a rattlesnake and just barely saw it slide away. That stopped her cold in her tracks, and they waited ten minutes just to make sure it was safe to proceed. Those cold drinks never tasted so good!

PCT Day #45

In the last three days we have hiked 52.3 miles! 16.9 was our day's total as we straggled into a corner of Vazquez Rocks County Park after hiker midnight. Let me start at the beginning.

The sunrise was amazing! Last night my Star Walk app told me there would be a "pink moon" setting in the morning. It was lovely. We didn't get out of camp early (9 a.m.) and we took a few stops to smell the roses (and filter water and hide from the sun and build sandcastles). To say our little kids are dirty is an understatement. I'm looking forward to showers and laundry tomorrow at "Hiker Heaven" in Agua Dulce! Adam's watch said it was 95 degrees around noon. Apparently, the official weather app says it was 86 degrees, but it sure felt like 95 in the full sun on the exposed ridge! We passed a major monument (which I accidentally hiked right past, but Adam stopped to snap a photo). It was a little pile of stones on the north side of the railroad tracks near mile 444.5. It marks the completion of the Pacific Crest Trail, officially, on June 5th, 1993. All our breaks set us up for hiking later into the evening than we normally do. Which is fine by me; I love watching the sunset as we hike! It was an awesome sunset. It reminded me of a favorite quote by Jo Walton: "There's a sunrise and a sunset every single day, and they're absolutely free. Don't miss so many of them."

We had to cross under Highway 14 through a very long, very creepy tunnel. Kaia said, "It looks like the gates of hell, but we are just trying to get to Hiker Heaven!" At one point towards the end of the tunnel, Adam started running. Kaia and I didn't know why he started running; we just knew we didn't want to be at the back of the pack. He was just teasing us, but we all ended up laughing at our imagined fears and clumsy scramble to get out of that tunnel!

It was a bummer to hike into Vasquez Rocks in the dark, knowing that we were missing out on some awesome rock formations (this area has been in 61 different films and about that many TV shows, according to my quick search on Wikipedia). We are looking forward to seeing it in the morning!

PCT Days #46–47

"Hiker Heaven, a Southern California paradise that, according to trekker lore, provided hikers with hot showers and soft cots, transportation for medical attention and gear, and laundry services where someone else washed and dried your grimy clothes. All free." —Backpacker Magazine, "Heaven Sent," June 2, 2015

Hiker Heaven was everything we dreamed it to be—and more! Immediately we were informed of the rules and set up with loaner clothes. We gave our dirty stuff to a volunteer to wash for us, Donna Saufley (trail name: L-Rod, short for lightning rod) gave us the two available rooms in the trailer, and we put our names on the list for a shower. The hiker box had many desirable treasures, and there were so many fun people to visit with. Adam got a ride to the store, and the rest of us just chilled (the rest felt so good to our weary bodies)!

PCT Day #48

"There is a quote in Hebrews," Donna Saufley says. "Something along the lines of, 'To show hospitality to strangers is to entertain angels.'"

Leaving Hiker Heaven was hard to do! We were so lucky to be given those two rooms in the trailer. Donna, her husband, Jeff (trail name: Mumbles), and their team of volunteers helped us with laundry, provided cold water to drink, provided access to laptops and sewing machines, and received and sent packages! A volunteer named Sugar Mama even surprised my kids with individual Easter baskets on Sunday morning (which caused me to shed a few tears of gratitude)! There was an owl's nest with a mama and three baby owls just about ready to learn to fly and a raven's nest, both in the same tree. They were so fun to watch!

They are on a septic system at Hiker Heaven, and water must be trucked into their house, so there are lots of signs warning people to be frugal with the water. The only bathroom with a shower accessible to hikers was in the trailer we were staying in. You write your name on the list on the dry erase board hanging on the bathroom door and wait for the person in front of you to call your name. Showers had to be ten minutes or less, on the honor system. The lid of the toilet has a handwritten warning saying, "No poop." There are six port-o-potties outside for that. On Easter Sunday, we were invited to dinner at the home of a family we met at church. After the lovely meal, Ruby asked me to join her in the restroom. (She is going to hate that I'm sharing this story.) All of the sudden, she looked up at me with wide eyes and said, "Does this toilet lid say, 'No poop'?" I assured her it didn't!

As we left town, we had to take a detour to the hardware store to pick up some Tyvek to go under our new tent. There was some water left out for hikers (which was great because the water tank was empty when we left Hiker Heaven). There were several benches outside the hardware store and a big sign that read, "Agua Dulce Bench Grumpies." An older gentleman named Bob and his little dog came to sit next to us there. Adam asked if he was part of the "bench grumpies" group. He laughed and said he was. He's lived there a long time and enjoys chatting with the hikers that pass through town. We saw Bob in his car two more times as we hiked out of town. He's a friendly guy! We also saw Donna's husband, Jeff, as we left the hardware store. He pulled his truck to the side of the road, jumped out to give Adam a fist bump, and said, "I think what you are doing is great. Thanks for staying with us, and good luck on the rest of the trail!"

It was a hot climb that afternoon, and we regretted not leaving much earlier that morning. At the top of the climb, we met up with Stork and Bye Bye Stick who were resting in the shade. We had read the trail register they just signed that read, "T minus 8 months and we'll be buying diapers!" We congratulated them and realized that Stork's trail name made a lot more sense (Kaia suspected all along). We hiked with them until we came to the water source, then visited with them there for a few more hours while we rested in the shade. Stork said she found out she was pregnant a week before starting the trail! Her midwife gave her the okay to start hiking though, so she proceeded because she's had her heart set on it for so long. Three weeks into the trail, she had a medical emergency and had to bushwhack off the trail to get to the hospital. The first house she came to asking for help was very unfriendly. The man told her she was lucky his attack dog didn't get her before she got to the door. She asked him for a ride to the hospital and he told her no. Then she asked to be pointed in the right direction to get to someone who would help her, and he said, "Well, I'll drive you off my property so you can get through the three locked gates." When she finally did find someone to help, they told her she probably walked into a drug operation and was lucky to have made it out alive! She got the help she needed at the hospital, and Bye Bye Stick came down to join her for the rest of the trail so she wouldn't be on her own. Stork said she studied botany in college, and as we passed a big patch of what she taught us was edible "miner's lettuce," we all started chowing down. Everyone enjoyed it, and later we used it in our "hiker fish taco." The kids finished off the giant bag of Skittles our friends the Strawbridges (the family of six that hiked the PCT southbound last year whom we met on social media) had mailed us, and Kaia filled it with miner's lettuce. We finally walked away from the water source (where our friends had decided to spend the night) and headed 2.6 miles down the hill to where we intended to camp. As we said goodbye Ruby said, "I feel like we are just leaving our friends' house."

PCT Day #49

"If you think adventure is dangerous, try routine; it is lethal." —*Paulo Coelho*

Today was our first attempt at a 5 a.m. wake up call. It was rough (Tristan had a really hard time waking up in the dark), and we didn't get out of camp until 6:45. We hiked for about four hours straight and made it 9.8 miles before stopping for our elevenses snack/rest. Our goal is to get 10 miles in before 10 a.m. during the hot desert section that lies ahead (then siesta until the cooler evening before hiking on). Now we know we will have to leave camp at least by 6 a.m. to make that happen. However, this section wasn't very desert-like at all. It was lush and green, and even though we were told it would be a 15-mile carry without water, there were streams flowing almost around every corner.

We arrived in Green Valley in the early afternoon and were able to hitch (in two separate vehicles) the two miles to Casa de Luna (another famous trail angel house). I heard Donna at Hiker Heaven say that some hikers complain that these two trail angel's homes are too close together. What's there to complain about? Terrie at Casa de Luna was so nice; she gave us big hugs and told us she was so glad we stopped by. The rule is that everyone must put on a Hawaiian shirt right when they arrive. The kids loved it. Terrie and her husband Joe have been helping PCT hikers for 30+ years! We set up our tents in the giant manzanita forest behind their house, painted rocks (where Stork gave Ruby the trail name "Ladybug" because she was painting a ladybug on a rock; plus, it fits so well!), and they fed us an awesome taco salad dinner. It was a blast visiting with old friends and meeting so many new ones. There were about thirty hikers there. Muir even had a few dog friends to run around with. We went to bed early, exhausted from our early start.

PCT Day #50

We got up at about 6 a.m. in hopes of leaving Casa de Luna before it got too hot. We happily ate the pancake breakfast Joe cooked up for everyone. We signed their giant 2019 register (a big white sheet) and all got the awesome bandanas they give the hikers.

One hiker chatted with us as we were waiting for a ride to the trailhead. He said, "It was nice to have you guys here. Everyone was on their best behavior because there were children around!" A few times I heard the trail angel say to other hikers, "Stop swearing; there are kids here." We had really debated about stopping into Casa de Luna because we heard it was a big party spot. But Adam talked with Sugar Mama, and she insisted we not miss it. I'm glad we listened to her!

We found a cave to have lunch in and hide from the midday heat. At first the kids were spooked, thinking there was a bear living inside. But after a while they got brave and explored all the way to the back. Some miners back in the day were looking for gold or something in here, but there were no bears. But when Adam fell asleep and started snoring, Sierra said, "It sure sounds like there is a bear in here!"

We found a great little spot to camp for the night. We tried something new for dinner: Bear Creek Country Kitchens Soup. The back label said it was made in Heber Valley, Utah (a beautiful mountain town we were lucky to live in for four years). It took me a whole hour to make three of those soup packets. But we all went to bed stuffed, having two servings each! Adam, Tristan, and I are "cowboy camping" again tonight, falling asleep under the stars (but not the girls; they like protection from creepy, crawly things)!

PCT Day #51

"A [family] on foot . . . will see more, hear more, feel more, enjoy more in one mile than the motorized tourists can in a hundred miles." —Edward Abbey

Today we had a 5 a.m. wake up! We got out of camp by 6:17, almost thirty minutes earlier than our last attempt. We were thwarted from getting 10 miles in by 10 a.m. because we had to go on a lengthy detour to obtain water. Lush green was the color of the morning! We walked through forests of miner's lettuce and lovely shade trees. It got hot in the afternoon, but we cut our siesta short because we were driven by the excitement of making it to mile 500! For a while now we've been saying that once we get past the 500-mile marker, this will all seem real (it still feels like a dream). This is the point where Adam feels ready to take on a trail name whenever he is presented with one he accepts.

PCT Day #52

What a sunrise! We woke at 5 but didn't make it out of camp until 6:30 because we got sucked into watching music videos on YouTube. We met a thru-hiker named Sam in Wrightwood whose husband's band just performed on the Ellen Show. We had to watch that because we had cell coverage at our camp. Sam got off trail for a few days to go to the recording in LA, and we think we spotted her in the audience! Well, that song reminded Kaia of one of her favorite songs, so she had to play it for Adam. We certainly regretted wasting the cool morning that way because the trail got hot fast. Even though it was mostly a "downhill" day, those uphill sections were killer! We made it to Hiker Town before 11 a.m. Shade, showers, bucket laundry, a trip into town for Sierra and Adam to get food, and visiting with our friends was just what we needed! There was no room in the cute tiny houses, so we set up our tents in the barn area (which we prefer anyway). The plan is to spend one night here at Hiker Town and hit the next section tomorrow evening when the temps drop. I'm super nervous about the next 134 miles. There are long stretches between water sources; thank goodness trail angels maintain a few water caches between here and there, without which it wouldn't be safe for us to cross.

PCT Day #53

"I believe that there is a subtle magnetism in Nature, which, if we unconsciously yield to it, will direct us aright." —Henry David Thoreau

This was another windy, sand-blasting kind of night. Kaia declared it to be her second worst night of sleep! That's okay, she got to hitch into the nearest town to do a Walmart run with Adam. They found an In-N-Out and brought back six double-doubles! Kaia was so excited to share two of them with Stork and Bye Bye Stick. Stork gave us big hugs and was so happy. Ants had gotten into some of their food last night—big bummer! It turns out it was her first taste of In-N-Out, and she loved it! We left Hiker Town at 5:30 p.m. to start the infamous LA Aqueduct section. We had so much fun walking along the pipe (then we jumped down to the softer dirt road). Our night hike didn't quite end as expected. We thought we would go the whole 17 miles to the next water source but stopped after about 11 miles. We were all exhausted, it was nearly 11 p.m., and an elevated slab of concrete looked like the perfect place to crash. We cowboy camped, looking up at the stars, the sound of flowing water below and a gentle breeze lulling us to sleep.

PCT Day #54

"Sleep that knits up the ravell'd sleave of care, / The death of each day's life, sore labour's bath, / Balm of hurt minds, great nature's second course, / Chief nourisher in life's feast." —*William Shakespeare*

Right here on this raised concrete slab above the LA Aqueduct we had our best sleep of the whole trail! We got up with the sunrise and started the seven-mile walk to water. I'm so glad we stopped where we did because that was the last of the raised concrete, and some meanie put a scary doll head in the bushes to frighten night hikers. No one in my family noticed it except me. Let me just say that if I would have seen that in the dark last night, I would not have gotten a good night's sleep! While we hiked down this stretch, a thirty-something-year-old hiker fell into step with Sierra and Kaia and started chatting with them. He said, "I know everyone out here on the trail thinks your parents are cool for bringing you guys out here, but do you think your parents are cool?" They didn't tell me their answer, they just said he gave them a long list of reasons why they are very fortunate to be on the trail at their age. I hope someday they believe him!

We made it to Cottonwood Bridge/faucet and spent six hours there hiding from the heat in the shade with about fifteen other hikers! Just as we were getting ready to leave, we heard someone shout, "Guys! There is trail magic up here! Cheeseburgers!" Turns out one of the hikers sent her location to her dad who is in LA on a business trip (from New York). He brought twenty-five In-N-Out cheeseburgers, fries, chips, pop, Gatorade, cookies, etc. He was awarded the trail name Uber Eats.

It was a fun surprise, and our second day in a row of In-N-Out! (Are you tired of me talking about what we eat? It is very important to us.) We were here with a great group of hikers. One goes by the name Professor. She is a geologist and enjoys talking to us about all the cool rock formations we have seen/are seeing. Plus, she knows the history behind the LA Aqueduct and told us all about it. We enjoyed walking through the giant windmill farms to get to camp!

PCT Day #55

"Thunderbolts and lightning, very, very frightening . . ." —*Queen*

At about 2 a.m., we got hit with a rain/thunder/lightning show! Luckily, there wasn't a lot of rain, and our tents were dry as we sauntered away from camp at 8:30 a.m. We had a 4+ mile uphill climb, but it went by so quickly because we were chatting with our friends Enigma and Professor.

You are not going to believe this: I sent a text message to a trail angel I found on a Facebook page just to see if we might find a place to crash for the night, and we hit the jackpot! JD picked us all up from the trail in his RV, drove us to Tehachapi and bought us pizza, then drove us another twenty minutes to his home in Stallion Springs. There is a herd of elk that live in this area year-round, which was so cool to see. Also, they have a pool and a hot tub, which we fully took advantage of! Their deck has an amazing view of the valley below, and the sunset was phenomenal. JD and his wife, Liz, have been helping hikers for four years. They are so unbelievably kind and generous! We plan to spend a few zeros here while we gather packages, resupply, and heal up. Tomorrow night is Taco Tuesday at their favorite local restaurant, and they are taking us with them for 99 cent tacos! Wooohooo!

PCT Days #56–58

We spent four blissful zero days with JD and Liz. Adam and I had time to make a backpack gear review video. JD is feeding us three meals a day (when he retired from firefighting, he was bored so he attended a cooking school in Louisiana for a year), and they are gourmet! Today's breakfast was pumpkin Belgian waffles, which Ruby piled high with fresh strawberries! Adam, wearing JD's firefighter pants, started weed whacking their big south hill. JD was going to hire someone to do this, but Adam insisted he would love to. We're so glad JD conceded! We've stayed here for four nights to allow Sierra's foot to hopefully heal up (most likely, it's tendonitis). We will see how she is doing in the morning and maybe take her to a podiatrist. JD is adamant that we are not a burden and that he loves having us (Liz has only been here one night because she is helping care for her mother with Alzheimer's, and she is a middle school math teacher in a district about two hours from their home). JD invited his friend, Joy, as well as the PCT hiker she is hosting named Bookworm over for dinner. We had a feast and loved visiting with them!

PCT Day #59

JD and Liz took us out to dinner tonight and said it was to repay Adam for running the weed whacker on their back hill. We tried hard to talk them out of it (because they've already fed us thirteen meals in the last five days), but they insisted. JD is a professional photographer and took us to their friend's property to get a few photos. It was so fun! Sierra's foot is feeling better, and we have our food resupply all set. We are so fortunate to get a ride back to the trail tomorrow and keep heading north to Canada!

PCT Day #60

Our Tehachapi trail angels finally kicked us out! Just kidding. JD and Liz kindly drove both their cars to drop us all off at the trailhead at 9 a.m. Sierra wrapped her foot in KT tape and insisted she didn't need to see a podiatrist. Hopefully five days of rest/ice/compression/elevation did the trick!

We had heard of the famous pumpkin bread that our trail angel Liz makes for hikers and were absolutely delighted when she sent us out the door with six loaves! We stopped (not long after they dropped us off) and ate them all in one sitting. They were unbelievably delicious!

Our friend, Rochelle, helped Adam and me get new shoes mailed to us in Tehachapi. We are now both wearing the Altras Timp 1.5, and they are awesome! About three years ago I started having trouble with plantar fasciitis, and it took me almost two years to find a good solution: heel cups. Well, when it was too late to turn around, I realized I had accidentally thrown away my heel cups with my old shoes at JD and Liz's house! My feet were hurting, and I had to play a mental game with myself all day (saying, "You can hike without heel cups, it's all in your head!"). I whimpered a bit to Adam, and he ordered me the same insoles he just got, which he thinks will do the trick. I just have to make it 135.7 miles to get them in Kennedy Meadows!

We have about 87 miles until our next resupply, and I heard this is the most water-scarce section on the PCT. We started the day with a huge climb! When we stopped for elevenses, it turned into a three-hour siesta, both to hide from the heat and because we lost our "trail legs" during our five days off. We tucked into a grove of giant Joshua trees to rest, and it was wonderful.

Aside from the obvious things, like don't let your kids get too hungry or too cold, I would tell families who want to do long distance hikes that they need to take every opportunity to chat with other hikers. If it is just one minute or for hours, involve the kids in the conversation. I heard a quote (and now I can't find it) about how much kids can learn just from talking with other adults. As we were setting up camp we met two hikers, Mosey and Mountain Time. They stopped to chat and laugh with us for at least thirty minutes. Mosey is from Georgia, and he must be in his mid-twenties. He's super clever and funny. Mountain Time appeared to be the same age and is from somewhere like Ohio. He told us his goal is to hike the last 100 yards of the trail into Canada on his hands. With his pack on! We laughed so hard as he described the training he is currently doing (and how Mosey says he feels so lazy at the end of the day while watching his friend take his cardio to the next level). Visiting with them was a highlight of the day. I'll say it once again: my favorite part of this trail is all the wonderful people we are meeting!

PCT Day #61

Happy Cinco De Mayo! We celebrated with Juanita's, tortilla soup (with mashed potatoes added in for extra calories, delicious!), and Little Debbie's Cosmic Brownies! But before this feast we had a difficult 16 miles. Sierra and Ruby each fell twice—no big injuries, just bruises and hurt egos. Adam has decreed that no one is allowed to fall anymore. This is a barren, burnt section with lots of spinning windmills. It's super hot, and I was not feeling "trail ready." (I'll probably keep complaining about how we lost our trail legs during those zero days for a few more days.) We took another three-hour siesta, and three ticks were found on our clothes (but none found their way to our skin or Muir).

Adam also keeps a daily journal and here is what he wrote for today: "PCT day 61, mile 593.0, 28,589 steps, 15.8 miles. We had a big water carry today; it'll have been 19 miles by the time we make it to water tomorrow. My feet felt good for the first time in a long time with new insoles and new shoes size 11.5, and I'm feeling like it was worth it. I bought insoles for both Mindi and Sierra; both are having foot issues, and I think this will fix it, plus Sierra is getting new shoes. We were dragging into camp today. I think it's because of heavy water carries and not drinking as much as we would like. We also had oatmeal for lunch, and I don't think it fueled us like it should have. I'm listening to *Men to Match My Mountains*, which talks a lot about the pioneers and the California gold rush. It is very interesting and humbling to hear about all the parties that tried or did make it over the Sierras, especially as we get closer to starting our trek into those mountains."

PCT Day #62

"Must we always teach our children with books? Let them look at the stars and the mountains above. Let them look at the waters and the trees and flowers on Earth. Then they will begin to think, and to think is the beginning of a real education."
—David Polis

This morning was misty and foggy, perfect for a long, dry stretch. The desert miles have taught us how much we love and appreciate the cool, misty mountains! Today we crossed the 600-mile marker! The Robin Bird Spring was a very welcome sight (and one of the few water sources in this section). We had lunch there and had a great debate about how to make "Hiker Pad Thai" (our daily lunch). Some like to start soaking in the morning, others prefer adding water to the ramen about an hour before eating. Some add the powdered peanut butter and honey with the water, others stir it in right before eating it (and some are mad we switched from regular peanut butter to powdered because they say it just isn't the same—but it saves weight).

We found a spot for dinner with benches and logs to sit on—luxury! Kaia entertained us by describing the plot to the Hallmark movie she had written in her mind while she walked. She is determined to direct it one day. I hope she does!

What everyone is listening to:

Adam—*Atlas Shrugged*

Mindi—I'm not good at listening while I walk. The earbuds bother me, someone is always interrupting me, and I prefer to write these nightly notes in my mind . . . then I forget 99% of it at bedtime.

Sierra—*The Call of The Wild*

Kaia—*Supernaturalists*

Tristan—*Mistborn*

Ruby—*Harry Potter*

PCT Day #63

"In the empire of the desert, water is the king and shadow is the queen."
—*Mehmet Murat Ildan*

We left the lush manzanitas and cool shady pines for about another 15 miles in the desert today. I wasn't mentally prepared for it. We said more than twice that we wish we would have been hiking this stretch in yesterday's weather.

We were so very thankful to find a water cache at mile 615.9! We saw the notes on the Guthook app that said this cache had 27 five-gallon jugs seven days before we arrived, and nine were left when we got there. We stayed here for a siesta under our umbrellas for longer than we intended to. It was so hot! As we walked away, a van pulled up. I asked if he was the trail angel who maintained this cache. He said he was one of them, so I did my best to thank him profusely!

We found a picnic bench along our path. It would have been a joyful rest spot if we weren't getting sandblasted with wind! We read the informative sign about the California Desert Tortoise, which increased our desire to see one! (But, alas, we didn't.) A hiker from Las Vegas named Flair Hair came up to us and said, "I finally caught up to the Bennetts!" and asked to take our picture. At dinner time we all huddled up against some brush and cactus to hide from the sting of the wind, trying to decide if that was where we wanted to set up for the night. After dinner the consensus was to stay put. It took four of us to get the girls' tent up in the strong wind. Adam, Tristan, Muir, and I opted for cowboy camping. We were in bed before the sun went down. I was up several times in the night and got to enjoy the star show.

PCT Day #64

"Rough winds do shake the darling buds of May." —William Shakespeare

We've really been fortunate with the weather on this hike, but the wind really gets to us. Often, I have the Queen lyrics "anywhere the wind blows" stuck in my mind and I'm convinced that's what the designers of the PCT were thinking too when they built this trail. When we woke after our night of cowboy camping in the wind, Adam looked at me and sweetly said, "You've got so much dirt on your face." We saw an old, rusty bus from way above on the trail. Adam said we needed to go get a closer look. Kaia refused because she didn't want to "hike all the way down there and all the way back up again." It was worth it. I wish there was an informational plaque there to tell us how this bus came to find its final resting place.

Sometimes when we are hiking uphill, the kids and I want to stop for water more often than Adam. Usually, we will try to drink as fast as we can before he catches up, but today he passed us and kept hiking about 100 yards. We were glad he was first to see a baby rattlesnake sunning itself on the trail. Later in the afternoon, when we were so hot and thirsty, we came around a bend in the trail and saw a big red shade tent! Trail Angel Jim used to be a raft guide and comes out here about twice a season to treat PCT hikers. His daughter section hikes the PCT, and that's how he found out about trail magic. We were so lucky to get his yummy sandwiches, ice cream bars, cold Coca-Cola, and Gatorade! It was a great oasis, and once again we stayed too long. It was a huge climb away from Jim's water cache (also known as Bird Spring Pass). This is our first 20-mile day ever! We pushed through the sunset and hiked 2.5 more miles in the dark. We arrived at McIver's cabin after hiker midnight and tried our best to set up quietly amidst five other tents. (We were apologizing in our minds to the previously sleeping hikers!)

I was thinking of providing a list of all the aches and pains we've got going on but decided against it. Everything hurts! I've been waking up so sore the last few days, which worries me because I never want to leave the trail. One hiker told us all our ligaments and muscles would be trail hardened by mile 750. We were chatting with a hiker named Atlantis at mile 350-ish, and he told us that we were lied to. He always finds new things hurting through the entire thru-hike. (He hiked the AT last year, and he was the first to enter the Sierras this year.)

Adam's notes: "PCT day 64, 20.6 miles, 49,190 steps, mile 643.9. It was our first day over 20 miles, and it wasn't that stellar of a day. We got out of camp late after a miserable windy night where Mindi and I didn't even blow up our pillows for fear of them blowing away; instead, Mindi gave me her clothes bag, and she used my 'arm pillow.' She is selfless. We got a late start out of camp leaving at 8:30 a.m. and pushed the 7.8 miles of a 15 mile water carry where we were pleasantly surprised to find Jim, aka Kim's Dad (he doesn't think he should have a trail name because he hasn't hiked the trail but anybody who drives 3.5 hours to set up trail magic for two to three days, depending when the food runs out, deserves to be sainted). We chilled there for three hours and then pressed on just 13 miles, and we made it. It wasn't pretty, and it was 9:00 by the time we got to camp and 10:00 by the time everybody got to bed, but we did it, and just two short days before Ruby's tenth birthday. This means she beat me to my first 20-mile backpacking day by 33.5 years."

PCT Day #65

"Take care of your body. It's the only place you have to live." —Jim Rohn

Just in case you are interested, I've improved my morning foot routine, and it has helped tremendously. Our new friends, the Strawbridge family, sent us some Slather. It's an awesome foot lotion that smells fresh and minty and works great for foot massages and blister prevention. So I apply that, put on my socks and calf sleeves, and then massage my feet again with a spiky ball for a few minutes. It feels great! I'm still trying to get into the habit of massaging everyone's feet at night, but I haven't quite found a good way to consistently make that happen. Last night was cowboy camping for Adam and I again, with Muir keeping watch. We set up our tents near McIver's cabin. As you can imagine, it was filled with all sorts of rodent poop, and no one slept in there. (But during storms we've heard reports of it being packed with hikers for the night!) There is a beautiful, clear spring running on the other side that we were grateful to see! A Jerusalem cricket was hiding under Adam's pack during breakfast. I've never seen one in real life before, so I was super excited!

We did eight miles in less than three hours, and we made it into Walker Pass Campground, our goal for the day. We had lunch and chatted with a hiker named Claire. She works as a park ranger in Denali National Park and told us so many awesome stories. I'll share just one: A tourist was taking pictures by a stream, and a grizzly bear came along. This lady remembered her "what-to-do-when-you-see-a-grizzly protocol" and curled up in a ball on the ground. A few rangers were watching this happen. They saw the bear curl up to take a nap next to the very scared woman. After a while they approached her and assured her that she could just get up and walk away. She did, and everything was fine. We thought that was hilarious. Claire said bears in Denali act a lot differently than bears in the Sierras. They are not used to humans being around and have no interest in them (unless they want a cuddle buddy, apparently).

After lunch, Adam and Ruby hitchhiked into town to pick up mail and resupply. The rest of us got to watch four guys in the Navy practice backcountry helicopter rescues. It was awesome!

I hiked up to the top of Walker Pass to try to get cell service. I had just enough coverage to get a call from Adam saying he heard there was a storm rolling in with lots of rain, thunder, and lightning, and he thought we should try to find a way to get out of the storm for the night. So, I walked back down to camp, about one mile from the pass, and found the note left by a trail angel at the water cache. Unfortunately, it didn't have a phone number, just instructions on how to walk about three miles to get to her house. That wasn't going to work. I walked a mile back up to the top of the pass to try to get service again to get on the Facebook trail angel page, but I couldn't get my phone to connect. I asked a hiker named Ash, whom we had met a few days earlier, if I could use his phone to text Adam, but it couldn't connect. I told Ash there was a storm rolling in and there was supposed to be quite a bit of lightning. He was just headed up over the hill and sounded surprised to hear bad weather was on its way. I wandered around for about ten more minutes, trying to call Adam, and turned just in time to see Ash coming down the trail and jumping in a car that had just pulled over. He must have looked at the storm clouds, got coverage, and decided to call an Uber to come pick him up and take him to safety.

I told the kids we needed to set up our tents before the rain hit us. I also added that the only way we were going to find a trail angel was if Adam and Ruby found one in town. I said something to the effect of, "If Dad can find a trail angel to drive him back here, tell us to pack up and jump in the vehicle, and drive us back to their house, that'll be the only way we are getting out of the storm tonight." Literally moments after we got the tents set up, while watching the rain and lightning get closer and closer, a trail angel pulled up with Adam and Ruby and said, "Take down your tents and jump in my truck! I want you to stay at my house tonight!" Kaia said, "This was exactly what you said would happen!" We broke camp and loaded into Frank's truck, quickly learning he is the nicest, most interesting man in the world. He is 83 and worked for the government as a Warfare Analyst for forty years before he retired. He and his wife, Debby, helped Mother Teresa care for orphans in India for two months. Then he went to PA school, and he just retired from that career three years ago. He also was on a ski patrol for twenty years, has climbed the highest peak in all fifty states (plus Mt. Fuji and more!), and he and Debby have traveled all over the world. He is a meticulous note taker and has shown us notebook after notebook of records of his adventures. We are absolutely blown away by what he and his wife have accomplished and their phenomenal generosity!

PCT Day #66

Today was a most delightful zero day with Frank and Debby. After printing out a weather report for us to study, Frank insisted we stay another night because of the storm. It was impossible to say no!

Debby drove us to Home Depot, Walmart, and Albertsons. Adam fixed a broken drawer in their kitchen, and they were so happy with him! We sat around and read their notebooks and watched TV. Frank talked Sierra into making cookies. He was so excited about those cookies!

At 5:30 p.m. on the dot, Frank announced it was martini, sardines, and the Great Lecture series time. He was the only one with a martini, but a few of us braved the sardines (Adam and Ruby like them). Every day at the same time Frank has this routine. We watched "The Celestial Sphere" and "History's Greatest Voyages of Exploration."

At dinner we told them about our favorite moments on the trail thus far. Debby made us chicken cacciatore with spaghetti, asparagus, and "happy salad" (their daughter-in-law's special recipe). I've missed vegetables so much!

Yesterday, Adam and Ruby had picked out a birthday cake at the grocery store that we thought we would eat on the trail. It was a Mother's Day cake, but we just took off "Mom" and wrote "Ruby" with chocolate chips. We sang happy birthday to Ruby, and Muir barked from the backyard (he just hates that song or maybe he is singing along)! It was so fun to be with Frank and Debby for this special event.

Here are some of Frank and Debby's stories, in their own words, from their "Adventure Notebook" they shared with us:

(1972) "After 11 months working in Korea, we came home 'the long way': Taiwan, Hong Kong, Thailand, India, and Nepal. We lived on a houseboat in Kashmir where our daughter Lisa caught pneumonia. We tried to get to a doctor in Israel, but the plane broke down in Tehran, Iran. Frank stayed with Lisa in Tehran's male-only Jam Hospital with the desert sheiks (each in flowing white robes with a golden band on the head, a sword, and escorted by two or more machine gun toting bodyguards). When Eric, Mark, and I (Debby) visited Lisa, I memorized the Persian numbers above the patient rooms. We went back to the hotel in a cab. The driver said the fare was so much. I looked at the meter and knew what the correct amount was and gave it to him. He was livid! Each morning Lisa would visit a different sheik and be given a little present (a stuffed toy, etc.)."

(1997) "Deb and I (Frank) decided we would like to work with Mother Teresa and Missionaries of Charity. We wrote a note to Mother Teresa saying we would come to Calcutta to help. We got a handwritten note back from Mother Teresa saying not to come to Calcutta but go to Madras and to take this note with us. That note is now framed and on my office wall. We did go to Madras and spent two months helping in a home for abandoned and orphaned children. We lived in the modest Woodlands hotel. Each morning after breakfast, we took an open rickshaw pedi cab taxi to work at 9 a.m. on the city streets crammed with 18-wheelers and buses. We were at the Missionaries of Charity Orphanage, run by Mother Superior, Sister Lin (who is about 60 years old), and 8 to 10 younger sisters. They're very energetic gals, like female Marines. The house also had a few older women who cooked the meals. Some street girls also helped with laundry, drawing water from the well, and making fires. Frank's job was to play with 15–20 young kids (ages 4–6). Deb's job was to work with the severely handicapped children upstairs. They wanted us to work until 3 in the afternoon. Then we returned to our hotel. After our stay in Madras, we went to Hyderabad (home of the royal Muslim kings). Then on to the Mother House in Calcutta—the sisters in Madras had made a cake and sent a huge jar of special pickles and handwritten letters for us to personally give to Mother Teresa. But she was quite frail and was not seeing any visitors as they were choosing her successor. She died four months later. While in Calcutta, we learned about the weekly Saturday opening of the fire hydrants hosing down the street kids, giving food, clothing, and a school lesson. We saw the preemie babies in their incubators (a young nun who ran this section told us she had never lost one), toddler rooms, sick and handicapped children, and mobile clinic vans. We also visited the leper colony (along the railroad tracks) (Frank had his backpack slit open while on the very crowded train going out there) and the Homes for the Dead and Dying."

PCT Day #67

"The best place to think things out is a long hike." —Frank Buffum

We had a wonderful breakfast feast this morning with the Buffums. Frank kept saying how happy he was that we were there because he got bacon two mornings in a row!

They took two cars and drove us all back to the Walker Pass trailhead. Very kindly, they offered to pick up Kaia and Adam in Kennedy Meadows on Tuesday around noon. That helps resolve many logistical issues of getting Kaia to the airport on time on Wednesday (this lucky girl gets to go visit family in Colorado and take a trip with her grandparents, aunt, and uncle!).

Adam had the brilliant idea to get Ruby a balloon to tie to her pack for her birthday! She loved it! Several hikers (and a whole Boy

Scout troop) that she passed on the trail today wished her a happy birthday! Even though we had a late start (we got on the trail a little after 10 a.m.), we still got over 16 miles in for the day with several big climbs. 4,430 feet in elevation gain!

PCT Day #68

"These blessed mountains are so compactly filled with God's beauty, no petty personal hope or experience has room to be." —John Muir

We woke up with all our gear soaking wet. We were camped near the Spanish Needle Creek, tucked in a cove, and the morning dew was plentiful.

While we were drying off and packing up, we met four hikers: Pace, Triple A, Blue, and Kanga. This fun tramily (a trail family that isn't actually related) has been together since they climbed Mt. Baden-Powell. Pace talked about losing 75 pounds on the AT last year. Afterwards, he gained 40 pounds back and felt like it took three weeks on the PCT to get his trail legs again. (I thought that was fast; it has taken me over two months to feel like I have trail legs!) He's looking great now and is the fastest one in his group. This has been a very memorable Mother's Day for me this year! I'm so grateful I have these kiddos and that we can adventure together!

Nine hikers passed us while we were filling up water at Chimney Creek (the massive bubble of hikers is quickly catching up to us). Aside from us, four of them were from Washington state (and two from the UK). We met Dan from Seattle (that's his official trail name), and he tried hard to persuade Muir to leave us to start hiking with him!

PCT Day #69

We got an early start, leaving camp around 7:15 a.m. Everyone was super motivated to knock out the 17-ish miles into Kennedy Meadows as fast as we could. Muir, as always, was making sure everyone was staying on task for the morning routine. We made it to mile 700! It is exciting to note that we made it from mile 600 to 700 in a week, even though we took a nero (an 8-mile day) and a zero in between there too!

We had a one-mile road walk to the Kennedy Meadows general store from the trail. I had heard, and we had seen on a few PCT related YouTube videos, that everyone out on the deck stands to clap for all the hikers walking in. Thus, I had big visions of a crowd clapping, maybe even singing happy birthday to Ladybug (her birthday balloon is still hanging on to her pack). Alas, only our friend Bernard was on the deck, and he is from Sweden, so he must have missed the memo that he was supposed to be clapping. That's okay; he played Jenga with the kids at the picnic tables and made up for it. Oh, and when we were walking to the main entrance, an employee did rush out to greet us, giving us a hearty clap and congratulations.

We had three packages waiting for us there. Unfortunately, they charge you $6 per package to pick them up! If only I would have read the hiker notes better and had them sent to Triple Crown Outfitters or Grumpy Bear's (where it is free to send packages).

From the general store we were able to catch a ride to Grumpy Bear's retreat, where there is free camping and laundry. Also, it's home to the legendary "Hiker Breakfast" that I've been daydreaming about for the last 100 miles. I told Adam that all I want for Mother's Day is that breakfast for the family. We also had a package waiting for us at Triple Crown Outfitters from the Strawbridge family. We got lots of yummy candy, new flavors of protein bars, toothpaste and toothbrushes, handy empty zip-lock bags, electrolytes, and more! We are so spoiled!

It was a fun night spent visiting with friends and making new ones. A guy named Delux who starts the trail in a week brought trail magic to us (watermelon, hot dogs, and a lot of laughs). After gathering intelligence here amongst hikers we've learned that our "plan B" isn't going to work (the Sierras are at 200% snowpack and getting hit with three more storms this week). So, we thought we could get ourselves up to Truckee in NorCal and start hiking north. Tiny Tim and Bowie were just there and told us that there is still a huge amount of snow and the small towns for resupply aren't ready for hikers yet. Plan C: find PCT sections without snow to hike on for a few months. We've heard more than twice from other hikers that the logistics for our family must be a nightmare. We've found that everything works out.

PCT Day #70

"It does not do to leave a dragon out of your calculations, if you live near one."
—J. R. R. Tolkien (In this case our "dragon" is all the snow hitting the trail ahead of us.)

The hiker breakfast at Grumpy Bear was beautiful, delicious, and very filling (Tristan was the only one who took advantage of the all-you-can-eat pancakes and had a second one). This is where we had a miraculous trail magic moment. Fred and Debby Buffum pulled up right at 11 a.m. (we had agreed on a high noon pickup time, but we figured the Buffums would be early, so we were ready). They gifted us a bag of tortilla chips, the pico de gallo we had left at their house, a gallon size bag of caramel corn their daughter had made, and a nine-page addition to their adventure notebook that they had written just about us! As they drove away, they saw a hiker named Blue (from Switzerland) who was hitchhiking into town, and of course they picked him up! That left Tristan, Ruby, Sierra, Muir, and I to spend the rest of the day at camp doing laundry, organizing gear, listening to books, and chatting with other hikers about their plans for the Sierras.

PCT Day #71

"Everyone has a plan until they get punched in the face." *—Mike Tyson*

Adam and Kaia rented a car (they ended up with a minivan because the car Adam reserved wasn't available) yesterday and spent the night with the Buffums. They left Ridgecrest at 4 a.m. to battle LA traffic and get to the airport by 8. Miraculously, the timing was perfect that Adam's mom, Le Anne, his two sisters, Meagan and Ellynn, and his niece, Bennett, were arriving at the same airport at the same time and heading to Disneyland (to celebrate Bennett's graduation). Adam got Kaia safely on her first solo flight and then drove the rest to the "happiest place on earth."

Meanwhile, Sierra, Ruby, Tristan, and I broke camp and waited for Adam to come pick us up (after he took a detour to REI). Since we had extra room in the minivan, I started checking with other hikers to see if they wanted a ride with us to the NorCal portion of the PCT. Our friend, Dan from Seattle, had suggested starting north from a trailhead near Burney, California. As we talked more about it, it started to sound like a much better option than what the other hikers around us were planning. Some said they were headed off trail for a week or more to see the beach or the Grand Canyon. Others were staying put in Kennedy Meadows to wait out three predicted snowstorms (hitting in quick succession), then heading into the Sierras to check it out for themselves. After much thought, Dan from Seattle decided he would join us. We left Kennedy Meadows at about 4 p.m. and took a winding mountain road to the main highway. We all get carsick easily these days (after almost 70 days of not being in a motorized vehicle). Ruby got it the worst and said, "Can I just get out and walk?"

As we drove up Highway 395, we had an amazing view of the Sierras. They look very beautiful but also very cold. As we entered the little town of Independence, we saw two hikers we recognized waiting at a bus stop. Adam flipped the van around quickly so that we could chat with them. Taz and Travis are super fast hikers, doing around 30 to 40 miles a day. They said the Sierras really humbled them! When they left Kennedy Meadows, they didn't have enough food. A storm or two came along, and they got hit with snow and hail. They would start hiking around 3 a.m., and by 10 a.m. the slushy, deep snow was super difficult to walk in. Their mileage dropped to about 10 to 12 miles a day, and they looked sunburned/wind burned. Their plan was to take a few zeros and head back in after a few more predicted storms passed. They said the hikers who were doing the best in this section were the ones prepared to do short mileage days and had about 12 days' worth of food. We were so glad we got to hear their firsthand experience (and that we were in a vehicle passing the Sierras for now).

We stopped at Taco Bell for dinner and bumped into Tony, a trail angel we met at Kennedy Meadows. Tony has a son and daughter on the trail right now; they both had gone into the Sierras recently, and he was so worried about them! He told us his wife is following us on social media and asked to take our photo. We arrived in Reno at about 11 p.m. and found an inexpensive hotel with complimentary breakfast. There was a "Little Fur Con" convention going on, so we got the last room available (Dan found a room at the hotel next door). We're looking forward to a great night's sleep.

PCT Days #72–75

"Give me six hours to chop down a tree and I will spend the first four sharpening the axe." —Abraham Lincoln

We weren't sure what to expect when we showed up at the Burney Mountain Guest Ranch. Adam drove us all there in the rental car, and we anticipated it would be a logistical mess trying to have him return the car an hour away and get back to us. Once again, the trail provides, and it all worked out. Linda and Mike are the owners here, and they are ultra trail friendly. Adam drove the car to Redding, took the $5 bus back to Burney, and Linda and I drove down to pick him up. They let us set up our tents on their property, sheltered from the wind, and fed us an amazing trail magic dinner of baked potatoes, biscuits (maybe the best biscuits we've ever eaten), and clam chowder. It was so filling!

There are three other hikers here, one from Holland and two from Switzerland. The next morning the weather report was calling for snow in our path, so we all decided to hunker down for a few days. Linda and Mike have a "work for stay" program set up, so we eagerly volunteered to help around the ranch. Adam helped build a gazebo and an outdoor fireplace by the pool with a few of the other hikers and Mike. He said it was an interesting experience to put together the gazebo with guys with construction experience but from a variety of foreign countries.

The kids and I helped pull weeds, move bark around their new playground, and clean out a few rooms in the cabins, the "goat shed" where laundry and showers are, and the dining hall. Linda is an amazing cook, and every morning she made us her fantastic waffles, eggs, potatoes, and sausage. For dinner we had pasta with very buttery sourdough, veggies, burritos, salad, taco soup, etc. Desserts included homemade cookies and brownies. It was seriously heavenly.

They have a Great Pyrenees puppy named Duke that Muir could have been much nicer to, but he was a grump. When we weren't working or eating, we watched movies in the dining hall, including all the "Lord of the Rings" trilogy! They've invited us back to stay with them when we return to hike south through the Sierras, hopefully in late August.

On Sunday, we found a couple from the local congregation to drive us to church. They probably went an hour and a half out of their way to take us there and back and were so nice about it. We were very, very grateful! We loved staying at the BMGR but are excited to hit the trail tomorrow!

PCT Day #76

We snapped a few photos with Mike, Linda, and Duke after a hearty breakfast (have I mentioned how much I love Linda's made-from-scratch buttery Belgian waffles?). Linda sent me a picture she took of us heading off down their driveway. We're really missing our daughter, Kaia, who is with our family in Colorado. I mean, we really miss her (and not just because she isn't here to help carry three days' worth of food).

The weather was nice and cool, with no rain, but four days off left us feeling like we'd lost our trail legs again. We made good time getting in the 9 miles to the Burney Falls, which was a spectacular sight! Crossing the Lake Britton Dam was exciting, too, with beautiful views! For the first time on the trail, I had to pull out my mosquito net. They were fierce at dinner time but disappeared right afterwards, and then the "monsoon" hit. There was so much rain, thunder, and lightning!

PCT Day #77

We had to call "uncle" to the weather and take the low road around Red Mountain today. It rained (and thundered and flashed lightning) on us all night. The weather app that told us there was a 40% chance of .09 inches of rain was way off! Poor Tristan failed to listen to his father's exact tent-in-the-rain etiquette and left his backpack too close to the edge, resulting in water entering his tent and soaking his sleeping bag and clothes. He also tucked one shoe only partially under the vestibule, resulting in a soaked shoe. It was a miserable morning for him.

We knew we would hit elevation above 4,500 today and would stay at that elevation for the next 35 miles. We'd been warned there was some snow up there. In fact, our buddy Dan from Seattle sent Adam some pictures the day before yesterday of his tent with a foot of fresh snow on it at mile 1,446. Dan from Seattle (who ended going home after this miserable day), along with two other hikers that were further up the trail, ended up turning around and hitching into town. Adam says, "In case anyone is wondering, we are more spirit of the law verses letter of the law. So, finding a low route that keeps us out of the snow and moving north as opposed to leaving the trail is totally acceptable." We found a forest road and followed it for about 17 miles (when we are off the trail, we can't track mileage on our Guthook app, so we are just winging it).

Our lunch break was intensely miserable. It was pouring rain, we were cold, and we didn't let our noodles soak long enough before we started eating them. We just forced it down because we needed to start walking again to warm up. We found three unopened Costco water bottles on the side of the road, tucked under a tree, and that greatly helped our situation (so we didn't have to filter water from a puddle). The trail provides! The upside to this day was that this forest is gorgeous, especially the blooming dogwood trees!

At one point, Sierra was walking slightly ahead of us and turned around suddenly with wide eyes. She walked back to us, double speed, saying "BEAR, bear! Did you see the bear? Bear!" A black bear had run quickly across the road in front of her and down the hill before any of the rest of us could see it.

We found a spot to camp and stopped a truck (the only other human we'd seen all day) to ask where the nearest campground was (10+ miles away, so we decided to stay put). Turns out the driver hiked the PCT last year but pulled off the trail at Truckee because he "just got tired." Understandable.

Adam, in the pouring rain, walked to the nearby bridge to hang our food bags in the most "bear-proof" way possible. Just as we were setting up tents, it started to dump on us again. Two out of three of our tents can be set up in the rain without the insides getting wet. We held the tarp over Sierra and Ruby while they set their tent up as fast as they could. If it would have been any colder, I might have declared this moment to be unbearable. As it was, we survived, even with only a Cliff Bar for dinner.

Adam's version: "PCT day 76, 29,570 steps, 15-ish miles. Ah… Tristan woke up with a puddle in his tent, his sleeping bag wet, clothes wet, etc. His pack had slid and pushed the tub of his tent beyond the fly, and water was just puddling. Then he took forever to pack up. It thundered and flashed lightening from about 11:00 p.m. to 3:00 a.m., and one bolt was right overhead. Muir was sick for some reason and kept pushing out from under the vestibule but was still leashed up. After waking up enough to clear the groggy stupor from my head, I realized he must need to use the restroom, which he did two other times that night. In the morning there was a nice present about a leash length away from the tent. We rolled up camp soggy, wet, and cold. Then it rained the whole day until 3:45 p.m., then for 75 minutes there was no rain and no blue skies, but the clouds thinned just enough to feel a little warmth from the sun. We got off trail and are hiking forestry roads to bypass an impassible snowy section of the trail."

PCT Day #78

We found plenty of lovely streams today from which we could get water (yesterday we crossed plenty of streams, but they all were difficult to get to). Early in the day, we took a turn onto a road leading to Iron Canyon Reservoir and saw signs next to a parking lot reading "No Camping" and "No Dogs." We crossed a bridge and saw another sign reading "Road Closed in 15 Miles." As we stood there researching how that would affect our path back to the PCT, a man named Doug pulled up on a 4-wheeler. He asked us if we knew about the hot springs on his property (over by the "No Camping, No Dogs" signs) and told us if we wanted to go, we could take our dog. We mentioned we had skipped the Deep Creek Hot Springs because of nudity, and he said, "Oh, well, you might find that to be the case here too. It just depends on who is in there." We politely declined the offer and kept chatting with him for a while. We told him about our hike thus far, and he said, "I'm so impressed. I'm going to mention your family at our next school board meeting—something new to talk about." He told that us a wolf has been sighted in the area, but not to worry, it won't bother us. White pelicans and vultures were something he said we might also see. Someday he hopes to have a PCT side trail to his property. He's a super nice guy; he arrived just in time to tell us the "Road Closed" sign doesn't apply to us, and we could move forward with our plans. The trail provides! I say this every day.

It was a long road walk to Iron Canyon Reservoir, but we found a great spot for eating lunch and drying out our gear. Even though we kept getting rained on throughout the day, the sun would make a bright appearance occasionally, which was enough to keep our spirits up! We tried to make it back to the PCT to camp at Ash Camp but had to call it a night about three miles short of our goal.

PCT Day #79

We ended up in an awesome camp spot off the forest service road last night. Aside from having Muir need to leave the vestibule at 2 a.m., then not returning right away when we called him (I was feeling quite panicked for about four minutes), it was a great night's sleep (I only imagined the worst; Muir was fine). Someone built a perfect bench to sit on while filtering water and overlooking the stream. It was heavenly! A mile before connecting with the PCT, we spotted the "Road Closed" sign. If it truly had been impassable to us, it would have been a long slog back to civilization to figure out a Plan D. Lucky for us, we could easily maneuver around the blockade.

Almost immediately after getting on the PCT here at mile 1,470, we walked into Ash Camp and met a hiker named Sody. He recognized Adam and said he was with Birthday Girl, HikerBro, and BikerBro (twins) that day we met them at the Cottonwood Bridge after the Aqueduct (it was that trail magical day when Birthday Girl's dad showed up in a black Cadillac with 25 In-N-Out burgers to share with hikers). Sody had taken some time off trail to let the snow melt and was heading south (his gear was spread all over camp, drying out). We found out he crossed paths with Ties (pronounced like "peace" but with a T) from Holland, and maybe Naudja (he just said a girl who looked cold, miserable, and in a big hurry passed him going north). We got a text this afternoon from Ties. He wrote, "Snow report. First snow at 5,000 feet. Patches and 1–2 inches fresh snow at 5,300 feet. All not too bad and most will melt fast. However, at 6,000 feet there is 6+ feet with half a foot of fresh snow. The fresh snow on top of compact snow is very slippery. So be careful." 17.7 miles today.

PCT Day #80

"He who distinguishes the true savor of his food can never be a glutton; he who does not cannot be otherwise." —Henry David Thoreau

Today was our first view of Mt. Shasta. It is a magnificent sight! We had a lovely hike through this section of the Shasta-Trinity Forest all the way to the I-5. At about 6:30 p.m., we stood at the intersection, wondering if we should continue walking to the Castle Crags Campground or try to get a hitch into Dunsmuir. A state park ranger pulled up and offered to give us a ride in his truck to Yaks (a highly rated restaurant in Dunsmuir). We happily accepted and tossed our packs (and Muir) in the back and piled in. We were given the royal treatment at Yaks! Between our waitress who was enamored to see a family on the trail and a waiter who loves dogs and wants to hike the PCT one day, they gave us six of the famously delicious sticky buns for free! We will forever be raving about Yaks; everything we ordered was so good. Plus, when a big group at the table next to us left their plates behind with untouched food, the waiter offered to put it all in "doggie bags" for us (it fed more than just Muir the next day!). 16.6 miles today.

PCT Days #81–86

"A surge of optimism overwhelmed me. At first, I couldn't quite identify the new emotion, but at last I realized what it was: I felt capable. Perhaps not capable of completing my goal, but at least capable of meeting challenges and solving problems as they came my way." —Heather Anish Anderson, *"Thirst: 2600 Miles to Home"*

It is tricky to keep track of trail updates on zero days, and we just had a lot of them! There's too much snow anywhere on the trail above 5,500 feet for us to safely proceed, so we are feeling stuck. Two families in the Mt. Shasta area took us in (thank you again, Pollacks and Andruses!), fed us, and provided shelter from the rain! We ended up getting a ride to Yreka, then took the bus (which was crazy fast on the winding mountain roads) to Seiad Valley. A few weeks ago, we heard that a PCT legend, Heather "Anish" Anderson (National Geographic's adventurer of the year and a "Fastest Known Time" record holder on the PCT, AT, and AZT), was going to be speaking at the Wildwood Tavern. She just published a book, *Thirst: 2600 Miles to Home,* and is on tour promoting it. When we arrived at the Wildwood, I noticed her book was in the hiker box, so I picked it up and read it in a few hours. It's so good! It was awesome to hear her speak about her experience on the PCT, although it is nearly opposite from what we are trying to accomplish. She hiked the entire trail in 60 days, averaging more than 40 miles per day! She didn't take any zero days! We bought her book, and she signed it for us. We are going to mail it home tomorrow so it stays nice and new (along with a few other things to lighten our packs). In the morning, we are going to attempt hiking north again on the PCT. There are no storms predicted in this area for a few days, and we are hoping all the warm temps have melted some of the snow.

PCT Day #87

"'I refuse to let this suffering be for nothing. In fact, I refuse to suffer.' I whispered to myself as I pushed each tent stake into the ground. 'I can adapt. I am adapting.' Another long day was done and I was forty-two miles closer to Canada." — Heather Anish Anderson, *"Thirst: 2600 Miles to Home"*

When we arrived by bus to the little town of Seiad Valley, we were delighted to find a group of other hikers there. Lullaby, Butch, and Patience were just headed south for a road walk to Mt. Shasta. We got a quick photo with them before they left. Another "tramily" was just taking off for a road walk too. Mountain Time was with them, and he showed us the progress he is making on his 100-yard hand walk (he can go about 10 feet). It was hilarious. That group headed south, but four hikers who just hiked in from Ashland joined us at the Wildwood. Good Cop lives in Colorado. Hot Lips just moved from California to Nashville. M and Chef (a real police officer, not just a good cop) are from New Zealand. It was great to visit with them. Fairytale and Sunshine arrived at the Wildwood the next day; we haven't seen them since Casa de Luna. They hiked a big portion of the PCT last year and just have 350-ish miles left. They are both teachers and have traveled the world. Sunshine was teaching Ruby math and jokes. She won't forget $7 \times 7 = 49$ because the 49ers are Sunshine's favorite football team. Both Sunshine and Fairytale use lots of praise when teaching and chatting with Ruby, and she loved it! It's so great to run into so many friends in Seiad Valley, and it goes to show how small this world is—at least our world on the trail.

Lingo amongst hikers is to call those going north, NOBO, and those heading south, SOBO. Adam coined a new phrase describing what we are doing as we hop around trying to avoid the snow: NoSnowBO. Maybe that should be his trail name.

We got shakes at the famous Seiad Valley Cafe. Poor Ruby didn't like the hazelnut flavor she chose, but the rest of us loved ours. I got the cheesecake flavor. It was the best!

The owner of the general store told Adam, "I know you are all trying to travel light, but those sticky lint rollers are really good for getting ticks off your clothes." We didn't take him seriously, but we should have! Poor Muir got the worst of it. Everyone except Adam had at least one tick removed.

It is a huge climb on the PCT as you leave Seiad Valley. Unfortunately, we got a late start because we needed to mail stuff home that we didn't want to carry. Hitting the trail close to 10 a.m., not drinking enough water, and taking lots of stops to take ticks off Muir and each other left us with headaches and slow progress. After 9.9 miles, we set up camp. Guthook shows we climbed nearly 5,000 feet, and it took its toll on us! We were exhausted and barely finished dinner before the rain and wind hit hard!

PCT Day #88

Our tents held up well in the storm last night, and we hit the trail around 7:30 a.m. We were camped near a stream, which disappeared into the earth underneath us. This section is full of springs bubbling up from the ground, causing us to be super curious about all the water flowing under our feet! We bought some dried crickets at a farmers' market, and we've been eating them for snacks in this section. Some facts about crickets: they have significantly more protein, Vitamin B-12, prebiotics, calcium, and iron than chicken, beef, or pork. Ruby said it best (while trying to convince Sierra to eat the crickets): "They taste like peanuts! Just don't look 'em in the eye!" The guy who sold us the crickets (from Evolution Ranch CrickEATS) gave us a discount if we promised to send him pictures of us eating them while hiking. He's trying to break into the hiker market.

On another note, our lunch was a complete failure. We had to quickly buy a few things to have enough food before we hit the trail and ended up with a few overpriced freeze-dried meals. The package said it served four, but that's a total joke! We had a "loaded baked potato" and a "cheesy macaroni," and we all ended up with maybe four bites. Good thing we had crickets though!

Today we got water from Bear Dog Spring. Seriously, some of the most delicious water on the whole trail was just bubbling straight out of the earth. Plus, Bear Dog should be Adam's trail name, am I right? (Adam's edit: "My third-great grandfather found his brother's body after he and a grizzly fought each other to the death. After that, he hunted grizzlies avidly. After chasing a wounded male grizzly into its den, he left to get a couple of other hunters to help him with his kill. He went into the den and killed the grizzly, as he started to haul the grizzly out, he saw another set of eyes. He quickly grabbed his gun and killed the mamma grizzly, only to find there were two cubs. He dragged the male out and then sent in the other two hunters to drag out the female, not mentioning the cubs. No sooner did they go in than the two hunters shot back out of the den running down the mountain, scared of the cubs. Later, they dragged the two bears down the mountain with the two cubs following. He built a den for the cubs and raised them to full size adults. The Native American people of the area would often stop by to visit Woodasatuck (their name for bear dog) and his bears and listen to his stories as he spoke their language and enjoyed their company." This story is from the life history of Ransom Asa Beecher). 14.2 miles today.

PCT Day #89

"In nature, nothing is perfect, and everything is perfect. Trees can be contorted, bent in weird ways, and they're still beautiful."
—*Alice Walker*

We camped near the snow line last night at about 6,300 feet. It was a beautiful spot, and Ruby got to build a snowman while we filtered water from the melting snow. We left camp around 7 a.m. with hopes of walking on hard ice and snow for as long as possible. At about 9 a.m., we met a group of guys hiking southbound who said they were Oregon State University students. They were backpacking for a few nights on their way to Seiad Valley. We were able to get valuable information from them about the trail from there to I-5. Turns out, the trail was super difficult to navigate when it was covered in snow. Fortunately, there were forest roads running nearly parallel, and those are much easier to follow. After hours of slowly trudging through slippery, slushy snow, we decided we needed a break! We found a snow-free intersection where the PCT crossed several forest roads. We took off our shoes, removed the insoles, took off wet socks, and set them all out to dry. Tristan and I made it over 800 miles with no blisters, but this day ruined my record. I had toe blisters forming in spots that are tricky to tape up.

As we were drying out and eating lunch, two four-wheelers pulled up. It was a member of the search and rescue team in the area and his wife. They were super kind and very impressed we were hiking as a family, and said something to the effect of, "Well, today is your lucky day!" We assumed this meant they left trail magic for hikers at the cabin that was about two miles ahead, but we were wrong. They rode off, and a few minutes later, a purple Jeep pulled up. A couple got out and said the other couple on the four-wheelers told them there was a family hiking the trail, and they wanted to come up and visit with us. We had a great time chatting with them for well over an hour. During that time another hiker walked up, and it turned out to be Blue, from Switzerland. We met him before in Kennedy Meadows, and when the Buffums gave Adam and Kaia a ride to Ridgecrest, Blue was hitchhiking and they picked him up. Blue said he had been following our footsteps today thinking, "Either the Bennetts are ahead of me, or it's a large tramily with a wolf following them!" (Muir's paw prints in the snow do look rather large.) We made it to the Donomore Cabin at about 3 p.m. Ruby was super disappointed that we weren't going to spend the night there. Someone has brought chairs and a cot to furnish it, and it is quite nice inside. Our friends, Good Cop, Hot Lips, M, and Chef got caught in a snowstorm here a week or so ago and spent about 24 hours in this cabin. They were so grateful it was here because about six inches of snow fell during that storm!

When we arrived at this tent site, .3 miles past the California/Oregon border, we had intended to keep hiking on. But Blue caught our attention, waving his arms and jogging towards us. He said he had hiked ahead about a mile and found there was lots of slushy snow. He doubled back, deciding to camp here and hit the snow early in the morning when it was harder. It didn't take any convincing for us to decide to do the same!

PCT Day #90

"The best way out is always through." —Robert Frost

I'm trying out the Injinji toe socks (under my Darn Tough Vermont socks) to see if they help with blisters. So far so good! We left camp at 6:51 a.m. Blue left at 6:30, leaving footprints for us to follow. After about a mile, we put on our microspikes for the first time. They work really well if the snow has an icy crust, but if it is slushy, they are useless. Observation Peak is right next to the trail, so we decided to go all the way to the top (about 7,400 feet at the summit). The views were breathtaking! From the peak, we did a quick descent to a forest road. There, it looked like the trail stayed dry, south facing, dropping in elevation. Wrong. We spent 45 minutes battling along, trying to find footprints to follow, slipping into tree wells, and only made it half a mile. We climbed straight up a ridge and over the other side until we got back to the road so that we could safely move forward. I wish I would have taken pictures during this part, but I was too focused on staying alive! It ended up being a 16.2-mile day. This is a big deal for us because the snow was tricky and really slowed us down. We've found hiking on snow to be so hard on our feet, ankles, and knees! We camped at an awesome shelter and were able to safely hang all our food/gear to protect it from the "mini bears" (mice). The sunset with Mt. Shasta in the background was phenomenal!

PCT Day #91

It was another great day with views of Mt. Shasta. It's funny how the trail takes a hard turn to the east in southern Oregon as we follow the "crest." This gives us a view of Shasta to the south for about 40 miles! We had planned to get to I-5, hitch a ride to Ashland or Medford, and then take a Greyhound bus to Portland. When I looked online two days ago it looked like the bus fare would only be $23 each, but I couldn't book it. When Adam called today, Greyhound told him it would be over $400 for the five of us! Our next plan was to have Le Anne come get us, borrowing Adam's sister Meagan's 15-passenger van. It was a huge hassle for them, but they so lovingly obliged!

As we came to a trailhead, about six miles from I-5, we met Judy and Jane. These sweet ladies were out for a day hike and asked if we were thru-hiking. When we told them our story, they said the nicest things, like, "Kids, you have awesome parents!" We talked with them for at least 20 minutes and asked if they would snap a quick photo for us.

We made it to I-5 and walked under the highway to get to the Callahan Lodge. Here they offer free drinks to hikers and a variety of "Hiker Services" (but ask that you don't take a bath in the bathroom sink).

We needed to get to Ashland where we were going to meet Le Anne. We tried to hitch, but to no avail. Lucky for us, a trail angel had left his number with the front desk at Callahan's. Even though it took him two trips, he happily got us all to the Ashland Albertsons. While loitering at the tables inside and eating chips, salsa, pickles, and a half gallon of Moose Tracks Extreme Chocolate ice cream, the manager stopped by to talk with us. She asked if we were hiking the PCT as a family, (with our selection of food, she must have figured we were all hikers), then sat down to tell us a great story. She said her daughter, Amanda, had passed away two years earlier. When the manager was pregnant, she was in a car crash, which resulted in health problems for her baby. Amanda had frequent seizures and never learned to walk or talk. One night, she peacefully passed away in her sleep. Her mom, Shawnna, had the idea to share Amanda's ashes with friends and family as they traveled the world. "Take Amanda with you" became the theme, and Shawnna was so surprised at how quickly it spread. Amanda's ashes ended up in several different countries and states. One morning, Shawnna thought it would be so wonderful if a PCT hiker would take Amanda's ashes along with them. That day she put a bag of ashes in her pocket and went to work. Long story short, she met a hiker from Boston and explained her story, and he said he would be honored to take Amanda's ashes. She said this hiker would send her pictures and updates often but was blocked from the last 30 miles of the trail because of a fire. He asked her permission to stop there and finish the hike the next year, which he did. By the time Shawnna finished telling this story, we all had tears in our eyes. "I think what you are doing as a family is awesome," she said. "I just felt inspired to come over and tell you about Amanda."

PCT Days #92–93

After taking care of zero-day chores on Wednesday (laundry, resupply, emptying out backpacks and washing them, etc.), Le Anne drove us about two hours south of her house to Lola Pass in Oregon on Thursday. It certainly is difficult for Le Anne to not be joining us on this section, but her broken foot from her time on the PCT in March still isn't healed up. We are so very grateful for her help shuttling us around instead (not as much fun for her, though).

Ruby was having a very hard time! It was hard to say, "See you later" to Grandma (her favorite tent mate) and hard to think about the cousins she was missing and all the "normal kid" things she was not participating in at this time of year. She also heard me say that rain and snow were in the forecast, and no one was looking forward to that. It took about 20 minutes and a lot of persuading, but we got her moving forward on the trail. Adam knows best how to help her "flip the switch," as we say, and improve her mood.

The flowers were so bright and vibrant! Bear grass, rhododendrons, trilliums, and others were in full bloom. It almost made up for the fact that our view of Mt. Hood (which should have been grandiose) was hidden by rain clouds. There were several stretches of trail that were snow-covered, slippery, and steep!

A barricade was blocking the Eagle Creek trail. We checked online before starting this section to see if this trail would be open and couldn't find anything saying it was closed. We had hoped to take this trail because it has beautiful waterfalls, and it cuts five miles off our route into Cascade Locks. There was a fire in this area, started by a 15-year-old throwing fireworks into the forest in September of 2017 during a fire ban. The fire burned over 50,000 acres and burned for three months! It was so sad to see all the destruction and the plethora of trails that may be closed to hikers for years.

That night at camp after we had finished dinner and set up, three section hikers walked in. We had met them earlier in the day while they had their lunch spread out on the trail in our way (something we do all the time, so we totally understood). One was limping badly and said he had slipped on the snow and overextended his knee. They found an area to camp not too far from us and started a smokey campfire (not illegal right now in Oregon).

We also met a thru-hiker named Gary who does daily online trail updates. He and two hikers from Australia in his tramily had also hiked to Kennedy Meadows and flipped north to avoid the snow in the Sierras. They were headed south from Cascade Locks, so we are interested to see what snow they encounter in Oregon. We covered 13.4 miles from 12 p.m. to about 6:30, which is pretty good!

PCT Day #94

This was a rain, snow, and hail with a speck of sunshine kind of day. I was afraid of what the change in weather would do to morale, but everyone did great. We stayed in our tents until about 8 a.m., waiting for a rain-free window to pack up. We hit it just about right. At about 7:40 a.m. we heard the group of three guys leaving camp. They came to my and Adam's tent, asking for advice for the best way to get the guy with an injured knee a hitch into town. Adam told them which road they should follow to a trailhead, with hopes that they'd find a day hiker to drive them into Cascade Locks. We arrived in the parking lot a few hours later, just in time to see that they did indeed find a ride (and were so very happy about it). Two other day hikers greeted us. One was smiling as the rain came pouring down and said to us, "It's a perfect Oregon day! What a great Friday to be out for a hike." I wasn't in a foul mood by any means but hearing that and seeing her giant smile certainly gave me a boost. I think her positive comments were infectious, and the kids caught on too. It is always so impressive to see the vibrant colors the rain brings out.

When we stopped for an afternoon snack, I popped a Milk Dud in my mouth (I never eat those), and moments later a crown on one of my teeth popped off. I saved it in a little zip lock, looking forward to visiting a dentist soon, somehow.

We sauntered into Cascade Locks at about 7 p.m., water sloshing in our shoes with every step. Wonderful Le Anne had dropped a resupply off here for us at the Ale House (she checked with four different places before finding this restaurant that would hold our box for us). Inside, a sweet trail angel named Jules greeted us, gave us our box, and showed us the Ale House's hiker box. It was like opening Christmas stockings! The hiker box had Trader Joe's chocolate covered berries, a huge variety of single-serve nut butters, a delicious trail mix from India, cashews, and more! Then we stayed and got pizza, and everyone was very happy. A campsite next to the train tracks and the Columbia River only charges $5 per tent for PCT hikers, so we had a place for the night (with a super loud train going past us on occasion).

PCT Day #95

Crossing the Bridge of the Gods into Washington was a highlight of this hike! Most of the bridge is a grate, so Muir had to be carried. The views were awesome! I was worried about Tristan, who has a fear of heights. I told him, "Don't look down!" so he immediately looked down. He surprised me by saying, "This is so beautiful!" Even though it was overcast, it was a hot day. We were sweating like we were in the rainforest. There was so much green! As we made the 4,655-foot climb away from the Columbia River, we passed several day hikers who asked us where we were headed. When we replied, "To Canada!" we got a lot of mixed responses. One guy said, "You are going the wrong way." We laughed and hiked on (but when he was out of sight, I quickly checked the GPS just in case). Maybe he meant the correct way to get to Canada is by car or plane, but what fun is that? Four groups told us about a bear sighting, but we never saw it ourselves.

PCT Day #96

The sunlight shining through the leaves onto our tents this morning will always be one of my favorite memories. I'm usually awake by 5 a.m., but this morning I slept in until almost 6, waking slowly to the sound of singing birds and sunlight on the tent. It was heavenly! Adam and I hiked this section of trail with his brother, Brind, his nephew, Jackson, and our brother-in-law, Jason, in 2014. We kept passing spots and saying things like, "Remember when we met Happy Feet right here?" or "Remember when we camped right here, and that group of thru-hikers passed us?" Adam said, "Remember when we were all out of water and Jason filtered water for all of us right here because he was the only one with a pump filter that could collect the water out of a small puddle?" Even though the wildflowers are different here in June than the ones I remember in July of 2014, it is still just as beautiful. I think if you have any desire to hike even a small part of the PCT, it should be this section from the Bridge of the Gods to Panther Creek. It's just amazing. You don't even understand green until you are in Washington and see ferns growing out of green moss-covered trees: green is crammed into every nook and cranny. Sitting here to filter water most certainly "filled up our senses," as John Denver would say!

I'm losing my resolve to eat crickets. I've been accused more than once that I believe everything I read. The back of the cricket package is very convincing that crickets are the perfect backpacking snack. But we ran out of the pesto flavored ones, and mixing just plain crickets with dried edamame doesn't do it for me. Plus, to get the 13 grams of protein, you must eat 8 ounces of crickets! That's a lot. I've been tapping out after two handfuls. Maybe I need to just go with the powdered version, so I don't have to think about the little legs and wings and such. Or it's time to find a new snack. 16.7 miles today.

PCT Day #97

"Ferns are my love language." —*Meagan Jean Bennett Allen*

5 a.m. wake up today! We knew we had a lot of trail to cover, a big climb, and a hot day, and we wanted to get away from this campsite near Trout Creek (poor Sierra had an unfortunate encounter with unburied human poo; I'll say no more).

My sister-in-law, Meagan, recently said that ferns are her love language. I'm beginning to feel the same! Today we had an awesome view of Mt. Adams! It is such a thrill to climb and climb and reach the viewpoint to see another breathtaking, snow-covered peak. It was another uphill day! I wish I could say these climbs are getting easier. 16.5 miles today.

PCT Day #98

I've never seen Tristan pack up so fast! He says it was because he got a lot of sleep and the night and morning were warm. ("It saved me at least 15 minutes because I slept in my shorts and I didn't have to pack my pajamas or my puffy!") We might have set a speed record, at least for our team. It was the lure of knowing that Le Anne was on her way to pick us up and that the kids were going to get to play with cousins! We made it just under 5 miles in just under two hours (with a water filter stop).

The battle against the mosquitoes was real while we waited for Le Anne. Sierra put on everything she owned! Tristan was distracted listening to his book, didn't react fast enough, and got at least 30 bites.

When Le Anne arrived, there was much rejoicing (she had giant homemade rice crispy treats). Now we zero for about five days, enjoy time with family, and watch the snow report to see which way is safe to head next! 4.8 miles today.

PCT Days #99–104

We had five blissful zero days in Battle Ground, playing with the Allens, Willmores, and Bennetts (Adam's family). I also got to visit a dentist to get my crown glued back in place. Thanks again, Discovery Dental!

It was hard to get back on the trail! On Monday, we told Le Anne we would be ready to roll at 8 a.m., but we didn't leave until 11:30 a.m. She patiently waited, allowing us to hijack her entire day yet again, and even made us a giant batch of her famous chocolate chip cookies!

We got to the trailhead at mile 2,198.4 and took off around 3 p.m., so excited to have our nephew Cole with us (and sad that Le Anne's foot still isn't healed enough to join us). The mosquitoes were unreal! We walked briskly to keep them at bay, and when that didn't work, we stopped so some could put on bug nets and long sleeves and pants (all the while frantically swatting the vicious blood suckers off of ourselves and each other). We know June is a rough month for backpacking, especially during wet years like this one, because of the mosquitoes. But we must press on! Adam saw one critical comment on a Facebook post about PCT hikers attempting to flip-flop this year, something to the effect of "These hikers are going to flip over the Sierras just in time to hit gnat season in NorCal, the ticks in Oregon, and the mosquitoes in Washington." That seems about right. Before Kaia flew home from Colorado on Saturday, she and Gram (my mom's mom) made a big batch of Gram's famous cinnamon rolls and stuffed them into seven empty Pringle's cans. It was a total success and brought much happiness to have such a treat on our first night out (some ate their portions much more quickly than others)! 7.4 miles today.

PCT Day #105

It was a cold morning! We managed to get out of camp around 7:30 a.m., moving as quickly as we could against the cold, misty wind. Patches of snow soon became huge fields of snow, making navigating tricky. We passed Mosquito Creek, and it truly lived up to its name! We always filter water with our bug nets on lately. They protect your head well, but the mosquitoes can certainly bite through clothing if you don't quickly put on multiple layers!

Tonight, we camped at the lovely Steamboat Lake. After dinner we were surprised to see a paddle board out in the water with an optimistic fisherman balanced on top. As far as we could tell, he didn't catch anything, but it was fun to watch. Silly Ruby ate all her candy (Swedish fish and sour patch kids) that was supposed to last for six days all at once and threw up right before bed. She started feeling sick right after dinner, kept asking me if we could hit the SOS button on my Spot device, then had me hold her hand until her body had expelled every bit of red dye #40. No more Swedish fish for trail snacks from here on out! 16.1 miles today.

PCT Day #106

"The farther one gets into the wilderness, the greater is the attraction of its lonely freedom." —Teddy Roosevelt

I just love getting water from these lovely Washington streams! We crossed mile 2,222.2 today! Trail conditions were dry until about 6,000 feet. Everyone was slipping and falling (except Adam). At one point Cole and Sierra both fell at about the same time, and their water bottles came tumbling out of their packs. Luckily, the water bottles didn't slide too far and were easy to retrieve. That slowed us down significantly, and everyone was extra tired and hungry when we got to camp. We met a hiker named Tough Cookie. She started March 26 at the southern terminus with her husband. They made it to Walker Pass, and he said he had enough. She was hiking south from Fish Lake, hoping snow would melt as she slowly moves along. A ranger for the Mt. Adam's Forest asked her which way she was going on the PCT, glad to hear she was headed south. The ranger told her there was still a lot of snow on the trail to the north. She also told us there was a 20% chance of rain tomorrow. We only got a quick peek at Mt. Adams before the clouds socked us in. 17.6 miles today.

PCT Day #107

"Snowflakes are one of nature's most fragile things, but just look what they can do when they stick together." —Vesta M. Kelly

20% chance of rain turned into 100% snow. It snowed all night, and it was dang cold! Lucky for us, there was very little wind. We've been rallying the troops around 6 a.m., but today we let them sleep until 7 (hoping the snow would stop falling, but it didn't). I think most were up around 6, dreading leaving their warm sleeping bags (at least that was what I was feeling). It took us two whole hours to break camp. Seven out of eight of us had frozen fingers and toes that wouldn't work fast enough (Muir was frolicking in the snow, playing with sticks, eating "snow cones," acting like it was the best day of his life). Adam and I had studied the map and knew of several "bailout points," where we could take trails to lower elevations and forest roads. Navigating out of camp was tricky. The trail at about 5,800 feet was already snow-covered in patches, and the freshly fallen snow hid the path even more.

We had intended to hike three miles to Adams Creek to see if it was passable (Adam, Muir, his brother and brother's dog, Dunkin, hiked this section of the PCT five years ago and had to turn around at Adams Creek when they couldn't get across). After .3 miles we were frustrated with the snow and worried about the cold, wet feet (everyone but Cole and Tristan are in non-insulated Altra trail runners). We took the Riley Creek Trail and quickly dropped elevation. As we hiked along, I heard Cole tell the girls this was like being in a video game (I think he said Halo 3) because of all the snow. Later he told me, "I love the snow. This is fun!" Morale was high, and everyone was joking and laughing.

We hit Forest Road 23 just in time for lunch. We spread out our wet tents, filtered water from a nearby stream, and had our Hiker Pad Thai. Several vehicles passed. One lady slowed down enough to give us the "okay" sign, and we just nodded that we were indeed okay. Since we have plenty of food (2.5 days' worth) to eat before we pick up the resupply we mailed to White Pass, Adam and I told the kids we weren't going to try to catch a hitch. As we walked down the road, the kids were sticking up their thumbs anyway at the passing cars. "It's no big deal; no one is going to stop to pick up seven hikers and a dog," I thought— until about an hour into our road walk a nice guy in a Sprinter van did stop. He asked Cole if we needed help, and Cole pointed to Adam and said, "Ask that guy. He knows everything." Adam chatted with the driver, Troy, for a while, while the rest of us hung back, trying not to get our hopes up. Long story short, Troy and his twin sons, who are seven years old, are on their way up to a Sprinter van convention (it has a better name than that; I just can't remember it) near Leavenworth, Washington. They are taking back roads, camping, and biking along the way. Troy has designed some kits to convert Sprinter vans into all sorts of things (like ways to store your bikes with a bed on top, etc.) and is looking at turning this hobby into a business. Sierra was so excited to be in the van, listening to all the design ideas and plans. Owning a Sprinter van like this has been her dream for years! Troy helped us load all our gear into the van, we squeezed in with his sons, and he drove us to a nearby lake with a campground. Tomorrow he is going to drive us to White Pass, where we can reconnect with the PCT (it just so happens to be right on his way to Leavenworth). He saved us from a 40+ mile road walk, several nights spent on the side of the road, and a difficult hitch when we got to Highway 12 into White Pass. The trail provides! Approximately 14 miles today.

PCT Day #108

Rolling in the sweet Sprinter van with our new friends was awesome! Our ride dropped us off at the restaurant at the top of White Pass named "Cracker Barrel." It's not a real Cracker Barrel with delicious pancakes, but this place did have awesome "everything" pizzas. It was here that Adam took on the trail name Kidnapper. I strongly dislike the name, but he thinks it is hilarious (and he's not a big fan of my trail name either. He says "Wildflower" is too common of a name and we've never met another Kidnapper on trail). He does have more kids on the trail than anyone we've met (and Cole is supposedly here against his will). We walked down to the trailhead and enjoyed drying out in the sunshine for a bit. As we were about to walk into the woods, a motorcycle drove up, and the driver said, "The Bennetts!" Turns out we had met Mona and her husband in Warner Springs, and she had been seeing our names on trail registers and was so excited to finally catch up to us! We headed south into the Goat Rocks Wilderness, and Mona went north. We hiked in a few miles and decided to stop at a lovely lake. Tristan and Sierra took a quick swim. The kids had a lot of fun tonight. I wish I could have bottled up their laughter to save for later. They played cards, made "hot chocolate" from protein powder that tastes like dirt, and watched a movie on Sierra's phone. The girls wouldn't let the boys in their tent for the movie watching, so they stuck their heads under the vestibule to watch from the outside.

PCT Day #109

It was a beautiful morning at Ginnette Lake. Do you think our socks will dry out overnight? Wishful thinking.

PCT Day #110

I honestly didn't take any notes on this day. I do remember the disappointment of entering Mt. Rainer National Park and not being able to see the massive mountain through the clouds. We also saw a lot of dog and/or big cat prints in the snow as we trudged through here. It was eerie to think a mountain lion might be following the hikers just ahead of us! Dewey Lake was a spectacular sight and a great spot to set up camp.

PCT Day #111

The sun came out today, and we've never been so happy to feel its warmth!

PCT Day #112

It was a rough night for me. I usually have no problem warming up once I get into the quilt I share with Adam; he is a furnace. But he was also cold (and he slept with his rain jacket on, thus keeping all his warmth to himself, I later learned). I couldn't get warm enough to sleep. I lay there thinking of how we could backtrack to Chinook Pass, hitchhike to Enumclaw, get a hotel room, warm up, and wait for someone to come rescue us (for the record, this is the only time in the four years of hiking long-distance trails that I contemplated giving up). Miraculously, when the sun rose the next morning, it was warm, and my attitude had changed. Cole was the first one packed up and ready! We hiked through a forest that had been victim of a recent fire. So many downed trees lay as obstacles across the trail. There were so many wildflowers blooming; the contrast between their bright colors and the black burned logs was striking.

We met five other hikers that had flipped north from the Sierras: Arc, Big Mama, Raspberry, Woodpecker, and their friend (whose name I forgot) all started at Snoqualmie Pass and were headed south. It was fun to chat with them, and they told us there was trail magic at an old cabin up ahead. The kids have never hiked so fast!

There were indeed sodas and small bags of chips waiting for us at Urich Cabin! We were able to wash some clothes in the stream and dry them over the wood stove. (The cabin filled with smoke, but we slept with the door open, and it was so nice to be out of the rain!) 12.8 miles today.

PCT Day #113

Rain hit hard in the morning, and we thought we would be in it all day. Then the sun surprised us and came out just for elevensies through lunch. We heard the thunder getting closer and the dark clouds approaching, so we wrapped up lunch and put on our rain gear. It was so hard for us to be cold and wet all afternoon, knowing that the forecast was calling for rain for the next three days! Washington has really been challenging this way: cold, wet, and with clouds socking us in when we know there are great views we are missing. It was a tragic dinner tonight. I was trying to balance the cookpot with Knorr rice (2.5 quarts full to the brim) on the tiny stove while holding my umbrella. Just as I was ready to dish everyone up, I accidentally knocked the stove over, spilling almost half of the precious contents. I started crying out of frustration and poor Cole did his best to help me salvage as much rice as possible. The rest we had to bury. 17.1 miles today.

PCT Day #114

"The best thing one can do when it's raining is to let it rain." —Henry Wadsworth Longfellow

I haven't heard Ruby complain for days, the bear grass flowers are phenomenal, and I'm doing my best to enjoy the rain. We walked an extra two miles searching for a camp spot big enough for our three tents tonight. 17.8 miles today.

PCT Day #115

"The forest is a quiet place if only the best birds sing." —Kay Johnson

Lots of noisy birds and forest sounds wake us in the early morning. Yesterday it was a crow and a raven (Adam said) at about 5 a.m. Today a plethora of birds started their songs at about 4 a.m., some sweet and melodic and some screeching. Then there was a sound like an elk with a cold blowing its nose several times nearby (we never found out what it really was!). We arrived at the much-anticipated Pancake House in Snoqualmie Pass only to be greeted by our YouTube hero, Dixie! She has the best videos about backpacking. I watched all of them while walking on the treadmill at the YMCA this winter prepping for this hike (check out her Homemade Wanderlust channel). She spotted the kids and came out to ask if they were "thru-hikers" and get trail condition info. It was so much fun to chat with her!

Adam had been telling us stories about this Pancake House for several days. When he was in high school, he taught ski lessons here at Snoqualmie every Saturday. He would drive a few of his siblings and friends up here, and after teaching they would all ski until the lifts closed, and then hit another resort for night skiing. Afterwards they would always stop by the Pancake House for toast and hot chocolate (because it only cost a dollar). The cost has gone up in the last 25 years, so instead of toast and hot chocolate (which none of us wanted anyway), we got desserts (which we don't recommend).

Then our friend Ryan Fredell pulled up in a big white bus he borrowed just to rescue us! He yelled, "Jump in!" and we all happily obliged, giddy about being able to go to the Fredell's house for hot showers, laundry, and a night out of the weather. Ryan even had a cooler stocked with pop, Gatorade, and water! He fed us fresh cherries too. It was so great to visit with the Fredells, eat a yummy, homemade meal with them (plus Ryan made us the best Snickerdoodle cookies I've ever tasted), get all cleaned up, and let the kids swim and watch tv with their friends. Whether they wanted to or not, the Fredells have obtained a very high trail angel status in our book! 11.2 miles today.

PCT Day #116

"You don't win friends with salad." —Homer Simpson

We have been so spoiled on this adventure by friends, family, and trail angels! We woke up, and Ryan said, "I'm going to make 'Bennett Heart Attack Hashbrowns' for you guys!" Years ago, when we lived in Colorado and would go on camping trips with the Fredells and other friends, Adam would make his famous hashbrowns (which are pretty much just potatoes and onions with bacon, sausage, and any other meat available). They were delicious. Lauren made pancakes and whipped up some fresh whipping cream to go with Ryan's homemade berry syrup. It was an absolutely divine breakfast. Cole said, "When you told me they were good cooks, I thought you just meant the wife! The dad can really cook too!" Not only did they feed us really well, but we also got to shower, do laundry, and sleep on luxurious mattresses. Plus, they gave us much-needed items like gallon-sized zip-lock bags, toothpaste, and individual bags of candy! Lauren even ran to the sporting goods store and got the fuel we needed for our stove. We have hot meals for another week! But better than all of that, we got a huge morale boost from visiting with awesome friends.

Ryan drove us back to the trail in the school bus, and we started hiking around 11 a.m. It was crowded on the trail, typical for a Saturday at a popular trailhead near Seattle, I suppose. Ruby had fallen asleep in the bus on the drive and was really dragging all day. If she slows down, the whole group must slow down, and that really annoys the faster, older kids. Plus, we did about 4,000 feet of elevation gain today, and it was hard work! We got to see some of the absolutely most breathtaking views of the entire trail!

One week before our wedding, almost exactly 19 years ago, Adam and I did a 50-mile backpacking trip here with his mom, brother, two sisters, a nephew, and friends. I think it was a litmus test to see how I fit into the family; I'm so glad I passed. 9.1 miles today.

PCT Day #117

I stand corrected. This day had the most beautiful views we've yet experienced on the PCT. I wish I would have taken more pictures! We had our first view of Mt. Rainier! We stopped here for a bit so Adam could explain to us the two different routes he took when he summited this mountain twice, many years ago. 17.5 miles today.

PCT Day #118

"May your trails be crooked, winding, lonesome, dangerous, leading to the most amazing view. May your mountains rise into and above the clouds." —Edward Abbey

We had another big climb at the end of a long day! These kids are so impressively strong; if they didn't have to slow down and wait for the adults, they'd be to Canada by now!

PCT Day #119

"Although I deeply love oceans, deserts, and other wild landscapes, it is only mountains that beckon me with that sort of painful magnetic pull to walk deeper and deeper into their beauty." —*Victoria Erikson*

A fast-flowing river crossing was the most exciting event of the day! We had been warned by other hikers that there were some tricky crossings ahead. Today's crossing was a lot of fun because we could jump over the river on big rocks without getting wet! Cole went across first, dropped his pack, and came back to help the rest of us. It was cold and raining when we got to camp. We had another night of making dinner in the rain. We are really looking forward to getting into town tomorrow!

PCT Day #120–121

"Traveling in the company of those we love is home in motion." —*Leigh Hunt*

It drizzled on us all night. We packed up wet tents in a hurry with a pep in our step, knowing we were going to be eating "town food" soon! The PCT goes right past the Stevens Pass ski resort. We stopped here for our elevensies snack. But the wind was fierce, so we didn't linger long. We split into two groups to hitch into Leavenworth. Adam, Tristan, Ruby, and Muir got picked up first, which caused much jealousy in the rest of us! It didn't take long, though, and Cole, Kaia, Sierra, and I got a ride. A very nice guy on his way to Wenatchee to visit his parents for the Fourth of July picked us up and told us all about the tomato growing contest he and his dad have going on between them.

We got to stay in a hotel! Hot showers! Laundry! Pool! Hot tub! Food! And best of all, lots of fun cousins, aunts, uncles and Grandma Le Anne met us there! Leavenworth is such a beautiful Bavarian town, one of my very favorite places to visit. They had a great event for the Fourth of July, too. Main Street was closed to cars, and they had it all set up with bouncy castles, games, free popcorn, snow cones, and cotton candy! If you ever get the chance to eat brats and pretzels at the München Haus, do it! I'd been daydreaming about this meal for 100 miles, and it was every bit as delicious as I'd hoped!

PCT Day #122

We are so excited to have Le Anne and Cole with us for this section! We slept in an RV Park at Stevens Pass that hadn't opened for the season yet. There were four RVs there, one of which had a great propane fire going and a few people sitting around. They asked us a bunch of questions about our hike thus far, and then offered us some water bottles. Later, they lit off a few small fireworks, which was exciting since those were the only ones we'd seen (they are banned in this part of Washington).

Our tent stakes wouldn't go into the road base, so we all had to scavenge around for rocks. It worked! A group of three hikers walked in and set up nearby. Adam asked if they were thru-hiking, and they misunderstood the question. "Yes, we are done hiking for today," one said. Kaia and I thought that was so funny.

It was a busy day on the trail headed out of Stevens Pass: lots of day hikers, southbounders, and people going out for a night or two. It was slow going with lots of fallen trees and obstacles in places. We hiked through a misty fog most of the afternoon and evening.

After we made it into camp, got all four tents set up, and were just finishing up dinner, a hiker named Sam asked if he could camp near us. He was a super nice kid who said he was from LA, I believe. He also started at the southern terminus but flipped up to Canada to go southbound a few weeks ago. I ended up making a double batch of dinner and had an extra serving no one wanted. We offered it to Sam, and he gratefully accepted. He was down to his last serving of beans and rice and was worried about being too hungry to fall asleep! We never have leftovers at dinner, so this worked out perfectly. The trail provides! He is headed into Leavenworth tomorrow to resupply at the Safeway. I told him he should stop by the München Haus for a brat and pretzel, too.

It was raining again while we ate dinner, but Sierra and Kaia stayed with me to keep me company and help clean up. Too often I feel badly that the kids are too cold and let them eat quickly and disappear into their tents to get warm for the night. I need to stop that because I get burned out, and "many hands make light work," right? 17.9 miles today.

PCT Day #123

I woke everyone up around 6:20 a.m., and we bounced out of camp at 8. The sun was trying so hard to peek through those clouds, but it was overcast (with a cold wind) until lunchtime. The sun coming out makes all the difference in attitudes and happiness levels (maybe just mine).

Ruby found a nest with four eggs next to the trail after the frightened mama bird rushed by and almost flew into her! There are lots of marmots around! Their high-pitched scream/whistle always makes me jump.

We decided to have dinner at Lake Sally Ann, 1.1 miles before camp. This worked out great because we had a lovely view of the lake and waterfall. We took our time to enjoy one another's company, read scriptures, have the dessert Adam prepared (chocolate chips on a spoonful of peanut butter), and get everything cleaned up without kids rushing off to get into their tents. Plus, we got to rest up a bit before the last climb of the day. (There was so much steep elevation gain today! It was exhausting!)

We camped in the clouds at 5,700 feet tonight. A hiker named Rattlebones rolled into camp and chatted with us for a while through our open tent flap. He's a teacher in California and was talking about how many other teachers he had met on the trail (as have we). He also spent a lot of time talking up the food in Stehekin. Oh, my goodness, we are looking forward to that bakery! I guess if you stay at the Stehekin Valley Ranch, the shuttle ride and a few delicious meals are included, but it costs over $100 per person per night. When we explained to Rattlebones how many people are in our group, he was astonished. He said he thought most thru-hikers were solo, and the biggest group he has seen is four guys. Our circus doubles that and adds a dog (who was doing his best to bark during the entire conversation). 14.5 miles today.

PCT Day #124

"We've got a motto here—you're tougher than you think you are and you can do more than you think you can." —Christopher McDougall

It was cold, and my hopes for a bright, clear morning were drowned in the fog. We were entering the famous Glacier Peak

Wilderness, yet no views could be seen. We met a hiker with the trail name of Locohontas, who recognized us from our YouTube videos. I told her I've really dropped the ball there because the trail in Washington has been so remote (plus there are so many other things to do during my down time). She said, "You've got to put your family first, of course, but when you can keep doing the videos because you'll inspire a lot of families to get out here!" So, we will.

Today was a big day: we climbed up and over the infamous Red Pass. We'd heard mixed reports about the snow conditions in this pass, and when we finally arrived, it was pouring rain. Fortunately, we didn't need our micro spikes and made it up and over the pass without incident. However, a few of the stream crossings before we hit camp gave us some trouble. Both Le Anne and Tristan fell into a stream (there were several very tricky crossings), and water flowed into their backpacks. Miraculously none of their sleep systems got wet (with the help of waterproof bags of course). About two miles before we camped, the trail turned into "the Pacific Creek Trail." This section is affectionately known for having a creek run through the trail, several inches deep. There was no way to stay dry today. When we finally got our tents set up, Le Anne reminded us of the dangers of hypothermia, and we changed into dry clothes (all but Adam, who graciously made us dinner in the rain). Everyone helped with cleanup and nighttime chores, and it got done in a hurry. I was impressed with the kids for keeping their humor and joking around together at dinner, despite having a wet, miserable day! 16 miles today.

PCT Day #125

It wasn't raining when we woke up! But nothing dried out overnight, naturally. Getting into wet hiking clothes, socks, and shoes still ranks as one of my least favorite activities. We had some exciting river crossings today too. Even though it was broken, we were so grateful to have access to a bridge at Milk Creek! This creek is glacier melt, filled with fine-grained particles of rock that is sometimes called glacial milk—according to Wikipedia. Some serious obstacles blocked our path (blown-down trees and washed-out bridges)! The mud was super slippery, and more than one of us fell. Today's biggest challenge was going up and over Fire Creek Pass. It was absolutely breathtaking! The snow wasn't bad at all—just small patches with nice, deep footprints to follow. I have a great video of Le Anne saying, "I can do this! I can do this!" And she did! Mica Lake is a glacial lake, almost completely frozen, and it's quite a sight to see! 15 miles today.

PCT Day #126

We didn't get the most level night's sleep, but we were so grateful to even have a tent spot! It was so exciting to come up over a rise in the trail and see both the top of Glacier Peak and a sun halo! Our friend Ricky Bobby, who we met in Wildwood, is headed southbound. It was so fun to run into him! We also met up with Kermit, a hiker from Poland that we hung out with at Hiker Heaven. He was there for 22 days with an injured leg but is now back on the trail headed southbound. 15 miles today.

PCT Day #127

Tonight, we camped by the Suiattle River. We arrived just as a southbound group was setting up their two tents and sweet talked them into moving over a bit so we could squeeze our four tents in too. Adam said it was the stinkiest camp thus far (very poorly buried poop), and we got out of there as fast as we could in the morning. Lucky for us, we hit Cloudy Pass on a cloudy day! 100 miles from Canada! 16.5 miles today.

PCT Days #128–129

"Injuries are our best teachers." —Scott Jurek

What a pair of eventful days! We had big obstacles (the bridge was washed out), and poor Le Anne was having trouble with her knee (at least that's what she thought). Before I try to sum up what happened today, I need to make sure you know there isn't a woman on this earth tougher than Le Anne! In fact, her trail name is Darn Tough. She knew she had hurt her knee yesterday and that we had to get to a ranger station to catch a bus into Stehekin (with buses only running at

3 p.m. and 6 p.m.), so she woke up very early and started hiking before the rest of us. The trouble was that she could only hike about a quarter of a mile per hour, and after a few hours, she had to slow down even more. We split into two groups: I rushed ahead with the teenagers to catch the 3 p.m. bus (to call Ellery to let him know Le Anne was injured and he needed to come pick her and Cole up from the Chelan ferry), and Adam, Ruby, Muir, and Le Anne stayed together (hoping to make it the 14.5 miles in time to catch the 6 p.m. bus).

After the teenagers and I passed Le Anne at 7:30 a.m., only about a mile from where we left camp, we knew she was going to need some serious help. There is no cell phone coverage in this remote area, which really complicated the situation. Adam and I were able to communicate by sending messages with hikers who were moving north and south. I sent a message back saying I would find help, and he sent a message forward telling me that they were about 10 miles back and to not try to bring them food.

At about 3 p.m. Adam knew they were moving too slowly, and he needed to get help. He set Ruby and Le Anne up with his tent and all his food, left Muir there to protect them, and started running. He made it 9.5 miles in about three hours but missed the 6 p.m. bus by less than five minutes (he said he could hear the bus doors closing as he ran down the dirt road to the bus stop)! Tristan and I were on that bus; if only we had known!

It all worked out though because Adam started walking into town and got to see a really big black bear and then was picked up by a local couple. When he explained our situation, they knew just what to do. They took him to Colter, a fourth-generation Stehekin resident who has horses and does backcountry rescues. His company is called Stehekin Outfitters (operating since 1947!) and they specialize in High Country Adventure (horseback riding trips and hiking) and occasionally help with backcountry rescue.

The next day, Colter, Adam, and two horses went about 9.5 miles south on the trail and found Le Anne, Ruby, and Muir. They had been hiking for several hours and only made it a half mile! Grandma told Ruby that they weren't going to just sit down and wait to be rescued, and if they only made it half a mile, that would still be a mile less that Adam had to hike back for them. Fortunately, Le Anne had sandals with her to wear because her boots had given her giant blisters. Colter put Ruby on his horse and Le Anne on the horse Adam rode. Ruby would later say this was her favorite 10 mile section of the PCT.

Meanwhile, back in Stehekin the teenagers were swimming in Lake Chelan and helping me with zero-day chores. Our friends, the Tomcos, sent us a care package in Stehekin. There was much rejoicing! Some of the treats were consumed before I even saw the box! Stehekin is so remote it can only be reached by ferry, float plane, or hiking. The general store is not very hiker friendly, and everything is so expensive (a pint of cottage cheese was $11). It was awesome to have this package of treats from the Tomcos to add to our resupply for the next five days (81 miles until we reach Canada)! 14.8 miles today. (P.S. When she got an x-ray, the doctor discovered that Le Anne had broken her tibia!)

PCT Day #130

"People think of deer as Bambi, cute and cuddly, but they can be extremely dangerous in some circumstances." —Steve Martorano

We spent the morning packing up and enjoying time with Le Anne and Cole before they caught the 2 p.m. ferry to Chelan. It was hard to say goodbye. We are going to miss hiking with them so much! The bus taking us back to the trailhead stopped by the bakery, so we got to load up on more treats. As delicious as the cinnamon roll and sticky buns were, their savory croissants with pesto and veggies were much better. They were so, so good. We stopped for the night, sooner than we had planned, at this nice campsite with bear boxes and picnic tables. (In case an explanation is needed, a bear box is a heavy-duty metal box that bears can't open. The forest rangers drop them by helicopter into areas where bears are actively getting into hikers' food.) There was a very odd doe there who kept getting really close to us and charging at Muir! She really wanted to trample him, and it took a long time to get her to go away. I had accidentally dropped my Smith sunglasses about a mile back, so Muir and I started to backtrack to look for them. The deer followed us, periodically charging. Finally, I gave up and ran with Muir back to camp. It was our strangest wildlife encounter yet! 5 miles today.

PCT Day #131

We had a nice, flat campsite at Bridge Creek—no incidents with bears (other campers said they had seen bears nearby) or that crazy deer. Today was a day of bridges! A southbound hiker said his dog refused to cross one bridge, and they had to go through the water. Muir looked a little nervous but went across the suspension bridges as quickly as he could. At dinner, we realized we had to have two shorter mileage days back-to-back. Adam will hitchhike into town tomorrow to pick up our passports and paperwork to enter Canada from the Winthrop post office. 12.8 miles today.

PCT Day #132

Tristan was excited to use his hammock again; it's been a while. Hanging the food to protect it from the mice and bears took about an hour last night, but everything was safe and untouched this morning. Adam and Kaia had a great time picking up our resupply in Winthrop. They said it looked like an old western town, and they found super nice people who drove them back to the trailhead (where Sierra, Tristan, Ruby, Muir, and I were patiently waiting). It was a lovely hike for the rest of the afternoon, and we found a great camp. The comments on tonight's campsite on Guthook said it is the most beautiful of all the PCT. I'm so glad the mileage worked out that we could camp here and that there was enough room for us! A super nice hiker named Siesta was already set up here when we arrived. It was fun to visit with her, and she was very kind about sharing this spot. Adam and I noticed that the sweetest lullaby birds were softly singing at bedtime. It was a wonderful way to fall asleep! 11.3 miles today.

PCT Day #133

The fog lifted later in the morning, and we had some sunshine to go with our views of wildflowers and mountains! Today was our first 21-mile day!

PCT Day #134

Harts Pass Campground had an old pit toilet that is now used as a bear box for us to store food in overnight—very convenient. We tried to leave camp early because rain was in the forecast. It was lightly raining by 5:30 a.m. and rained on and off throughout the day. It was a bummer to not be able to see the views in this section, but the fog with the colorful wildflowers was just stunning.

We got to see Professor! From the back of the pack, I saw Kaia giving a hug to a hiker, and it turned out to be our dear Professor. She said, "I kept wondering when I would run into you guys!" We last saw her in SoCal, right before Tehachapi, where she took two months off to work and wait for snow to melt. I told her how much we loved all that she has taught us about geology thus far on the trail. She then told us all about the conglomerate rocks we would see ahead and explained that glacier ice (which formed these valleys we are hiking through) is nine times more dense than regular ice. I wish Professor could be with us every day! It was raining just softly enough that the mosquitoes were still a problem. Just yesterday Ruby asked me if we were going to see any elephant head flowers on this hike. Today we entered a sub-alpine meadow just before Rock Pass, and there they were! These are my very favorite flowers. Up close, the petals look just like tiny elephant heads. We've only found this flower on a hike one other time—at Lackawaxen Lake near Guardsman's Pass, Utah.

Rock Pass was very windy, and the rain poured down on us in bucketfuls, not the usual drizzle! We finally found a place to camp, setting up our tents on top of puddles and hoping for the best. Kaia got her trail name today: Honey Badger. She was trying to get some cold honey out of the jar, feeling frustrated about many things, and the name just stuck. 19.2 miles today.

PCT Day #135

"With glowing hearts/ We see thee rise/ The True North, strong and free/ From far and wide/ O Canada!" —Canada's National Anthem

It was a rough night! The rain was coming down so hard, and we kept hearing rockslides from the cliffs surrounding us. Kaia said it sounded like dragons tossing rocks at one another. Oh, that view when the sun came out though! The sunshine didn't last long; before we got packed up it started snowing on us. We could feel the temperature drop as we stuffed our tents, and then tiny snowflakes were fluttering around. As we hiked up and over Woody Pass and gained elevation, the snow picked up in intensity. I guess it is only appropriate for the day we enter the Great White North! That's right, we made it! For the last three days we've hiked over 19 miles a day to make it into Canada.

We stayed at the northern terminus for about two hours, taking pictures, signing the logbook, eating our lunch, and visiting with the two other hikers that arrived. They both had to turn around and hike back, one to get to Harts Pass and hitch to the airport because he had just finished his section hike of Washington and the other to begin his southbound PCT journey. We were very grateful to have gotten permission from Canada five months ago so that we could walk across the border (looking both ways for any border patrol agents riding moose, but we saw none) and hike the 8.8 miles into Manning Park. The trails in Canada also have fallen logs and obstacles to climb over, eh? The only difference really is that the trail signs are now in kilometers. 19.4 miles (and a fraction of a kilometer) today.

We had hoped Adam's parents would be in Manning Park to pick us up, but we hadn't had cell coverage in several days to let them know we were arriving on Thursday evening, not Friday like we had planned. I kept sending the family our GPS locations from my location device, hoping they would be able to see our impressive progress, but some of the emails didn't go through. Adam got us a room at the lodge, and we all enjoyed hot showers, the pool, steam room, sauna, hot tub, soft beds, and a night protected from the rain!

PCT Days #136–141

After five blissful zero days (getting spoiled by Adam's family), we are back on the trail! We hit Costco and Winco (several times) and gathered an 80-ish day supply of food (a task of epic proportions). Imagine a cart filled with 282 Knorr packets in addition to ramen, dried fruit, and a variety of protein. It took much longer than we thought to organize all our resupply boxes, but hopefully it'll pay off as we try to pick up our pace in Oregon (a state notorious for having tricky and expensive resupply options).

We set off from the amazing Timberline Lodge at about 1 p.m. First, we had to go in and get photos holding the ax used in "The Shining" movie. After hiking 11 miles, mostly downhill, we came to a camp with a picnic table and pit toilet (luxury!). There were lots of northbound hikers we chatted with; everyone has been flipping this way and that on the trail. We learned from an informational sign that the flowers we saw all over are called Bride's Bonnet or Queen's Cup. It is the first time we've seen this lily on the trail. It's beautiful! 11.3 miles today.

PCT Day #142

"Feeding people is a way of loving them." —Shauna Niequist

Today was a double trail magic day! I wish I would have gotten pictures of us with Trail Angel Brian and Trail Angel Connie, but I just wasn't thinking straight! Brian fed us pork loin sandwiches (because we caught him before he had his grill going for the hamburgers and hotdogs he planned to cook for hikers, but he insisted on feeding us!). Then we hiked about .2 miles and followed a sign to Trail Angel Connie. She had a huge variety of food and camp chairs in the shade, and we really enjoyed visiting with her.

We ran into Firekeeper, who is headed north. Kaia gave him his trail name, way back at mile 100. We heard he took a bad fall on Mt. Baden-Powell and was off the trail. He told us he had indeed fallen 300 yards down the ice but is all healed up now and will be in Canada in no time at all (he is fast).

Today we had a "flat" section in the trail, and it was a new experience for us. Adam and I noticed that we had new sore muscles, probably from the distance of the day but also from walking on level ground. The kids didn't complain though! 22 miles today.

PCT Day #143

We met a dad and his two sons that are hiking the Oregon section of the PCT. The mom has been hiking most of it with the boys while the dad works, but they had swapped places for a few days when we crossed paths with them. It's awesome to meet other families on the trail! We ran into our friends Good Cop and Hot Lips at Olallie Lake. I saw their names on the PCT register in the General Store and set out to find them. We caught them for a photo right before they jumped back on the trail. Earlier today, we crossed paths with Biz, a hiker we met near Big Bear. He was going to push a 40+ mile day to get to the Timberline breakfast buffet the next morning (I'm really wishing we hadn't skipped that one). Tonight is Tristan's birthday dinner; luckily for him, the general store had chocolate donuts. 19 miles today.

PCT Day #144

"When clambering a mountain, we always hope the hill we are on is the last. But it is the next, and the next, and still the next." —Thomas Jefferson, 1786

Today was filled with awesome views of Mt. Jefferson! Wow, what an impressive mountain! We found a spot for dinner near a small lake, and a few family members went for a cold swim. There are so many varieties of wildflowers blooming right now. It's hard to keep a good pace because I want to stop and snap pictures every few feet.

PCT Day #145

Today we crossed paths again with Claire, who we met way back at Walker Pass. She loaned us her solar charger while she went into town for supplies, but when she returned, we were gone (that's when Trail Angel Frank told us all to load up in his truck and he rescued us from the rainstorm). Don't worry, we saw Claire again in Kennedy Meadows (south) and returned her solar charger. She is one of the very few hikers we know this year who were able to hike straight north, no flips. Her stories from the high Sierras had us all entertained for at least thirty minutes. It was so great to see her again! It was an exciting day, running into so many trail friends! Also spotted today: Mosy, Mountain Time, Tiger, and Travis Looper. The best part about flipping and heading southbound has been seeing all these awesome thru-hikers again!

PCT Day #146

Today we hiked near a peak called Three Fingered Jack. We crossed the 2,000-mile marker on our way into the Big Lake Youth Camp. We haven't quite logged 2,000 miles, but we are getting close! Kaia found an Osprey pack in the hiker box there and decided to ditch her pack and start using that one. 14.4 miles today.

PCT Day #147

"Hot, tired and just a bit discouraged, we sat on a trail-side log, sweat dripping from our faces. Four north-bound hikers came past and shared a half-liter of their water. That was our total water supply for the next three hours. Getting up and moving, eventually we found ourselves slogging south on a gravel road, under a very hot sun, headed for someplace called Big Lake Youth Camp. We didn't know what it was, or what we'd find, yet it had a lake and we wanted to be there!" — Minnesota Hiking Viking (who hiked the PCT in 2015 and sponsored the PCT Welcome Center here at BLYC)

We had a great time at Big Lake Youth Camp! It was wonderful to visit with other hikers, eat the delicious food, do laundry, get showered, and wake up to an epic sunrise!

PCT Day #148

North Matthieu Lake and the Three Sisters Wilderness were awesome! We met lots of hikers and stopped to chat with almost all of them (especially Adam). One couple was hiking a loop to celebrate the wife's retirement. The husband said, "Thanks for taking the time to stop and talk with us!" We absolutely loved Obsidian Falls. This area was amazing; there was black, sparkling obsidian everywhere for about a half mile! We were so excited to see Butch and Lullaby again! She just loves Muir, and he loves her right back. Today we saw lots of blooming lupine and sego lilies! Too bad I can't share sounds and smells through this book. This area was delightful. 17.4 miles today.

PCT Day #149

Ruby kept asking me if she could eat the berries we kept seeing along the trail. I didn't know, so we didn't partake. Then we met a hiker named Forage who told us all about the huckleberries, thimbleberries, raspberries, and salmon berries in this area. Now we know what we can eat!

We had a great stop at Elk Lake, where we picked up supply boxes. Adam and the kids swam while I worked on our resupply. A few people looked at the pile of packs, food, and gear surrounding me quizzically. Two couples asked what we were up to and were blown away by my response. Today we've learned that lots of lakes means lots of mosquitoes. Tristan loaned Muir his bug net to try and help him out (Muir didn't leave it on long). 20.9 miles today.

PCT Day #150

"Anyone who thinks they are too small to make a difference has never tried to fall asleep with a mosquito in the [tent]." —Christine Todd Whitmann

I failed to take notes today, but I took lots of photos of PCT signs, and we enjoyed a quintessential Oregon lunchtime swim. Tristan filled his mosquito net with goldfish crackers and discovered he could snack, walk, and be protected from biting bugs. Brilliant! The mosquitos are thick out here.

PCT Day #151

"If nobody comes back from the future to stop you, how bad of a decision can it be?" —Kaia Bennett

It was fun to cross paths with Shredder again as she headed north. She made it through the Sierras with a few other hikers we met in SoCal, and it was great to hear their stories. Shredder is from Germany but spent a year in Minnesota during high school. It's fun to hear her German/Minnesotan/English accent. She's a tough one!

We had a fun swim in Rosary Lake, slipping and tripping over logs and rocks under the water. There was a great view today from the overlook above Odell Lake, our next stop! We arrived at Shelter Cove just in time for the first annual PCT Hiker Olympics put on by a thru-hiker named The Mayor. We all had so much fun roasting hot dogs and s'mores over the fire and playing games with this group.

The most exciting news of all: Meagan and Wilohm (Adam's sister and nephew) arrived tonight to hike with us for the next six days! It was late when they pulled up, but the excitement level was very high all around!

PCT Days #152–153

It was complicated to get out of camp today. Adam and Meagan took off early in her van to find a place to park it at Crater Lake, then hitched back to us. After several hitches they finally returned at about 3 p.m. While they were gone, the kids and I were working on chores: laundry, showers, and gear repair. We decided to hit the restaurant at Shelter Cove before we took off and enjoyed the "hiker special": burgers and fries. Thus, we didn't start hiking until after 5 p.m.

We heard there were reports of cougar activity on the PCT and a lengthy water carry, so we took an alternate route several hikers had mentioned. Even though it was a big climb, we got about 6 miles in before setting up camp for the night. We left camp early the next morning and battled against mosquitoes for most of the day! We were having so much fun laughing and chatting with Meagan and Wilohm that we passed a horse camp, completely missing some trail magic set up there (which we learned about later from some hikers that passed us). Today we crossed paths with School Bus, Fat and Sassy, and Tree Trunk. 21 miles over two days.

PCT Day #154

Finding flat spots for four tents is tricky, but the trail provides! Chores include "vacuuming" out the tents each day (which means picking up the tent and shaking it, so all debris falls out through an unzipped door). We covered fewer miles today because we had a long water carry, and we decided to take a side trail to a lake. We got there at about 2 p.m. and enjoyed a leisurely afternoon of swimming, playing games, and eating. It was definitely one of my all-time favorite days on the trail! There was lots of laughter and merriment. 13.4 miles today.

PCT Day #155

We were up to see the sunrise at Maidu Lake and were on the trail by about 7. We met several hikers here that we had met before, like Kanga (from Alaska) and Kicks (she's from Australia; she got her name because she accidentally kicked a bird). It felt like we were hiking in a green tunnel for miles and miles. We were excited to climb up a set of rocks and get a great view of the forest and far-off mountains. Aunt Meagan loaned Ruby her hat because Ruby refuses to wear the two bucket hats she has in her pack.

Today we hiked in the shadow of Mt. Thielsen, an impressive peak! Our lunch break was next to the creek that comes directly from the glacier on Mt. Thielsen. That water was so unbelievably cold. I couldn't keep my feet in there for longer than five seconds! It was a long day on the trail, but the miles just flew by because we were having so much fun with Meagan and Wilohm. 18.2 miles today.

PCT Days #156–157

"I expected something remarkable but was not prepared for a scene of such wonder and beauty . . . It seemed a blue gulf . . . No where else had I ever seen such a shade of blue . . . How exquisite, rare, unreal!" —Zane Grey (speaking about Crater Lake)

Crater Lake! We've been waiting to see this National Park for our whole lives! It did not disappoint. Did you know it isn't a crater? It's a 2,148 feet deep caldera that was formed when Mount Mazama collapsed about 7,700 years ago. We enjoyed swimming, cliff jumping, meeting Oh Lordy and his 6-pound base weight pack, and playing with two of the funniest people on the trail, Meagan and Wilohm! When it was time for them to leave, they took our beloved Muir with them (a monumental favor). We just didn't feel good about bringing him with us into hot NorCal in August.

PCT Days #158–159

"Good friends are like stars, you don't always see them, but you know they're always there." —Unknown

Three friends from Utah joined us from Fish Lake to Hyatt Lake, Rochelle and Makayla Richards and Angela Longman, and it was a non-stop party! We got to see giant trees, got rained on with lightning and thunder right overhead, collected and ate lots of berries, and dried out in a shelter with twenty other hikers. Having friends and family join us on our hike seemed like a logistical nightmare, but it was totally worth it. These are some of our most treasured memories of the entire trail!

PCT Day #160

We saw a lovely sunrise at Howard Prairie Lake! I can't say enough how much fun it was to have Rochelle, Makayla, and Angela join us. It was a huge sacrifice and effort on their part to pull it off, but they did, and we are so grateful. The size of old growth trees in this forest was phenomenal: a fallen log is taller than Ruby! Kaia, Makayla, and Tristan had a great time swimming in Little Hyatt Reservoir. There is a resort nearby where we got delicious pizza for dinner, and the waitress told us we could camp here for free (as opposed to Hyatt Reservoir, which isn't free). It was beautiful! It was so fun to have a short mileage day and enjoy dinner next to the water with our friends. Poor Tristan realized he left his tent stakes where we camped last night. Luckily for him, Rochelle had her car and was willing to drive me back there to find them (which we did). We had a fun dance party during our lunch break, and Rochelle taught us some sweet new dance moves! It was the most memorable lunch break of the entire trail, I'd say. Rochelle and Angela are both yoga instructors, so they guided us through a wonderful session (and taught us a few new stretches). I wish we had them with us every day! 9.2 miles today.

PCT Day #161

"As long as I live, I'll hear waterfalls and birds and winds sing. I'll interpret the rocks, learn the language of flood, storm, and the avalanche. I'll acquaint myself with the glaciers and wild gardens and get as near the heart of the world as I can."
—*John Muir*

Our friends were up at 5 a.m. and drove off into the sunrise on their journey back to Utah. We took our time getting on the trail, repairing some gear, and enjoying the view. More thimbleberries were to be found along the trail. They were delicious! The temperature was rising as we hiked the big climb with a view down into Ashland. Excitement levels always vary. It was hot. Ruby was mad. We had to go about a mile off the trail on a road to get water. But conditions improved once we found camp. There might have been a fire way off in the distance, causing tonight's sunset to be extra spectacular. I'm so grateful we were positioned with a view tonight! 11.1 miles today.

PCT Day #162

There is a big event called PCT Days that takes place in Cascade Locks, Oregon, every year. We didn't think we would be able to attend because we were going to be in southern Oregon, but the Homeboys of the PCT, trail angels we met in SoCal, offered to pick us up in Ashland and take us there! We had time to slowly make our way into Callahan Lodge (where we flipped from on June 5) because our ride wouldn't arrive until tomorrow morning. We got to the Callahan Lodge just as a hiker was dropping off three big boxes of food she didn't need! It had Pop-tarts, beef jerky, freeze dried meals, etc. We were excited to snatch that all up and leave some ramen behind! 11.5 miles today.

PCT Days #163–166

PCT Days was awesome! Our trail angels, Andrew and Jamie (aka Homeboys of the PCT), picked us up in Ashland in their Sprinter van and drove us all the way to Cascade Locks. We stopped at Multnomah Falls because it is a must-see. We ran into a plethora of our hiker friends, including Second Chance Hiker and Smoky the Bear! Pa brought Muir and a bunch of food and gear for us. Three kids won NEMO Equipment Switchbacks, which replaced their worn-out ones! We missed winning the Osprey pack Sierra wanted in the raffle by one ticket number. But we got lots and lots of free swag (stickers, hats, etc.). We were spoiled rotten by trail angels who made pancakes for the hikers every morning during the event. Not just any pancakes either! They added chocolate chips, berries, and sprinkles (and even gave Tristan a baggy of sprinkles to take on the trail). Ruby made a new friend her age named Jaxon. His family also has four kids, and they want to hike the entire PCT someday. It was fun to chat with the parents and answer their questions about how we are making this dream a reality.

PCT Day #167

After PCT Days, our trail angel friends were headed back to Lake Tahoe and offered to drop us off at Burney Mountain Guest Ranch. This is where we started hiking north on May 20th. So now we head south from here to the Sierras. The BMGR has an awesome pool that the kids got to swim in all afternoon. Mike and Linda own BMGR and were so kind and welcoming to have us back a second time. We got a late start on our hike because it was a hot day, and Linda fed us a trail magic dinner. (Her cooking is legendary!) We hadn't made it far when the sun started to set. Baum Lake was a slight detour but so beautiful! We stayed there watching osprey catch fish and take them back to their nests. Our original goal was to hike 10.5 miles tonight, but once it got dark, we called it a night at three miles. We found a good spot to camp, next to the last water source for 13.4 miles, and crawled into our sleeping bags.

PCT Day #168

A kind hiker from the Czech Republic was set up in the campsite last night when we arrived. He didn't mind that we squeezed in. Adam asked him what time he planned to take off in the morning, and he said around 5 a.m. He asked when we were planning to leave, and we told him closer to 6. I noticed he waited until I was up and waking the kids before he started to pack up. I felt bad because it wouldn't have disturbed us at all for him to leave earlier, but he packed up while we were getting ready. He was so fast! Before I even had my socks and shoes on, he was walking away telling us to have a good day. Believe it or not, it takes our circus way too long to get going in the morning (our fastest pack up time to date is 60 minutes. It's usually takes more like 75 minutes to get everyone totally ready and walking).

We were all in a bit of a funk, but some awesome trail angels left coolers of trail magic near the trail, and nothing lifts our spirits like trail magic! Adam found me some powdered hummus in a hiker box, and I've been adding it to cold soaked ramen. It's delicious!

We took a five-hour siesta/lunch today. This area is called the Hat Creek Rim, and it is notoriously hot. I wish we weren't out here hiking it in August, but that's just how the trail must go for us. We had fun during our rest, and the views were great! We made it to a water cache, affectionately known as Cache 22, just before sunset. It was time to have a late dinner, fill up our water bottles, then hike three more miles in the dark. Kaia is always out in front of the train (the six of us hiking in a line looks like a crazy train) and gets to see the most wildlife. A raccoon ran across the path, and for a moment she thought it was a skunk! A few mice were darting across the trail. One kept running right in front of Kaia. I heard her yelling "Hey mouse! You're too slow! Get to the back of the line. I'm trying to get to camp." She's a funny kid.

Our camp destination was at the top of a big climb at what Guthook called a communications tower. There was supposed to be a flat cement slab for us to set up on, but we couldn't find it in the dark. It was about 10 p.m. when we all finally got settled for the night. 16.1 miles today.

PCT Day #169

"A mouse can be as dangerous as a bullet or a bomb." —Lamar Smith

The sunrise was one of the most spectacular we've seen on trail, and we had a great 360-degree view! There were cows mooing near and far, but none came too close to us while we slept. Adam, Tristan, and I cowboy camped. At one point in the night Adam felt a mouse on our sleeping quilt by his feet and kicked it off. In the morning there was a hole where the mouse was probably chewing on our expensive bag (it's called a "quilt" because it doesn't have a zipper). We hung all of our gear because of the number of mice seen on the trail the night before. Conveniently, this communication tower had a nice fence for us to use. Another kind soul left water and apples under a picnic table where we had lunch. We've been so spoiled by trail magic here!

We took a quick side trip to see the Subway Cave. It was only about 1,000 feet long. We learned from the informational signs that this lava tube was formed less than 20,000 years ago. It stays 46 degrees year-round! It's a great way to cool off on a hot day.

We are getting close to Lassen Volcanic National Park. PCT hikers are not allowed to camp within the boundaries of the national park unless they have bear canisters. We do not. So, we had to cut our miles short today and stay in Old Station, which no one complained about (there was ice cream and charging of the electronics involved). 14 miles today.

PCT Day #170

"There is considerable overlap between the intelligence of the smartest bears and the dumbest tourists." —Yellowstone Park Ranger on why it is hard to design a bear-proof garbage can

Another short day as we hiked to an area where we were allowed to camp without having bear canisters. I should explain what bear canisters are, for those who don't know. We met the guy who invented the most popular canister. He must be awfully rich because canisters are required in certain areas, like the national parks in the Sierras. It's just a big, cylindrical tub that weighs about three pounds (which is a lot!), and you store your food in it. Supposedly bears can't open it, and you are supposed to store it a quarter-mile from where you sleep. Most hikers use them the least amount possible because they are awkward to pack around. We plan to get ours right before entering the Sierras (they are expensive, and one will only hold a two-day supply of food for the six of us).

There was an impressive volcano, Mt. Lassen, in our view as we walked today. We met a nice couple as we hiked along who wanted to chat. They said now that they are retired, they would like to do the whole trail. They are just waiting for their "dogs to kick off." Ha! I haven't heard that one before. We took another nice long siesta next to Hat Creek (which had a lovely waterfall). We played cards (the kids created their own card game), rinsed out clothes in the creek, and rested.

The sunset tonight was off-the-charts magical! We set up camp here just before it got dark. Another hiker rolled in about 10 p.m. and was gone before 5 a.m. It is amazing how fast some people hike this trail! Even though we are taking longer than we had planned, I'm happy with our pace. We're taking plenty of time to soak it all in. 10.2 miles today.

PCT Day #171

"The land is positively alive at Lassen Volcanic National Park. Home to all four types of volcanoes—shield, composite, cinder cone, and plug dome—this park in the northeast corner of California literally bubbles, steams, and roars. But for all its hydrothermal activity, Lassen has a restive side too, with crystalline lakes and meadows filled with summer wildflowers." —visitcalifornia.com

Boiling Spring Lake is so cool! Terminal Geyser was a fun side trip (it's not really a geyser, the sign says, like Crater Lake isn't really a crater). Our journey through this section of Lassen Volcanic National Park made us feel like we were in Yellowstone except without the crowds. We didn't see another soul until three hikers stopped to get water at the same stream we were at in the evening. 17 miles today.

PCT Day #172

"If I be waspish, best beware my sting." —William Shakespeare

We hiked past Cluster Lakes, Silver Lake, and Feather Lake: all beautiful, but sadly, this forest looks recently burned. We stopped for lunch at Upper Twin Lake, and Ruby entertained herself building sandcastles. We camped at the campground in Warner Valley (where bear boxes are provided). We are having a lot of trouble with wasps. We rarely see a mosquito these days, but four out of six of us have been stung (multiple times) by wasps. Poor Adam has the worst reactions: the area of the sting swells, gets hot, and hurts like crazy. I think he even gets a low-grade fever to boot. He has gotten stung three times recently! The wasps are everywhere; they're the annoying kind that dive right into your food. Tonight, I didn't see one land on my spoon as I shoveled dinner into my mouth, and I bit it! Somehow, I didn't get stung. I spit it out right away because I knew that wasn't what my mashed potatoes were supposed to taste like! Kaia had us all laughing by impersonating what I would have sounded like with a swollen tongue. 12.5 miles today.

PCT Day #173

We made it to Chester, California! The kind people of this town allow hikers to camp behind a church with access to port-o-potties, a hand-washing station, shade, a hiker box, a deck with chairs, etc. There is a laundromat with pay showers attached that we are way too excited about.

I want to share our hitch story: Sierra and I got picked up first by a sweet woman named Lisa. She saw us by the side of the road, pulled over, and flipped around, interrupting the caravan of the family members she was leading to the lake. She couldn't take us all the way into Chester but dropped us off at the next junction. Before she left, she opened her cooler and offered us some of the fresh-cut local peaches she had! Her daughter and son-in-law were in the car right behind her, and they pulled over too (very kindly asking us if we had enough water or if we needed anything else). Next, another kind lady picked us up and brought us all the way to the grocery store in Chester. She had two happy dogs in her vehicle, including one with a mohawk that sat next to Sierra—too cute. Adam, Kaia, Tristan, and Ruby took longer to get a hitch, but a tourist eventually got them to town in an RV. Meanwhile, Sierra and I waited at the grocery store and visited with a woman on a motorcycle trip with her husband. She said her mother was born in Battle Ground, Washington (where we will live after the trail), but it was during the Depression, so they moved to California for work. We got to hear all about how her parents met while working at an apricot orchard. I love hearing people's stories like that; they're so interesting and endearing. 6.8 miles today.

PCT Day #174

Adam and Tristan got some much-needed haircuts with the clippers provided at the church! Post-haircut showers were in order, so we headed back to our favorite laundromat. We started chatting with the owner, Steve, and he offered to drive us back to the trail! He's so awesome. Back on trail, we ran into two friends, Steady and Oh Lordie! We met Steady on day two of this adventure; he's such a great guy. Oh Lordie walked up, eating a Cliff bar, with a big smile on his face. This is the fourth time we've run into him (he's headed straight southbound, fast, and we keep flip-flopping into his path).

We got to the PCT "midpoint" monument! Thank goodness we only have 600-ish miles to go, not 1,325. It was a hard night; we had to push into the dark to get to camp. But we got to enjoy a phenomenal sunset! This morning a hiker named Tent approached us. He asked the girls their names, and when he realized we are the Bennett family, his reaction was the best we've ever encountered. He said, "I don't want to get all 'fan girl' on you, but can I take a picture with you guys?" We chatted with him for a while, but he had to rush off to catch a bus. He quickly told Ladybug, "Sometimes when I'm having a hard day, I just say to myself, 'There is a 10-year-old girl out here kicking your [butt]!' You guys are awesome!" It was a huge morale boost to hear him say all those nice things.

Ruby was having a hard time as we hiked late into the evening to get to camp (we tend to see hikers we know and stop to chat for too long). Our friend, NoID, sent a message and said, "Man, she is such a trooper. Tell her no matter how hard it is, or how hard it gets, she will make it! Fix your ponytail and keep pushing." Kind words do wonders! 10.5 miles today.

PCT Day #175

The trees had great motivational messages for us today! On one, someone had written, "Be Happy!" and another said, "Keep on Truckin'." Tomorrow is the big descent into Belden, and then the climb back out is going to be brutal! 15.4 miles today.

PCT Day #176

Today we walked far and saw pretty things. Kaia walked right past a rattlesnake without noticing it was there. It scared her to death when it hissed at her, but it never did rattle. We all slowly shuffled by without incident. We saw an informational sign today that read, "In the early 1930s, Clinton C. Clarke offered to the world his vision of a continuous trail stretching from Canada through three states to Mexico. Along the summit divide of the mountain ranges, traversing the best scenic areas and maintaining an absolute wilderness character. The virtue of such a trail, said Clarke, would be in helping to preserve wild areas and in encouraging people of 'our too-artificial civilization' to return to a simpler life and an appreciation of nature and the outdoors."

We made it to Belden! Adam picked up some cookies and chips in the "general store," our friend Viking let us fill up our water bottles in the room he was renting for the night, and we sauntered off to camp down by the river (eating Knorr, not government cheese, for dinner). 19 miles today.

PCT Day #177

"Life is not a straight line leading from one blessing to the next and then finally to heaven. Life is a winding and troubled road. Switchback after switchback. And the point of biblical stories like Joseph and Job and Esther and Ruth is to help us feel in our bones (not just know in our heads) that God is for us in all these strange turns. God is not just showing up after the trouble and cleaning it up. He is plotting the course and managing the troubles with far-reaching purposes for our good and for the glory of Jesus Christ." —John Piper

We've never experienced switchbacks like the ones coming out of Belden. The kids did awesome! We finished the climb and found a nice flat spot in the shade to relax next to a stream (with tiny fish that the younger kids attempted, but failed, to catch). The view down to Silver Lake was phenomenal.

We had a package waiting for us in Quincy (and a new insulated mat for Adam and I; ours has been going flat each night for a while now). There was very little traffic at the road where we were trying to get a hitch, but fortunately for us, a guy was parked up there trying to get cell service. He graciously allowed all six of us to pile into his Honda Civic (picture a clown car scenario) and took us to the Quincy Safeway. In no time we were feasting on rotisserie chicken and potato salad, forgetting all about our car sickness! 18.6 miles.

PCT Day #178

Last night, as a last-ditch effort, we found a church lawn to camp on. When the sprinklers turned on at 2 a.m., we took shelter behind the dumpster. Surprisingly, we had a great night's sleep! (It was a very clean dumpster area because we are still in black bear country). We went to the hospital next door to use the restroom and fill our water bottles. A kind woman at the front desk was so excited to hear our story. She said she wished she would have known we needed a place to stay last night. She would've gladly housed us and let us shower and do laundry! Oh well. She called the local newspaper, and a reporter did a quick phone interview with me. That was an exciting first!

The hitch back to the trail was fun. Sierra, Kaia, Tristan, and I were picked up by a nice retired forest service employee. He insisted on dropping us at one location, even though I said Adam and Ruby would be meeting us at another location. So those two had to hike an extra three miles to meet up with us. While we waited for Adam and Ruby, Kaia read Sherlock Holmes to us (there was a fun hiker box at this location full of books). Trail magic comes in many different forms! 14.9 miles today.

PCT Day #179

Somewhere lost in a shoebox, there is a picture of Adam's great-grandfather in Europe with a couple baguettes strapped to the side of his backpack. A few generations later, it's still fun to strap a few baguettes on a pack and head out on a great adventure! Our gourmet trail meal last night: sourdough, brie, and balsamic glaze. While on the trail, this is pretty much what we are eating every day:

First breakfast: Gatorade bar
Second breakfast: Cliff bar
Elevensies: Nature Valley bar
Lunch: cold soaked ramen with peanut butter and honey
Afternoon snack: dried mango and trail mix
Dinner: Knorr pasta

We reached the Middle Fork of the Feather River, a much-anticipated sight. It was too early in the morning to swim here, which was so sad because we heard it was the best swimming hole on the whole trail! 19.1 miles today.

PCT Day #180

We reached 7,000 feet this morning! It's hard to believe that Mt. Whitney is our end goal, and it is over twice this height. Way off in the distance, we are getting our first views of the Sierras, which are absolutely breathtaking. We had a funny experience at camp tonight. As I was filtering water, everyone else was setting up tents. I kept hearing bells ringing off in the distance. I thought maybe a hiker with several loud bear bells on their pack was headed our way. But the sound stayed the same distance away from me. I was baffled. It took me about an hour to figure out there was a herd of cows nearby, all with bells on. These cows were curious and came close to our tents, ringing their bells almost all night long (that part wasn't funny)! 17.9 miles today.

PCT Day #181

We were up bright and early, enjoying the morning light filtering through the forest! We hiked to Packer Lake right after lunch and couldn't resist taking a swim (even though the wind was blowing something fierce). It was a long descent into Sierra City with a plethora of switchbacks. We got a hitch into town from a kind father/son combo, Cedar and Miles. They picked up Adam, Sierra, and Ruby first, took them to the PCT camp spot in town, and then came back for the rest of us. As I was making dinner in the dark on a crooked picnic table, I noticed the fuel can must have been running low (the noodles just weren't cooking right). Moments later, I knocked almost the full 2.5 liter pot on my lap while trying to reach a water bottle. Thank goodness the water in the pot was only lukewarm and I wasn't dealing with burns (just a few tears of frustration and a sticky mess). Don't worry—no one went hungry, and the kids helped me clean up. 21.7 miles today.

PCT Days #182–184

"Does this make me a trail angel?" —PA Tony Smith

Our cousin, Tony, is a PA, and he just saved our hike! Poor Sierra has been complaining of a painful spot on her tailbone for a few days (Sierra is not a complainer, more the suffer-in-silence type, so when she says something hurts, she really means it). Tony diagnosed it over the phone as a pilonidal cyst. He was able to call in a prescription for some strong antibiotics to the nearest pharmacy. We had to hitch into Truckee, but it was all worth it to get her feeling better.

We spent two nights at the Donner Memorial State Park. The stones on this monument are 22.5 feet tall, the height of the snow in 1846 when the settlers were arriving in this area. There are lots of sad stories in the museum about the Donner party, the Chinese railroad workers, and other aspects of this area's history.

We learned how the first convenience store came to be: "Around 1920, after the monument to the Donner party was dedicated in Truckee, tourists began removing rock from the pedestal as souvenirs. T. C. Wolhbruck came up with an idea and offered to lease the site for $1 a year. He provided a caretaker, a fence, landscaping and set up a very popular souvenir and refreshment station."

Another informative sign caught my eye with the story of Elizabeth Keagan, a 12-year-old girl who faced unbelievable hardships. "No one knows the strength of kindred love until it is tried," she said. We were back on the trail on September 5th with Sierra feeling better. 15.5 miles today.

PCT Day #185

It felt good to hit the trail bright and early this morning! The sky was filled with colorful clouds, and the sunrise was phenomenal. Aspen trees are my favorite, and they are everywhere today. This is the first time we've seen a PCT trail marker on an aspen. Ruby was proud to be the first one to spot Lake Tahoe and was always quick to point out when it was in view. You really grasp how big this lake is when you hike next to it for four days.

We visited the third ski resort we've hiked to in the past two days, with more to come. Sierra said, "In all our years of skiing, I never imagined we would hike to the top of ski lifts!" Leaves are turning yellow and falling on the trail—brace yourselves, fall is coming! The PCT combines with the TRT (Tahoe Rim Trail) in this section. It felt like we ran into twice as many hikers here. It is such a beautiful area, I can see why! Adam and I went on a "date" and left the kids at camp while we went to the creek to wash our feet together.

Tonight, we celebrated six months on the trail with the Little Debbie's Cosmic Brownies that sweet Aunt Darla sent us in a care package. We counted our zero days, and in the past six months we've taken 29 zeros, so that explains why we are going past our schedule by three weeks. But Adam reminded me that we had hiked every bit of snow-free trail that we could and we had to take those days off while we waited for the snow to melt (plus intermittently letting some injuries heal). It's a crazy snow year to be out here on the trail, for sure! 15.8 miles today.

PCT Day #186

"My best memories are some of the worst days."—*Trevor Pyke (aka Crunchmaster)*

Today we ran into a hiker who goes by the trail name Crunchmaster. He just completed his third PCT thru-hike and was on a "victory lap" with some of his friends when we caught up to him. On his final day (slightly over 24 hours of hiking), he did 71 miles (which included four passes in the Sierras).

We were lucky enough to spot a sun halo above Richardson Lake! This is the second sun halo we've seen on the trail. We passed by lots of lovely lakes today, but Fontanillis Lake was the most beautiful (in my opinion). There was a group of college-age guys jumping off a cliff into the frigid water. If it hadn't been so windy, I think our family would have jumped in too. We got to the lake later in the evening than we wanted to and spent a long time chatting with a friendly ranger (it was the first time we've had to show a ranger our PCT permit). We found an awesome spot to camp, slightly protected from the wind (good thing, too, because it was a very windy night). 14.3 miles today.

PCT Day #187

"Life's not about how hard of a hit you can give . . . it's about how many you can take, and still keep moving forward." —*Rocky Balboa*

Most arguments between our three girls involve who must get out of the tent first in the morning (so the other two have more room to get ready). Ruby has really been digging in her heels lately, insisting that she will not be first out! Kaia is the only one with a bear canister right now. She hides hers from bears each night and says it is like an "Easter egg" hunt every morning when she finds it.

We hit the trail early, knowing we had a big climb to get over the pass. We took a quick lunch break at Lake Aloha and visited with our friend Good Cop. Everyone was in a rush to get to the highway and catch a hitch into South Lake Tahoe (much to Ruby's chagrin; she really wanted to swim here!).

Just before reaching the highway into South Lake Tahoe, we met three ladies who had come up for a day hike. They couldn't give us a ride because they were headed in the opposite direction, but they did give us a bunch of food they didn't need and gave us lots of sweet compliments (it's amazing what an apple and a few kind words will do to lift our spirits). We found a ride for all of us into town but had to split up for the lengthy hitch out to Homewood where our friend, Travis Looper, invited us to stay with him for the night. He and his partner made us a delicious dinner and let us shower, do laundry, and stay in their six spare beds! Travis finished the entire PCT a few weeks ago, and we had run into him three separate times on the trail. It's amazing how this common bond of thru-hiking builds such great friendships!

A few moments after our ride dropped us off, I realized I had left all our trekking poles in her trunk. As fast as a cartoon character, Travis grabbed his keys, and we jumped in his car (shoeless even) and rushed to intercept the driver before she got on the highway. Travis took some side streets, knew exactly where she would pull out, and parked right in front of her before she could turn. I hopped out, explained the situation, and safely retrieved all the trekking poles. They make movies out of these kinds of moments! 15.5 miles today.

PCT Day #188

"He is richest who is content with the least, for content is the wealth of nature."
—*Socrates*

Travis drove us into town to get our resupply package from the post office. He had two extra bear canisters and gave one to us and one to Good Cop (somehow hers got lost in the mail). He also gave Sierra and Kaia a pair of gloves each, which they were so grateful for because it got cold today. Travis had to leave to go to LA, so we split into groups to hitch back to the trail. It took until about 2 p.m. for all of us to end up in the same place, but all's well that ends well.

There are awesome granite boulders everywhere! We sure wish we could hike with our geologist friends every day. Ruby identified a conglomerate rock; she was excited about that. We got our last view of Lake Tahoe as we kept heading south; it's so magnificent! 10.5 miles today.

PCT Day #189

It was a cold, cold morning, so we stayed in our tents until about 7:15. We didn't get out of camp until 8:40, but it is hard to move fast when your fingers won't cooperate! It warmed up in no time and was a beautiful day to be outside. We stopped by a visitor center in Toiyabe National Forest where they filled our water bottles, gave us oranges and tiny Snickers, and let us sign the logbook. We learned from the informational sign that this area is called Elephant's Back, and it is a massive lava dome. Nearby were peaks named The Sisters and Round Top, which are craggy lava vents. Geology!

We met this Australian couple in Oregon and ran into them again today. They said they talked to their friends with kids about our family, saying things like, "Just because you have kids doesn't mean you have to stop doing cool things!" Our kids had already passed them, but Whitewalker told Adam, "Give all your kids hugs from us and tell them how proud we are of them." 18.8 miles today.

PCT Day #190

Tristan says this was his last night of cowboy camping for this hike! We were about 200 feet from a small lake and woke up to frost on everything. He says he slept fine though. 16.1 miles today.

PCT Day #191

I didn't take notes today, but we hiked 18.8 miles with 4,019.7 feet of ascent and 3,884.8 descent.

PCT Day #192

We were up early, super excited because today is a "going to town" day! The big obstacle was going up and over Sonora Pass, about 10,500-ish feet above the sea.

Poor Kaia started to get an ocular migraine as we started up the pass. She took some ibuprofen and laid down to rest when we got to the trailhead. Adam, Sierra, Tristan, and Ruby hitched a ride to Kennedy Meadows with a nice lady who was just dropping her husband off for his PCT section hike. She said her daughter had started hiking the PCT this year but pulled off at Tehachapi because of the high snow levels. Turns out we met the daughter, Katie, during the first few weeks of our hike! Kaia started to feel better (to the point that she didn't think she would throw up during the winding mountain road drive), so we found a hitch with two ladies who just finished their day hike.

The General Store at Kennedy Meadows (north) lets you fit as much soft serve ice cream as you can into the cup for $2.25. Our kids took this contest very seriously.

Our sweet friend, Janel, arranged for her parents to pick us up at Kennedy Meadows and take us back to their cabin. This was a tremendous undertaking because their cabin is about an hour and a half from the trail. They let us shower and do laundry and fed us taco salad (I think most of us had at least three servings) and delicious pie! It was so much fun to visit with them and enjoy their lovely cabin. 11 miles today.

PCT Day #193

John and Ramona spoiled us with an amazing breakfast of French toast, fresh fruit, bacon, and eggs! On the way back to the trail, I asked John if he would take our picture by a Big Foot statue. Apparently, this area has a lot of sightings of the legendary Sasquatch.

At the trailhead, Adam developed a system for measuring whose pack is heavier (just by holding one in each hand). Tristan is carrying all the dinners, so he was heaviest today (but we ate out of his bear can first). We all learned a lot about "food as fuel" today. Yesterday we didn't really have lunch because we rushed to get a hitch, but we had a big dinner. Today we had a huge breakfast and a small lunch as we rushed back on the trail. The extra calories from dinner and breakfast fueled us for 13 miles. Adam reminded us that when we are not hiking 13–20 miles a day, we won't be able to eat the way we are now (without negative consequences, that is).

We entered the famous Tuolumne County! In college I had a North Face backpack that was the Tuolumne version. A guy from California that I was dating noted that he enjoyed hiking in those mountains, and ever since then I'd always wanted to hike there too. Now here we are! An informational sign at the trailhead told us that we would be seeing "a mixed conifer forest dominated by Jeffery pines, Lodgepole pines, and red fir . . . higher elevations support junipers and hemlocks." 13 miles today.

PCT Day #194

Our "formation" for hiking these past few months has been Kaia, Sierra, and Tristan in the front, then Ruby and I, with Adam as the caboose (honestly, it takes the creativity and long-suffering of both parents to keep Ruby moving forward on the trail some days). Today the teenagers were about fifteen minutes ahead of us because Ruby had stopped for a lengthy potty break. When the three of us came to a stream crossing, it became confusing which way the trail went. We went left, but I checked my app and quickly realized that we should have gone right to stay on the PCT. We backtracked and found the older girls sitting next to Harriet Lake, waiting for us to catch up.

Tristan wasn't with them. This began the most frightening hour on the trail for us thus far.

We figured that Tristan also got confused at the unmarked split in the trail, went left, and just kept walking because he thought he was following Kaia and Sierra. Adam and I dropped our packs and ran to the other side of the lake. The trail split again, so he took the higher trail, and I took the lower one. I ended up at a campsite, and then my trail ended. I backtracked and found Adam, who also had no luck finding Tristan. We were both starting to get worried; a storm was supposed to hit that night, and I think we had "worst case scenarios" running through our minds. There were many splits in the trail, and we feared Tristan would hike a long time, deeply absorbed in his audiobook, before he realized he was lost. The wind was also blowing hard, muting the sound of us yelling Tristan's name (which he probably wouldn't hear anyway with a headphone in). We sent Sierra on a trail heading south, Adam went north, and Kaia and I went east (Ruby stayed put). Fortunately, Tristan came walking up to Kaia and me a few minutes later. He was in tears; I hugged him and burst into tears. Kaia is such a tender heart that she cried too. Our prayers were answered!

I ran south to find Adam and bumped into another hiker. "I'm looking for my husband who is looking for my son. Have you seen him?" I blurted out. The hiker said, "Yes, he's not far behind me. Is everything ok?" I told him we found Tristan, and Adam came walking up shortly thereafter. Adam gave Tristan a big, long hug and told him he loved him. I wish I would have captured a photo of that tender moment! We sent Kaia to find Sierra, and they both returned about ten minutes later. Sweet Sierra ran 1.5 miles uphill looking for her brother before turning around. We had an early lunch there at the lake; we needed to rest after all the running and let our nerves calm down!

We have a new system of hiking now. Kaia and Sierra still want to be in the front, but they stop more often to wait for us to catch up. I'm ahead of Tristan, always keeping an eye on the girls ahead and those behind!

We were passed by a group of hikers heading north with big packs and matching walkie-talkies (I was wishing we had those this morning!). Then seven horses and two riders came along. One rider leaned over and handed Kaia two candy bars, saying, "These are the last of my mule treats." Adam chatted with them for a while and learned they were with the backpackers. We have no idea why their packs were so big when they also had seven horses carrying gear!

We passed the beautiful Dorothy Lake, named after the daughter of Yosemite's superintendent from 1902 to 1912. Other lakes in this area are named Bonnie Lake, Lake Harriet, Lake Ruth, Stella Lake, Lake Helen, Avonelle Lake, and Wilma Lake (I'm not sure if these were all the names of the daughters of the superintendent). We camped at Wilma Lake and learned this interesting fact: "The lake was officially designated 'Wilma Lake' in 1964, though it was previously known as 'Wilmer Lake' due to an error perpetuated through map designations." All the signs say Wilmer Lake . . . poor little Wilma got the raw end of the deal! 17 miles today.

PCT Day #195

We woke to a lovely sight of Wilma Lake at dawn and set off for the day. It started out bright, clear, and cloud-free. We had high hopes of getting in 17 miles today. But right as we got to the top of Seavey Pass (9,129 feet), it started to rain, snow, hail, and sleet on us. Adam wisely told us to find the next tent site and set up. We were all in our tents by 4 p.m. and waited out the storm for a few hours. At about 6 p.m., we handed out some beef jerky, dried mangos, and Cheez-Its and called it good for dinner. The temperature dropped, and we were so grateful to be protected from the wind by the rocks and trees around us! 11.4 miles today.

PCT Day #196

It was a very cold morning! Some tears were shed, but once we got hiking, we started to get the feeling back in our fingers and toes. Kaia made a quick stop to build a tiny snowman. We had a big climb up and over Benson Pass. Wonderland, Siesta, Jolly Rancher, and Sour were a few hikers we ran into this morning. They all had a rough night in the storm too. We stopped at Smedburg Lake for lunch. Tristan took a quick swim, not making it out to the island he set his sights on because the water was too cold! We got to visit with our friend, Siesta, who we camped with way back in Washington and have bumped into several times since. She said our family is her inspiration to keep going on the trail! So sweet.

We hiked until twilight to make nearly 16 miles for the day and camped on a hill above Miller Lake. The sunset and the stars were breathtaking! (And it was really cold.) 15.8 miles today.

PCT Day #197

Today was a big day! We've been in Yosemite National Park since Sunday, and of course everything is astonishingly beautiful. Today is the day we hike into the "more than famous" Tuolumne Meadows. We passed so many awesome waterfalls! My favorite one is next to the Glen Aulin Sierra Camp and is the lower level of the Tuolumne Falls. We sat there and cooked up some dinner for lunch (we had extra dinners, and no one wants ramen for lunch anymore), and it was a perfect setting.

A day hiker stopped to chat and asked if we knew the latest weather report. Of course, we didn't, so she told us that a storm was supposed to hit tonight, bringing snow and cold temperatures. Sitting in the warm sunshine, it didn't seem possible (but we know from experience, it is). We paused at Soda Springs to read the informational signs and see the carbonated water bubbling up from the earth (we didn't try to drink it). We picked up our resupply box at the Tuolumne Meadows General Store (and borrowed a Home Depot bucket filled with goodies from the hiker box), then went to the backpacker section of the sold-out campground. Kaia made us all peanut butter and Nutella sandwiches (all from unopened jars in the hiker box). It was dark by 7:15 p.m., and we all hunkered down in our tents, ready for the storm. 17.2 miles today.

PCT Day #198

The storm hit through the night in several waves, as promised. It really wasn't all that bad. We had thought about taking a side trip to the Yosemite Valley to see Half Dome, the Ansel Adams gallery, etc., but decided against it. (1. Because of the storm. 2. Because it would have cost $132 for the six of us to take the bus there and back.) By the time we got electronics charged, resupply sorted, camp packed up, and ourselves back on the trail, it was 10 a.m. It was then that I discovered we had to rush to get to the next town, Mammoth Lakes, to pick up our next food resupply before the post office closed for the weekend! Even though we had such a late start, we needed to push to get at least 20 miles (plus go over two passes). The kids were up for the challenge, and Adam and I could barely keep up! We had a big breakfast at the campground (hot Spanish rice with dehydrated beans, a luxury!), so we opted for protein bars for a quick lunch.

The PCT and the John Muir Trail merge in this section. It snowed lightly on us while we went up and over Donohue Pass. The sun was mostly shining, and Kaia said it felt just like we were in a snow globe. It was magical! We entered the Ansel Adams wilderness; he happens to be one of our very favorite photographers. I've heard a few hikers say this section is their very favorite of the whole trail. I can see why! I'm so grateful we were there just in time to see one of the best sunsets yet (which is the front cover photo of this book)!

PCT Day #199

It was a cold morning at 1,000 Island Lake, but we were up early. For the first time on the trail, we had to get into town as fast as we could to get two packages of food from the post office before it closed (at 4 p.m. on a Friday; it's not open Saturday or Sunday). We all hitched into Mammoth Lakes (split into two groups), made it to the post office on time, ran errands, and spent the night in a hotel. There was a dune buggy convention going on in town. It was so fun to see hundreds of them driving all over!

PCT Day #200

The Meyers Manx (dune buggy) convention in Mammoth was so much fun! We decided to leave town a little later in the day so that we could walk through all the cars on display. We took a free trolley back to the trail. Leaving town, we had nine days' worth of food! Usually, we are strained carrying six days' worth. But somehow, we fit it all in and started walking.

The first lake we passed was McLeod Lake. It looked like it should have been surrounded by palm trees, not pine, since the color of the water was tropical. It was amazing. Before we lost coverage, we checked the weather and got nervous about the cold snap headed our way on the final leg. The upcoming weekend temperatures were predicted to be single digits! 10.5 miles today.

PCT Day #201

Today was a big mileage day for us! We had to make up for the lack of miles yesterday. We went up and over Silver Pass with an impressive amount of gain and loss of elevation. The trail followed the Silver Pass Creek and the North Fork of Mono Creek. Both were beautiful and full of ideal swimming holes. At one point I looked across the creek and saw a perfect set-up that I hope to recreate one day. A man had strung a line to dry socks he washed in the creek (something we used to do but lost motivation), had set up his tent (I'm always envious of the backpackers who have camp set up before 4 p.m.!), was sitting in the sunshine next to the creek, and writing in a journal. He smiled and waved at us as we passed. Something about that scene—maybe it was the afternoon sunlight or my longing to be the one sitting and writing—just felt like the quintessential backcountry moment. As for us, we hiked until it was past dark, nearly past hiker midnight, until we finally crashed for the night. 20.4 miles today.

PCT Day #202

Our camp last night was not exactly flat or ideal, but it was better than anything else we could find in the dark. Instead of the regular PCT sign, this area had a brand they burned into the trees. It was very cool. We took a brief lunch by the lake; we are missing our siestas we've had in the past that lasted for 2+ hours. Now we must eat quickly and try our best to be up and moving in less than an hour.

We spotted our first coyote! It was a cute little guy, about the same size as Muir (we are all missing our dog), but it didn't hang around long. The granite rocks all around us are so impressive; we particularly enjoy seeing "waves" in the rocks. It was a beautiful walk into the Muir Trail Ranch, and everyone working there was so friendly and helpful. This spot is famous for its hiker box set up. A lot of PCT and JMT (John Muir Trail) hikers stop here to resupply. Many have too much food (usually JMT hikers, judging by the quality) and leave it behind for other hikers. We are a bit late in the season, so most of the buckets were picked through, but we got a five-day supply of oatmeal for the six of us and a few other goodies. (Even though we left Mammoth with a nine-day supply, we really need ten days to make it out safely. If we couldn't gather enough here, we would have had to hike out of Kearsarge Pass into the town of Independence.) We decided that was good enough and kept hiking on. 18.1 miles today.

PCT Day #203

"Another glorious Sierra day in which one seems to be dissolved and absorbed and sent pulsing onward we know not where. Life seems neither long nor short, and we take no more heed to save time or make haste than do the trees and stars. This is true freedom, a good practical sort of immortality." —*John Muir*

The 19-mile climb from Muir Trail Ranch to the summit of Muir Pass was definitely in the "top five most beautiful days on the PCT" category. The aspen leaves were turning gold, the waterfalls were lovely, the lakes were breathtaking, there were lots of curious deer, and the sunset was so phenomenal we couldn't stop taking photos until it was over and dark (the view of the Milky Way and the night sky was the best we've had on trail!).

PCT Day #204

A kind hiker stopped to chat with us as he was headed northbound. He gave us an updated weather report and a few tips for climbing Mt. Whitney: "If it is so windy up there that you are holding on to the rocks with both hands, don't try to summit." Roger that!

PCT Day #205

It was a scramble to get into camp tonight. We were determined to get to an area that had a bear box to store food and would set us up best for the big climb tomorrow. We crossed a suspension bridge in the dark and stumbled into camp around 8 p.m. A kind hiker we met the day before was keeping an eye out for us and showed us the best places to set up our tents and where the bear box was. 21 miles today, and we climbed up and over both Mather (12,099 feet) and Pinchot Pass (12,107 feet)!

PCT Day #206

When we were on the suspension bridge last night, it was dark, and we failed to notice the sign saying, "One at a time." It got a little wobbly with our circus on there (I was second in line; I'm certain Adam wisely waited until we were all off before he crossed).

There are three beautiful lakes we passed on the way to Glen Pass that I would love to visit again. They are all named Rae Lake (upper, middle, and lower), after the wife of conservationist William E. Colby. The top of Glen Pass was quite a sight to see. We met an awesome mother-daughter duo up there, Brenda and Lacy. They visited with the teenagers while Adam, Ruby, and I slowly climbed up. Very kindly, they offered us the extra food they were carrying since they were almost done with the loop they were hiking. Of course, we eagerly accepted. 16.4 miles today.

PCT Day #207

It was an extra chilly night and a frigid climb up Forester Pass with the wind biting any exposed skin. I did my best to get photos with everyone in front of the famous Forester Pass sign, but no one wanted to hang out at the top for very long. Just a few weeks before we arrived, a hiker died from slipping on the snow and falling, which is so sad. Fortunately for us, we didn't have any snow in our way on the descent.

PCT Day #208

"Believe you can and you're halfway there." —Theodore Roosevelt

Icicles formed on the water bottles as we hung them up to filter this morning! Despite the cold, I saw Kaia smiling and heard her tell Tristan, "Can you believe it? Today is our last day!"

On our way to the summit, we met our friends Little Legs, Good Cop, Crazy Eyes, and Uncle Dom. They all woke up at 1 a.m. to get to the summit by sunrise. It was so very cold that some of them regretted going so early in the dark. At 5 a.m., about two miles from the summit, they found a day hiker who spent the night huddled under a rock. Apparently, this woman had summited Whitney yesterday, but on her descent her phone died, and she had no way to navigate. These friends gave her an external battery pack so she could charge her phone and massaged her muscles until she warmed up. Good Cop was surprised the woman survived the night at such low temperatures! They sent her on her way back down the Whitney Portal, and then they summited. We don't know what happened to her; hopefully, she made it back to her car safely. It was a scary situation.

When we finally reached the summit, it was windy and cold. We visited with other hikers while we huddled together in the warming hut. One creative hiker had made her own Mt. Whitney sign, and she let us borrow it for our photo. The descent was brutal for us. It was 9 hard miles, Ruby wasn't feeling good, and it was lots of hiking in the dark. We went from 14,505 feet to camp at 8,374 feet. It was rough finding three tent sites, but we did and were all tucked in by 10:45 p.m. (and totally tuckered out!).

That's the end of our official PCT journey! I want to note that we safely hitched to Lone Pine the next morning, got a lovely hotel (with a hot tub), and slept great! Good Cop, Little Legs, Crazy Eyes, and Uncle Dom came to visit us at the hotel the next morning. We love those guys! Adam's amazing parents drove all night to pick us up and surprised us by bringing Adam's nephew, Jackson, along (we haven't seen him in two years because he'd been serving a mission for The Church of Jesus Christ of Latter-day Saints). We all drove to Death Valley because we felt we should visit the lowest spot in the US since we had just been to the highest! We went to Universal Studios for two days (Adam told the kids about halfway through the hike that we would hit Harry Potter World to celebrate all their birthdays this year). Hindsight being 20/20, it was not the best idea to hit an amusement park after being on foot for 6 months (those rides are so fast!). What an adventure this was. We are so grateful that we were able to saunter along the PCT, overcoming so many obstacles, avoiding disasters, and spending quality time in nature together.

Post-trail thoughts from Tristan: "Hi, I'm Tristan, the only son and third child of the Bennett family. My trail name is Turtle. I had been hiking and backpacking almost all my life even before the long trails, and I learned to love nature from a very young age. I had pretty much always known that I'd hike these trails. My parents told me when I was 6 or 7, and my little kid brain went 'Cool! That sounds fun!' My perspective didn't change much from the childish neutral excitement I displayed back then. As the time to hike the trails drew nearer, I began to feel slight nervousness that I wouldn't be able to actually do it. The reality of what I was about to undertake started to sink in: I was about to hike one of the longest trails in the world. The momentum of the preparations and sacrifices we had made to hike these trails, buying thousands of dollars of gear, moving from Colorado to Utah to Washington, and acquiring permits for the trail, was too great for my mild hesitation to stop. Before I knew it, I was on the PCT, beginning a trek of over 2,000 miles that would take me 7 months. I loved it. I saw so many new things: cool rocks, bugs, plants, and small animals. I met so many new people: trail angels and fellow hikers, some of whom we are still in contact with. I had so many new experiences: sleeping through windstorms, hiking through snowfall, bitter cold, and blistering heat, and seeing towering cliffs, shady forests, and expansive plains. I read so many new books, probably more than I had read in my entire life leading up to the trail. And most of all, what drove me onward was the knowledge that I was doing it. I, Tristan Bennett, 12–13 years old at the time, was conquering one of the hardest backpacking challenges in America. It felt amazing to feel so powerful, to learn for an absolute fact that I can do hard things. I remember at the end of the PCT telling somebody, probably my Mom, that my four favorite things about it were the people I met, the things I saw, the books I read, and the knowledge that I had done it."

Part 2: Pacific Northwest Trail

July–September 2020

We didn't intend to hike the Pacific Northwest Trail in 2020. Yet, along with almost the entire world, we had to make changes to our plans because of COVID-19. The Appalachian Trail was our original goal, but we quickly changed our minds when our friend Travis flew out to Georgia and then almost immediately flew back home to LA. His reasoning was that the unknowns of COVID made him feel like it was a bad time to thru-hike. If people were too worried to pick up hitchhikers, getting food would be extremely problematic. It didn't take us long on the PCT to realize how dependent we are upon trail angels. So, we decided to stay closer to home and take a shot at the PNT. The success of this adventure hinged on the fact that we had Adam's parents, Le Anne and Ellery, to help us. Le Anne hiked with us more than 600 miles, and Ellery ran the supply car. The time we got to spend with them is priceless, and in my opinion, this was our most enjoyable hiking season because of them.

PNT Day #1

"Above all, do not lose your desire to walk. Everyday, I walk myself into a state of well-being and walk away from every illness. I have walked myself into my best thoughts, and I know of no thought so burdensome that one cannot walk away from it. But by sitting still, and the more one sits still, the closer one comes to feeling ill. Thus, if one just keeps on walking, everything will be all right." —Soren Kierkegaard

Logistics to get on the trail were complicated, per usual. Adam, Tristan, Ruby, Kaia, Muir, and I drove our little Volkswagen Jetta from our home in Washington to Lincoln, Montana, where we spent the Fourth of July with our awesome friends, the Fairhursts. After the celebrations, we drove to Eureka, Montana, 3.5 hours away. Unable to gather intelligence about the trail conditions in town, we decided to hike east from Eureka to Polebridge. All we knew was that we couldn't get to the official eastern terminus because the Blackfoot Tribe had closed its land due to COVID (and set a very hefty fine if any hikers were caught there).

After stocking up at the grocery store, we started the seven-mile drive to the trailhead, mostly on rough dirt roads outside of Eureka. On the way, we met a thru-hiker named Catwater (she was taking a break in the shade on the side of the road as we drove by, so we stopped to chat). She gave us an update between Polebridge and Eureka (she is super nice, about Adam's mom's age, a 20-mile-a-day type hiker, but was slowed significantly by the blow downs and snow). She has done the PCT and CDT and was supposed to be on the AT this year too.

We parked our car at the trailhead and noticed the car next to us was a firefighter from Colorado with PCT, AT, CDT, and Great Divide Trail stickers (a Triple Crowner+!). The trail started with steep switchbacks, which were super tough. One switchback touched against the "49th Parallel," and we got to touch Canada. Ruby had a meltdown when she couldn't get her book to play on her MP3. Kaia needed to take breaks to use her inhaler. Tristan has accepted the trail name Turtle (on the PCT he went by Gancho).

Perks of this hike thus far: Kaia keeps reminding us that she hasn't complained, we are getting hours of exercise, and we are seeing beautiful sights outside! We stopped for dinner near Blacktail Creek. Our stuff was spread out all over, and we were surprised by three hikers: Cervesa, her dad, Mosey, and Matt. Cervesa is the Triple Crowner+; it was fun to chat with her, and she gave us a big compliment when she said, "You guys look like thru-hikers."

Dinner was awful. We didn't have enough water to presoak the couscous, so we only let it sit for about ten minutes. (I need to remember that the day you start a hike isn't the day for backpacking food! Just bring town food because you are going to eat it right away.) Kaia was cracking me up (and herself) saying it tasted like sand. She took a big fall today when she rolled her ankle on a rock and then the weight of her pack smashed her head into another rock on the trail. She didn't cry, just laughed it off. I guess that's the way we start big hikes! We ended up hiking 6.9 miles with a 3,000-foot elevation gain!

PNT Day #2

"I don't know where I'm going, but I promise it won't be boring." —David Bowie

Today we met Not A Chance, Gasket, Click, Iron Husk, and One Gallon. One Gallon is a quadruple Triple Crowner—you read that right, he has hiked the CDT, AT, and PCT four times each! Plus, he's done a bunch of other trails. He was so humble and genuine. He told us, "I don't really see myself as a hiker. I'm more of a canoe guy." He builds his own canoes in the off-season! Ruby spotted two very old, dilapidated cabins; we wondered who would have built them in this remote location so long ago. We dealt with lots of slippery snow, and it rained on us too.

I told Kaia to look up at the cliffs we were hiking under, and she lost her balance and almost fell backwards. She yelled, "Never tell me to look up again!" Her pack is too top-heavy, and that's a problem. We hiked a steep trail about a mile off the PNT to a lookout on top of Stahl Peak. We hung everything to protect from mini bears (mice) and settled in to spend the night. Kaia enjoyed dinner more tonight (because of hiker hunger and the longer soak time for the couscous). We don't have a stove with us this time, so we are experimenting with "cold soaking." At lunch Tristan laid down on spilled ramen noodles and tuna to put on his rain jacket and got a lengthy lecture from both parents about how bears want to eat him now that he smells like food. We are in grizzly country! There was rain and fierce wind all night (another bad night's sleep for me).

PNT Day #3

"If at some point you don't ask yourself, 'What have I gotten myself into?' then you're not doing it right." —Roland Gau

It was so disappointing to wake up to no view this morning from the lookout—it was a total whiteout. But we got to sleep in a fire lookout! How cool is that?! Our socks, shoes, and clothes didn't dry a bit overnight. Collectively, we can agree that one of the worst feelings in the world is putting cold, wet socks, shoes, and clothes back on! Even when it wasn't raining on us, the plants were so overgrown on the trail that it was like walking through a carwash. We met a hiker named Cruise, who we met on the PCT near Snoqualmie, Washington. He was also on Kaia's hiker Olympic team in Shelter Cove! We also met his friend Goose. Tristan had a bad fall yesterday while climbing over blown-down trees and landing on some broken branches sticking out like daggers. He seems to be well enough to keep moving forward.

I asked everyone before bed what was their favorite of all God's beautiful creations they saw today:

Kaia: waterfall

Ruby: other hikers

Me: flowers that look like fireworks

Adam: the beautiful turquoise stream by our camp

Tristan: the parting of the clouds for a moment of sunshine

13.7 miles today.

PNT Day #4

"I am always doing that which I cannot do, in order that I may learn how to do it." —Pablo Picasso

Another not-good-night's sleep on the tiny Klymit mats we switched to save on packweight. (I miss my Big Agnes mat!) But we had a much warmer night and morning, and I let everyone sleep in until 7 a.m. We camped on Flathead National Forest land and walked on Highway 114 for about 14.5 miles. We only had a few cars pass, two dual sport bikes, one forest service worker (who stopped to ask if we were okay), and a nice older gentleman who stopped on his four-wheeler to chat with us. He couldn't believe we were headed to Polebridge because he said it was 17 miles away and very busy this time of year. He counted 187 cars or trucks pulling boats passing his house yesterday! He was funny and asked which one of us was bear bait and if the dog was packing his own weight. We told him we were hoping to camp for the night on forest service land, and he told us where we could go. I'd been praying for help just like this! Fortunately, we were very close to the campsite (we'd been passing private land signs for over an hour and were getting nervous).

We ate dinner in a little meadow and backtracked to some tent spots. I found a small antler shed during dinner and gave it to Muir. He's so happy with his new toy. Kaia's knee is swelling and bothering her. I'm hoping we get a hitch into Polebridge tomorrow so she can rest. I've noticed how I'm spending a lot of time pondering, praying, memorizing, and enjoying podcasts, and what a change that brings. I love it out here!

PNT Day #5

"Nature never did betray the heart that loves her." —William Wordsworth

We need to remember that a 10% chance of rain means 100% while backpacking! Tristan decided to use his hammock last night. At 3 a.m. it started raining, and I got him out of the hammock and into the girl's tent. We left camp by 7:45 a.m., knowing it was a 15-mile road walk into Polebridge. We stopped for a break at an old cabin the forest service has for rent (there are a lot of them around here). Glacier National Park was right next to us, on the other side of the river. After about seven miles of walking, a very kind man named Mark pulled over and offered us a ride. He was the leader of a big line of trucks, all caravanning on a family rafting/camping trip. The kids and I loaded into one truck, Muir went in the back of another, and Adam went in another. They dropped us off at the famous Polebridge Mercantile where we got bear claw donuts, a loaf of their huckleberry bread, and a few sandwiches. Yum!

Adam and Ruby were able to hitch all the way back to the Jetta at the trailhead in Eureka (in three hitches, one of which was an 18-year-old kid who went 110 miles out of his way to get them safely to the car!). They drove back to Polebridge and brought us fried chicken and veggies for dinner, and we camped out on National Forest land (next to the same group who gave us a hitch into town earlier; they're great people). The clouds parted momentarily during the sunset, and we caught a glimpse of the beautiful mountains in Glacier National Park. This area is breathtaking!

PNT Day #6

"'You do not understand,' said Pippin. 'You must go—and therefore we must too. Merry and I are coming with you. Sam is an excellent fellow, and would jump down a dragon's throat to save you, if he did not trip over his own feet; but you will need more than one companion in your dangerous adventure.'" —J. R. R. Tolkien, "The Lord of the Rings"

We left Polebridge early and made our way back to Eureka. Highlights were eating at McDonalds, getting Kaia a knee brace, picking up some Little Debbie's Cosmic Brownies and non-ramen food for Kaia's birthday, and swimming in Lake Koocanusa.

It was a big climb to the top of Webb Mountain, 3,333 feet in 4.5 miles. Ruby spotted some blueberries and huckleberries and had a great time picking them for all of us. As we sat eating dinner, a guy on a fat-tire bike came along. He is bike packing around Montana, mostly on roads but taking side trips on trails. He noticed Ruby's ration cup full of berries and excitedly asked if we had just foraged them. Ruby showed him where the blueberries were, and he said it is the first time he has ever eaten blueberries in the wild.

After a long, slow slog to the top, we hung out and enjoyed the view from the lookout. We thought it was strange that no one else was there. Our trail app noted that the forest service rents this one out for $35 a night, and it is nearly always booked. We decided to hang our food in the pit toilet for the night to keep it safe from bears and mini-bears. Right after securing our food, a tiny car with a giant canoe on top drove up the rough dirt road. I stopped to chat with the driver, who kept saying, "That's odd," when I explained that we were camping nearby and had hung our food in the bathroom. I asked him if he wanted us to move our food, and he thought for a moment, then said, "No," and apologized for being so frustrated. He had gotten lost trying to find the lookout, and the road was rough on his car. Tristan and I helped him unload his car. He offered us water, Gatorade, dark chocolate, and a hot breakfast with him in the morning!

PNT Day #7

"We're merely one tree with various types, shapes, and sizes of leaves that all wave differently in the breeze." —Rasheed Ogunlaru

True to his word, trail angel Joe from Minnesota provided us with an amazing breakfast: eggs, hash browns, sausage, cherries, yogurt, and fruit cups! We used his binoculars to see the next lookout, and it turns out that's where we planned to camp tonight. I thought we'd do a 14.5-mile day and camp by a lake, but Adam talked us into going all the way to the lookout, and I'm so glad he did. Awesome wildflowers were in bloom all along the way, including some we'd never seen before! We hiked from 8:30 a.m. to 8:30 p.m. (with a few hours' worth of rest stops in between), staying at the Mount Henry lookout with a hiker named Wook. Another big climb day. Ruby wants to now be called

"Piggy Bank" because she's found 11 cents on the trail. 16 miles, 5,000 feet of elevation gain.

PNT Day #8

"In the presence of nature, a wild delight runs through the man, in spite of real sorrows." —Ralph Waldo Emerson

We survived the night in the Mt. Henry lookout. Four out of seven of us were convinced the wind would topple us over. I kept thinking of that movie Twister where the barn was torn apart by the wind. Good thing this lookout was built better (and anchored by thick cables and concrete, Adam reminded us). We awoke to a beautiful sunrise, way above the clouds!

Just yesterday, Tristan was talking about how much he appreciated having dry shoes, admitting that if he hadn't spent so much time hiking with wet shoes, he wouldn't have the same level of gratitude. Well, today we got another dose of wet shoes as we hiked through wet bear grass. We got to see the lovely Turner Falls and hike through plants taller than Ruby!

We hoped to get into town to get Kaia a hot birthday dinner, but we were having no luck getting a hitch. A friendly guy named Marty drove past us on his way to go fishing, saw us again on his way home, and brought us all into Yaak. He joined us for dinner and ended up buying our food (and ice cream for the kids!). He is originally from Iowa, used to be a firefighter in Montana, and is currently working at a boarding school for troubled teens. He is renting a cabin from a lady who runs an "oasis" in this tiny town. She let us set up our tents on her property, do laundry, and use her outdoor shower, all for $40. She breeds Akita dogs and has a whole gaggle of cute puppies that she is selling. ($1,000 each! "Mom, can we please get one?" Nope.)

PNT Day #9

"The world is big and I want to have a good look at it before it gets dark." —John Muir

Adam left early to hitchhike to our car parked near Eureka. The rest of us did zero-day chores, including patching too many holes in Tristan's gear. Muir got us kicked out of the "oasis" by barking too much. So we got lunch at the saloon and hung around their shaded outdoor eating area. They are super hiker-friendly and are allowing us to set up our tents in the back of their property. We are waiting for Adam, his parents, and Sierra to arrive tonight, and we will hit the trail again tomorrow.

PNT Day #10

"Nature is not a place to visit. It is home." —*Gary Snyder*

Adam, Sierra, Le Anne, and Ellery arrived last night with Costco pizza! We camped for free behind the saloon in Yaak, and Ellery spent hours shuttling us up to the trailhead. It was our first "slack pack" (where the bulk of our gear stays in the car, and we only take the bare essentials). We climbed up to the awesome Garver Mountain lookout (it costs money to spend the night here, but it was open for us to just look around). They had puzzles, maps, magical twinkling lights, and a desk with a drawer that has a checkerboard drawn underneath! It was so cool. I wish we could hit all the lookouts, but the next one involves miles and miles of bushwhacking. Le Anne led us back to the car, and we did three miles in an hour and ten minutes! (A personal record pace for this group!) We are so happy to have Sierra back and Le Anne and Ellery joining us.

PNT Day #11

"Security is mostly a superstition. It does not exist in nature, nor do the children of men as a whole experience it. Avoiding danger is no safer in the long run than outright exposure. Life is either a daring adventure, or nothing." —*Helen Keller*

We left camp at 7:45 a.m. with a big climb ahead of us to Rock Candy Mountain. (That's its real name; I didn't make it up!) Avalanche lilies were in full bloom by the pond. There were plenty of patches of snow—always a slippery adventure! Ruby slipped but recovered quickly.

Today we reached the Montana/Idaho border! There is no official marker, so a hiker ahead of us drew a line with rocks and spelled out the states with pine branches. We will hike all the way across Idaho (all 92 miles) on the PNT.

Super embarrassing moment for me: I found a 2.5 pound weight in my pack—nearly 200 miles into the trail! I'd been adding weight to my pack while training for this hike, and this one was hidden in the Camelback pocket I never use!

Poor Ellery had a hard time finding us tonight. We had some miscommunication through the InReach and had asked him to meet us at a forest road that was difficult to find. He has a very hard job taking care of all of us!

PNT Day #12

"My wish is to stay always like this, living quietly in a corner of nature."
—*Claude Monet*

Our day started with two teenage-looking moose crashing through the trees near where we were packing up camp. There was no sign of the mama. We saw a sign that read, "Attention Motorcyclists: National Forest Requirements in Effect during Fire Season!" Then there was a list of things required: Forest Service–approved spark arrester, a shovel at least 24" with 6" or wider blade, and a one-gallon water bucket or crash helmet. We laughed for a long time about the "one-gallon water bucket or crash helmet" requirement. We asked a ranger about it later, and he said, "Well, you have to have something to collect your huckleberries in!" Foraging for berries is Ruby's specialty!

The Feist Creek Resort is right off the trail, so we treated ourselves and met Ellery here for lunch. Le Anne stayed with Ellery to help him find the next meeting point while the rest of us started a monster climb (while slack packing). It started to rain, thunder, and lightning, and that put extra pressure on them to find us (even though the "Old Jeep Road" they were on was way too rough for their car). Eventually we were reunited, and we felt so badly they had such a stressful time getting to us!

PNT Day #13

"Study nature, love nature, stay close to nature. It will never fail you." —*Frank Lloyd Wright*

We had two trail runners run through camp as we were packing up this morning. They were super nice guys and stayed for about twenty minutes to chat with us about trail conditions. This is where we left Le Anne and Ellery to drive down the awful "Old Jeep Road" while we hit the trail. Tristan was looking at the map and said, "We have 10 miles to bushwhack. It isn't as the crow flies, it's as the crow walks." We laughed and laughed.

My kids are appreciating and identifying wildflowers (they are so abundant in this area), much to this mama's delight! Ruby's collection of berries today: wild strawberries, huckleberries, and blueberries.

Our Guthook app gave us two options for getting to Brush Lake. We chose the red line alternate option, a bushwhack. This turned out to be a mistake. It added 3.5 miles of hot road walk/bushwack and made us two hours late for meeting Le Anne and Ellery. However, our frustration was soon forgotten when we found the perfect camp and swam in the awesome lake.

PNT Day #14

"They sat there, feeling happy together." —*Arnold Lobel, "Frog and Toad are Friends"*

Today was a zero day with not much to report except that I put my foot down and said I could no longer get an awful night's sleep on the Klymit mats. I need the three-inch Big Agnes mat back. Lucky for me, Le Anne and Ellery brought it out with them! We had another "fire in the sky" sunset tonight!

PNT Day #15

"In nature, nothing is perfect, and everything is perfect. Trees can be contorted, bent in weird ways, and they're still beautiful." —*Alice Walker*

The trail crosses the Kootenai River and starts the climb up Parker Ridge. It is cool to see the way the river snakes through this beautiful valley! Last year, hikers were leaving comments on Guthook that there were 200 to 300 blown-down trees on the trail in this section because of a fire. We were very grateful that some trail crews had been out before us to get it all cleaned up! There was also a spring five miles up from the road (it was a hot climb of 5,180 feet elevation gain in 11 miles). Tonight was one of the best sunsets yet! Parker Lake down below us was reflecting the beautiful evening glow.

PNT Day #16

"Passion is lifted from the earth itself by the muddy hands of the young; it travels along grass-stained sleeves to the heart. If we are going to save environmentalism and the environment, we must also save an endangered indicator species: the child in nature." —Richard Louv, "Last Child in the Woods"

Ruby and Le Anne worked together this morning to get the bear bags down from the trees. Tristan prefers to hammock over setting up his tent–I don't know how he survives the mosquitos! He says he doesn't mind them. We got to take a lunch break and go swimming at Pyramid Lake. The PNT is known for being extra difficult, and this is one of the reasons why: bushwacking! Today was the beginning of the five-mile Lion's Head bushwhack. It was sketchy, and we ended up setting up camp about halfway through, way before our intended stop for the night. It was hard to take photos/videos while bushwhacking, but I got a picture of Adam's bleeding leg, and that sums it up well (he got several deep gashes from a dagger-like broken branches). This day was very hard on our gear, our bodies, and our schedule!

PNT Day #17

"The trick to happiness wasn't in freezing every momentary pleasure and clinging to each one, but in ensuring one's life would produce many future moments to anticipate." —Brandon Sanderson, "Oathbringer"

It was a miracle that we survived the bushwhack, all in good spirits even! Five miles took us 11 hours! When we finally got back to the trail, Kaia got on her knees and kissed the ground. We saw beautiful sights though and are all the better for it. It was by far the most difficult section of trail that we have ever hiked. After chatting with other hikers, we learned about the many injuries that have happened here. I'm so grateful we made it out safe. Taking a rest next to the Lion Creek with its natural water slides was awesome.

Thru-Driver (the trail name we gave Ellery) met us on a dirt road (after being lost for several hours and getting some directions from a local). When he got to us, he said, "In all my 50 years of working, I've never had as much anxiety as trying to find you hikers!" He made us homemade pasta and chicken salad, cut up watermelon and cantaloupe, and got a dozen doughnuts per Ruby's request. We got to bed at 11 p.m., way past hiker midnight, but we were all safe and sound and well-fed!

PNT Day #18

"I have learned that to be with those I like is enough." —Walt Whitman

Ellery provided a feast for breakfast (cold cereal and fruit) and a lunch to-go. We repacked a three-day supply of food and hit the trail at 10 a.m. Along the way, we met a thru-hiker from Seattle named Fifty who has hiked the PCT and CDT. Nowhere in all of Idaho is there a PNT sign, which makes navigating frustrating, but for a few moments we collided with their Centennial Trail. A 3.5-hour lunch break at Priest Lake was just what we needed!

Later that afternoon we came to a sign that read "Boundry: Natural Research Area." We think this sign meant that they were researching mosquitoes (the kind that don't care what repellent you use and can bite you while you are hiking, no matter how fast you go). Whenever we can, we eat dinner several miles before finding home for the night–just another attempt to make sure bears don't smell our food. We found a super flat, nice camp spot right off the forest road in a lovely little meadow.

PNT Day #19

"The tree which moves some to tears of joy is in the eyes of others only a green thing that stands in the way. Some see nature all ridicule and deformity…and some scarce see nature at all. But to the eyes of the man of imagination, nature is imagination itself." —William Blake

This morning's walk was filled with sights of fields of daisies (that match perfectly with Ruby's Kavu hat) and giant cedars. The mosquitos out here are big trouble! Ouch! There was much rejoicing when we crossed the state line from Idaho into Washington. However, there is no marker for this monumental achievement on the trail.

Lots of blowdowns to maneuver around today. Muir jumps up on fallen trees and looks at us like, "What's the big deal?!" We ended the night with a double rainbow and a tough time finding a spot to camp.

PNT Day #20

"Whether you think you can, or you think you can't—you're right." —Henry Ford

This will go down as one of the most difficult camps we've ever had! We just couldn't find flat ground, so we did the best we could. Tristan lucked out and was able to hammock, but it was still tricky to find trees close to us and spaced apart correctly. Sierra's pants got destroyed today in blowdowns; they had so many holes. We passed a dilapidated cabin next to Noisy Creek, which was so cool. I wish there would have been an informational plaque to tell us about its history. Ellery was waiting for us at the Noisy Creek Campground. He was so fortunate to get a spot in a busy campground, and we were so grateful!

PNT Day #21

"Someone get that kid an apple pie!" —Cory Allen (Tristan's uncle who noted that a boy who talks about apple pie so often should have one for his birthday)

It was a lazy zero-day getting some much-needed rest. Today is Tristan's 14th birthday! Sullivan Lake was the perfect spot to relax and celebrate. Ellery even brought up a Costco apple pie for the occasion!

PNT Day #22

"I would have never started this trip if I had known how tough it was, but I couldn't and wouldn't quit." —Emma Gatewood

We had a big day today. Ellery was able to help us avoid about 70 miles of road walk (on dangerous, busy highways), but it took a lot of logistical planning and driving for him. Le Anne came up with the idea that Adam, Sierra, Kaia, and I would ride with Ellery early in the morning to the trail while the rest stayed behind to clean up camp. There were 11 miles of trail sandwiched between two big sections of road walk that Adam didn't want to miss. It would have been so hard to shuttle all of us to the trail, so we divided up. On the way up, we stopped in the super cute town of Metaline Falls to look around and briefly take advantage of the cell coverage. Then it was about 10 miles up a rough dirt road to drop us off at the trail (we scouted out this area yesterday, so it was the second time Ellery had to maneuver his car up there).

We started hiking at 10:15 a.m., and it was a three-mile uphill slog. We took a side trail to summit Abercrombie Mountain, and the views were awesome. There was a logbook in the geocache box at the top that was fun to look through. Some were PNT hikers and some just there for the day hike. The logbook was a "Rite in the Rain" brand, the same as the journal Adam had just bought for me. The one in the box was completely filled in, so Adam suggested I donate mine as the next logbook. I did, and I look forward to going back someday to see all the entries.

PNT Day #23

Tristan had heat stroke symptoms yesterday, so he got to go to Spokane with Ellery and rest for two days. The logistics of getting him off trail if we didn't have our "Thru-Driver" would have been so difficult. We are extremely grateful for his help! Today we spotted a PNT sign. Very exciting! We ran into three hikers here at the water source (one of which was Not A Chance, who we met on day two). Another hiker named Sweetblood was going eastbound for a three-day section. She hiked 1,800 miles of the PCT last year. She told us she has run into twelve westbound hikers in the last two days. Wow, we are in the bubble!

PNT Day #24

Ruby filled in a page in the register at the top of Cooper Butte. I wish I would have taken a picture of what she wrote; it was so cute to see how she signed all our trail names (Darn Tough, Kidnapper, Wildflower, Amazon, Honey Badger, Turtle, Ladybug, and Muir).

PNT Day #25

Today we passed through an area burned by the White Mountain fire, caused by lightning in 1988. Guthook offered us two routes today, another choice between a red line (bushwhack) and a blue line (also with a bushwhack but shorter). We took the blue line, and it was still hard. A group of hikers passed us as we were getting into our tents. One of them was Not A Chance, and she said she lost her phone during the bushwack. Poor girl! She had paper maps with her, but I think it would be so hard to navigate this trail with just maps.

PNT Day #26

We got everyone up at 5 and were on the trail by 6. It was predicted to be a hot, hot day (and it was). This is the moment Kaia told us she was having heat stroke symptoms. Ruby ended up with two bloody noses, and Tristan got stung by a wasp. It was a slow moving, very hard day. Four of us are wearing Altra Olympus shoes, one is in Oboz, one is in Hokas, and one doesn't need no stinkin' shoes (Muir). So far so good with the footwear. Thank heavens we found a muddy little stream, both for our water and a spot for Muir to cool down. We enjoyed an evening swim in Swan Lake to wash away the trail dust and have some fun.

PNT Days #27–28

We got two much needed zero days at Swan Lake. We swam, used our bear cans to shampoo everyone's hair, put together puzzles on top of pizza boxes, slept a lot, and ate and ate and ate (thanks to Ellery for picking us up some food at the nearest town). Also, there were some very memorable sunsets here (especially while swimming at sunset—pure magic).

PNT Day #29

We said goodbye to Ellery and Bear Box (the trail name for Le Anne's car). They get to return home for a two-week rest! There was lots of road walking today, but it was along beautiful dirt roads with very little traffic (maybe four cars passed us all day). We took a 2.5-hour dinner break by Granite Creek to hide from the heat.

Tristan has created several different dice games and is always trying to recruit players during down time. He also spends a lot of mental energy calculating the probability of rolling all sixes or all ones—stuff like that. It must be the cold-soaked ramen that makes him so smart (ha!).

Today's climb was a big one, and it was so hot it felt a bit like walking on the surface of the sun. We were all sweating buckets! The view towards Republic at the summit was awesome though.

PNT Day #30

The "Sturgeon Moon" was unbelievably bright last night! What a sight to see. The sun was just starting to rise when I sounded the mom alarm. We are trying so hard to hit the trail early, but it seems like the earlier I wake them the longer it takes to get out of camp! 5 a.m. has been our norm, hoping to be hiking by 6 (but usually it's 6:30). I'm so glad we camped where we did last night. The other spots we were considering had lots of unhealthy-looking trees that seemed like they could topple over any time. We hiked past a good flowing spring about a mile back because Guthook comments made it sound like Pass Spring was better. It wasn't. We should've passed, but we needed the water! It was a very slow trickle from the pipe, and it was the worst colored water we've seen on the trail thus far! But we drank it and lived to tell the tale.

We saw lots of trees that had been cleared and a few chainsaw "drawings" in logs, proof that the Pacific Northwest Trail Association was here in 2011 doing trail maintenance. Our map led us right to private property. We were looking for a way to avoid it but found none. The kids saw a sign that said, "No trespassing! We are tired of hiding the bodies!" There were skulls and weird statues like a grim reaper with the baby doll head. The only way out was to toss our packs through the fence and crawl under (which we did as quickly as we could). Fortunately, we didn't see anyone on the property.

We stopped at Cougar Creek for a lunch break. As we were packing up, a local came over to chat with us. He was nice and looked like Santa Claus, but we didn't talk long because Muir was barking at him. Later, he drove past us in his truck while we were road walking. He said another group of hikers had stopped right where we did to take a lunch break soon after we left. He told us, "You sure did pick a hot day to do this hike!" and asked us where we were headed. We told him Bonaparte Lake, and he told us about a "short cut" on a dirt road (which is where the trail was leading us anyway). We thanked him, and he drove off in his air conditioning while we continued sweating in the heat.

We were all so excited to jump in Bonaparte Lake after a long, dusty day, and it felt so good! The campground hosts were very kind and let us have the "Double Site" for just $6! We met two other hikers here, Lumberjack and Stretch. They are 30+-miles-a-day guys, so we'll probably never see them again. They had seen our names on trail registers and were happy to meet us. Lumberjack shared some homegrown tomatoes a trail angel gave him near the highway (they were so good; they tasted better than candy!). 21-ish mile day.

PNT Day #31

5 a.m. wakeup call! Putting on cold, wet clothes from last night's swim didn't feel so good. Goodbye Bonaparte Lake! We watched it fade away as we climbed up, up, up to the top of Bonaparte Mountain. The lookout at the top is one of 30 remaining lookouts in WA that are still manned by a fire ranger in the summer. The original lookout was built in 1914! We met Jim, a ranger who works three weeks on, then two days off (in that order, all summer). He was a super nice guy; it was obvious he loves having company when hikers come up to visit. Because of COVID, he could only have two visitors in the lookout at a

time. When it was my and Kaia's turn, he pointed out all the mountain ranges we could see and the route he thinks the PNT should have gone (he said he would never hike the PNT because there was "too much road walking!"). Kaia said later that she wanted a summer job in a fire lookout someday (but that she would have to have someone with her, so she didn't get lonely). By the time we made it down Bonaparte Mountain and found a place to camp, we were at a 17-mile day.

PNT Day #32

Rain hit at 3 a.m. Sierra and Kaia didn't have their rain fly on, so they scrambled to get that attached and got Tristan from his hammock. He got to sardine in with them for the last few remaining hours of sleep.

The trails we followed out of this area are all part of a snow park in the winter for cross-country skiers. It looks way fun! The kids were noticing all the fish in a pond, and Ruby was lamenting that she didn't have a fishing pole. A few moments later, we met a couple with fishing gear that were headed to this pond. They offered us some cherries and chatted with us for at least twenty minutes. The husband asked us what our favorite piece of gear is. I said, "My umbrella," and Adam said, "Well, the piece of gear I'm glad we don't have with us is a stove!" Then we chatted about cold soaking and what we've been eating. The wife pointed out a plant on the side of the road. She said it is called plantain weed and that it is edible. Then she picked a leaf, half-heartedly wiped off the dirt, and popped it in her mouth. "It's a little gritty," she said, "from the dirt." I appreciated her willingness to prove that it was edible, but the sight really grossed out Kaia because of how many cows had obviously trampled that plant.

Just before Havillah, there was a random bench on the side of the road chained to a big pine tree. It was a very nice rest stop for us weary travelers. Usually the church in this little town of Havillah allows hikers to come in and get water and food, use the restroom, camp on the lawn, etc. We had heard they would be closed to hikers because of COVID, but they did leave a large informative sign by the road telling us where the nearest water was located and some trail angel numbers in case of emergency. That sure was nice.

After a lengthy lunch break, we got hit with rain just as we were packing up. We haven't had a drop of moisture on this trail in three weeks! Our map showed that Summit Lake, which is one mile off the trail, one way, had a campground. Someone had described it as "disgusting," but we felt it was worth the risk (we needed water and the next closest source was eight miles ahead). I was hoping for pit toilets and a shelter to protect us from the rain. No such luck. It wasn't even a campground, just a road to the lake. We crawled in our tents early to warm up and hide from the rain. 16-ish miles today.

PNT Day #33

Last night we heard two dirt bikes and one truck pass us (the person in the truck probably wanted to go fishing but was deterred by four tents in the parking spot). Otherwise, it was a peaceful night. It rained off and on, but we woke up to clear skies. It was super hard to get moving when we were cold and putting on wet clothes. We didn't get out of camp until 7 (in spite of waking at 5). Filtering water from the lake took a long time, and it was not delicious.

The thimbleberries are finally ripe! No one is more excited than Ruby. The couple we met yesterday told us we could also eat the serviceberries (which they call Saskatoon). Those have a lot of seeds and aren't our favorite (no one tried the plantain weed, either). Our friend Wook fell behind when he stopped to work at a dude ranch near Republic for a few days. We found him at an overlook, just packing up his camp. I told him I liked the patch on his shirt. (It read "Hiker Trash: National Trail Addict." We need to get a few of those!) It was great to visit with him again.

We came across a sad sign about an accident that took place here in 1946. It read, "In Memory of Forest Judd," and a smaller sign that had fallen to the ground read, "Judd was killed when his log truck rolled here. He is buried at Loomis Cemetery. Harry Haney was at the scene of death and put up the above sign. Forest was 29 and was killed at this location on December 23, 1946." The old road was now an overgrown trail. I can only imagine what road conditions and logging trucks looked like back then.

We had a beautiful view of the Osoyoos River and surrounding valley! On the road walk into Oroville, Tristan found a case of conchas (a Mexican dessert he likes) on the side of the road. Some of them were still sealed, so he gathered them. That was some exciting and unexpected trail magic!

We met the owner of the only hotel in town (who was out front hanging a sign to welcome PNT hikers. He used to live in Yakolt, Washington, near where we currently live). He tried to get us to stay for $60 a night and free laundry. It was tempting, but he was adamant about only four to a room and we knew we could fit our whole group in one campsite if we just walked a half mile more.

Adam's brother Geof and his daughters Dayne and June arrived with Costco pizza and our next food resupply. We're so grateful for their help, and it was very fun to see them. The wind really picked up as we were setting up our tents! We are looking forward to swimming in the lake, doing laundry, eating town food, and using coin-operated showers tomorrow! It was a 17-mile day with the walk to Osoyoos Lake.

PNT Days #34–35

We had a few zero days at Osoyoos Lake visiting family, cooking up yummy food over the fire, and roasting marshmallows. It's such a beautiful campground!

PNT Day #36

Last night Le Anne dropped us off at Cold Springs; she isn't going to join us for this next section because of poor trail conditions in the Pasayten Wilderness and logistics. We thought it was one of the best campsites thus far, well-cared for by hunters, most likely. The first climb of the day was crazy steep, and we lost the trail for a bit. Bushwhacking through thick sage is harder than it looks! We came across a rare PNT sign after we found the trail again. Sierra said, "We really could have used this sign back there when we were lost, rather than here in the open." Oh well. We took a nice long break while Adam and I used the last moment of cell coverage to book backcountry permits for North Cascade National Park (coming up next week! Yeah!). 19.9 miles today.

PNT Day #37

The Apex Mountain area is so beautiful! It was especially cool to see the Tungsen mining cabins. Cathedral Peak was an unbelievable sight with a giant snow and ice crag running down the middle. We took a detour down below Cathedral Peak to see a deep slot canyon. Another hiker had suggested we take that route, and I'm so glad we did. Upper Cathedral Lake was also phenomenal; this whole section is gorgeous. We stopped to inspect the locked Spanish Camp Patrol Cabin. Apparently, there are rangers here on occasion, but it was empty when we arrived. We are almost done with the 40-ish miles of burn in the Pasayten Wilderness (fires hit this area hard in 2015 and 2017, we learned from a trail crew member).

This was our biggest mileage day of our hiking careers up to this point, 23 miles! We had intended to go about 20, but where the app showed a camp, we found none. So, we hiked on into the night, about an hour past dark, and finally found a spot to drop our tents.

PNT Day #38

What a sunrise! It was a welcome sight on a very cold morning (today was the first time temperatures have dropped below freezing on us this summer). We are using hanging water bladders (CNOC brand) and Sawyer filters to get drinking water these days, a hands-free solution to the multi-daily chore.

Today we faced so many blowdowns! Our pace slows down to 1–1.5 mph during these obstacles. We had hoped to hike 20 miles today but only made it 14 because of those darn blowdowns. Crossing the Pasayten River at the end of the day was a great time for all of us to wash the blood and dust off our legs!

Today just so happens to be my and Adam's 20th wedding anniversary! It was a perfect way to celebrate: an epic day in the wild with our four children and dog (our treasures!).

PNT Day #39

Because of all the dead trees falling everywhere, it was tricky to find a safe place to camp last night. But we did. We were out on the trail early in spite of the cold! We passed a fire weed plant that was taller than Kaia, and I kicked myself for not snapping a picture. The Pasayten Airfield might have been constructed in 1931 by the Works Progress Administration (although some sources say that is a rumor). It is amazingly flat! A ranger cabin is nearby, and we stopped there for a lovely lunch.

We reached the Pacific Crest Trail and pretty much lost our minds with excitement. I've been looking forward to this moment since we started the PNT. Kaia wondered if we would recognize the trail once we got there. Right away we were flooded with memories! Last year, exactly in this spot, we had stopped for a snack break on the PCT when we saw two rough-looking hikers come out of the woods. They had a tough time in the Pasayten and didn't have many nice things to say about it. They were only using paper maps and didn't even carry a phone or GPS. I remember thinking, "Yikes, that PNT sounds too hard. I don't think I want to hike that one." And here I am. We walked past the same campsite where we slept the night before we saw the Canadian monument last year, which was so cool! We enjoyed the big climb over Rock Pass. It was pouring rain last year, and it was so wonderful to see the amazing vistas this time around!

PNT Day #40

We stopped to check out the remains of an old cabin on our way to Devil's Pass. I'm so very grateful that trail maintenance crews have recently been through this section!

The biting horse flies were out in full force today, and they particularly love Adam. We took the Jackita Ridge Trail to meet up with Adam's parents for a resupply. At the trail junction, we stopped for a moment to chat with a trail runner. A few minutes later, we realized he told us he was headed to Ross Lake, but he took the trail in the opposite direction. I was worried he got lost, but there was no way to track him down to find out.

This area is called Jack Mountain, named for prospector Jack Rowley in 1859. It is an impressive sight. We had a very memorable camp with a long-lasting "wowza" of a sunset.

PNT Day #41

We woke to a sliver of a moon and Venus above our camp at sunrise. The stars were amazing last night! Tristan took the lead for this steep section. Usually Ruby is in front, but sometimes it seems like Tristan has so much energy that it is painful for him to go our slower pace. At Devils Park trailhead, we met up with some bear hunters who entertained us with hunting stories. Le Anne and Ellery arrived, and three of us piled in with them and three caught a hitch with the bear hunters. The trail provides!

PNT Day #42

When we were hiking the PCT last year, Adam and Kaia hitched into the awesome town of Winthrop to resupply. Turns out, it is a resupply town for the PNT too. We had to recreate a photo they took last year sitting on some saddles in town, but this time with buffs over their faces because of the mask laws. Aside from a lot of food and rest, we also got to swap out some old gear for much-needed new gear this weekend (especially shoes).

PNT Day #43

We took off from the Ross Lake trailhead mid-morning. It was fun to walk across the dam on a bright, clear day. There were such beautiful views! COVID restrictions prevented us from visiting the Ross Lake Resort. We would love to go back someday. We took our lunch break in a cove, and Tristan and Ruby caught little fish while Sierra and Kaia swam. The trees were so big and beautiful that it brought tears to our eyes!

PNT Day #44

We had a backcountry permit for 39 Mile Camp in North Cascades National Park last night. The ranger gave us the "stock camp" because of our group size. When we got there, another group was spread out in the best spots. We did the best we could and found decent spots for our four tents (just not all together). There was a bear box and a toilet. One of the other backpackers said, "It's an outhouse without the house—so just an out."

We took a lunch break at the Beaver Pass Shelter. A few miles after lunch, we crossed over a ground hive of bees and wasps (maybe just one or the other, maybe a united army of both—we don't know). Muir and I got stung once and ran away as fast as we could. Ruby and Kaia made it past with no problem. Adam and Sierra decided to bushwack in a wide arch around the hive. Tristan was listening to a book and instead of heeding our warnings, he walked right through the angry swarm. Le Anne went off trial but stepped into a different hive. Le Anne and Tristan both got stung about 30 times each. It was beyond awful! Then we saw a small black bear but didn't get a picture. Next, Ruby got a bad bloody nose. We slowly made it to Twin Rocks Camp, mostly in a green tunnel, but with a few glimpses of the views we would have tomorrow.

PNT Day #45

Tristan did well with Benadryl overnight to help with all his stings. Le Anne didn't sleep much because she had an itchy allergic reaction, and no medicine seemed to help. She said in 32 years of backpacking she's never had a run-in with bees or wasps like that!

Today we got to cross the river on the cable car. We highly recommend this activity; it's fun for the whole family! The only hitch in the cable car system was getting Muir down the ladder at the end. Adam carried him down safely by using the handle on Muir's backpack and carrying him like a briefcase.

PNT Day #46

Rain woke me up in the night. I hopped out and got all the tent flies zipped up, with a few sleepy people whispered "thank you!" from inside. Morning hit and we were off, walking through wildflowers and foggy skies.

We ended up at the Hannegen PNT trailhead at 1:30 p.m. From here, things got interesting. Adam and his parents left to go find a campsite. The kids and I thought they would be gone for about an hour. Eight and a half hours later, Adam came back for us! We watched a movie, ate almost all the food, and set up an emergency plan. I hadn't received any messages on the InReach, even though I sent five out. We set up our tents and tried not to worry too much. Our plan was to call Adam's sisters in the morning if we hadn't heard back from our missing party. Turns out, Adam and his parents drove about 45 minutes until the road they were on abruptly ended. Then they realized they would have to drive about three more hours, all the way around Mt. Baker, to get to Baker Lake. On the way, they stopped in at the Pacific Northwest Trail Association's main office. Adam got us some stickers and chatted it up. Sounds like our kids will be the youngest kids to ever hike the PNT. He also heard that there is a dangerous river crossing that we need to avoid. So, they set up at Baker Lake, and he came back for us around 10 p.m. Luckily for us, he also brought pizza!

PNT Day #47

After much searching, Le Anne and Ellery located a spot last night to set up our tents. The group that was here before us left a huge mess, and Le Anne put on a rubber glove and cleaned up a lot of yuckiness! Adam, the kids, and I arrived at 1 a.m. Ruby had Le Anne's tent poles and ground cloth in her backpack, so we were worried Ellery and Le Anne were without shelter (it was raining so hard). Fortunately, Le Anne is super resourceful and found Adam's tent and got it up (it has a tricky set up). Our slack pack around Baker Lake was extremely beautiful (and memorable because it was raining cats and dogs). We didn't see many other backpackers, but we did scope out some backcountry campsites that we would love to return to in the future.

PNT Day #48

The day started out with some magnificent sunshine! We attempted another slack pack, but it went terribly wrong. Early in the morning, Ellery dropped us off at the Park Butte Trail, a very crowded trailhead with access to a plethora of trails up and around Mt. Baker. We took a side trail to the Instagram famous Park Butte lookout (#worthit). We had a beautiful 13-mile walk with several big obstacles, and we were very grateful to not have our packs. When we got to the meeting spot, however, we instantly knew something was wrong. The Pioneer Horse Camp parking lot was completely overgrown. I turned on our InReach, and a message from Ellery popped up: "Hey guys, big problem. The road is closed nine miles away from where I need to pick you up!"

All we could do was start the nine-mile road walk. It was 8:30 p.m. Fortunately we had one headlamp and one flashlight. We came across two big washouts in the road, one of which we had to climb/ fall 10 to 15 feet straight down then back up again (that was fun and muddy). A group of big-sounding animals (probably elk) moved in the woods next to us at one point. We never saw them, and Adam started whistling along with the music Sierra was playing loud on her speaker (that's how I knew he was nervous too). All our prayers were answered at 1 a.m. when we saw Ellery's car. He had food for us and seemed even more relieved than we were to know we were all safe and sound! There were three different locations he could have been waiting for us at; fortunately for us, we picked the right spot to start looking for him! We are grateful that Le Anne had taken a rest day to help him instead of slack packing with us. It was a 24-mile day. Whew!

PNT Day #49

Sunday: a day of rest! Le Anne and Ruby built us a fire, and we hung out at camp until 2 p.m. Our trail friends, Port and Starboard, hiked past our camp, and Adam called them over to chat. They have their godson, Henry, joining them for the rest of their hike. We persuaded them to join us for s'mores. It was so great to visit with them and get some of their intelligence on the trail ahead (Olympic National Park is going to be tricky for PNT hikers this year). After our friends left, we packed up camp and sent Ellery, Adam, and Sierra off to find our next campsite. When Ellery returned for the rest of us a few hours later, we were shocked to find out that he was driving us to a hotel! It's our first time sleeping in a bed in six weeks! Turns out, as our trail leads us into more civilized areas, it is going to be increasingly difficult to find places to camp (especially with a group our size).

PNT Day #50

We had trouble getting back on the trail today. Obviously, we couldn't hop back on where we left (at the Pioneer Trailhead) because the road is closed, so we tried to enter on logging roads. The "No Trespassing" signs (and a guy in a logging truck) told us to move on. Next, we tried to bushwhack to the trail, but there were too many blackberries—and there is no bushwhacking through blackberries. Despite all the obstacles, we got in about 10 trail miles today.

PNT Day #51

The morning started on logging roads but merged into lovely trails. Soon we were seeing lots of PNT signs! Ellery helped us with a yellow blaze over I-5. We connected with the trail again near Oyster Dome, and the views were amazing! We camped at Bay View State Park (logging three more miles after dinner). We enjoyed an amazing sunset over Padilla Bay!

PNT Day #52

We walked into Anacortes on this awesome bike/foot bridge (reading all the informative signs along the way). We got to hike through the Anacortes Community Forest. Our Guthook map was way off in this area, so we relied on the Gaia app. We took a picnic lunch to Cape Sante Park to enjoy the views. Then we hiked through the amazing Deception Pass and North Beach. We ended the day with Thai food in Anacortes!

PNT Day #53

Whidbey Island day! We had a blast slack packing along the beach, checking out the lighthouses, and exploring Fort Casey. We got our first bald eagle sighting. Finally, we took a ferry from Whidbey Island to Port Townsend (our only ferry ride on the PNT!).

PNT Day #54

We found a good deal on two hotel rooms in Port Townsend and gratefully got all cleaned up. The PNT cuts through Port Townsend on eight miles of paved Olympic Discovery Trail, so we got that covered today. We also made a lot of calls to Olympic National Park to get permits and try to figure out the tide chart for the final leg of our adventure.

Just a side note about maps and tide charts for this area: it took studying three different maps, three different types of tide charts, and talking with three different rangers before I grasped how to navigate this area and set up our backcountry permits. If you go (which you should), be sure to get the "Green Trails" map for the Olympic Coast Beaches because it has the most helpful information about how low the tide needs to be in order to cross the "danger" or "caution" areas. Be sure to calculate that sometimes you'll be doing fewer miles per hour (we dropped to an hour per mile or less in the slippery spots), and always check for tide levels before you book your permits!

PNT Day #55

We had a bit of trouble getting out of Port Townsend. We decided the road walk would be too dangerous for seven hikers and a dog, so Ellery shuttled us. The campground was full, so in a wild twist of events, we ended up in another hotel (where the little kids played putt-putt, for a moment forgetting all about the trail and feeling like normal tourists).

PNT Days #56–57

The Allens came to hike with us for a few days! They brought delicious, fresh peaches that we ate with cream, no sugar needed! Luxury of luxuries! The eleven of us hiked through Deer Park Camp and Blue Mountain in Olympic National Park (enjoying the best sunset on the trail thus far). We rented two shelters to sleep all of us. Tristan made a rookie mistake and left some trail mix in the side pocket of his backpack. At 3 a.m. a mouse (or pika) chewed through his pack and noisily enjoyed a snack. This woke up everyone (except for Tristan), and there was a flurry of activity. Some cousins decided to set up a tent and sleep in it for extra protection from the rodent.

PNT Day #58

We were so fortunate that the Allens could join us on the trail from Hurricane Ridge to PJ Lake today. Nothing puts a pep in the kids' step quite like hiking with other kids their age, especially these fun cousins. Ellery was able to hit a Costco today and surprised us with giant pizzas and a watermelon. We were quite a sight, snarfing all that down on the side of the trail. The kids all had a blast swimming (very briefly) in the super cold PJ Lake.

PNT Day #59

We had to say "goodbye for now" to our beloved family, and the rest of us continued the trail west (Le Anne is with us too). We hiked down to the Elwha River, and Adam pointed out all the King Salmon to us. We set up in a shelter by the river and had a great night's sleep (no rodents because extra reminders were given to store food properly).

PNT Day #60

We started out bright and early and took a quick tour of what was once the Elwha River Dam. It was removed in 2011, and a cool outdoor museum of sorts is in its place with lots of informational signs and displays. Unfortunately, the only way to see this is to hike or bike to it because the river washed out the Olympic Hot Springs Road (the National Parks Service paid $450k to fix the road, then flooding destroyed it again). We did see a few people on bikes. It is such a beautiful area. We took a break to enjoy the hot springs (although it was a very hot day, so we used our umbrellas to shield us from the sun as we sat in the hot water). After that we crossed paths with the legendary One Gallon again. He told us he never filters his water—unbelievable, yet true. We finished off the day hiking through fireweed taller than our heads up to Appleton Pass, where we set up camp and witnessed an off-the-charts kind of sunset!

PNT Day #61

Bear! A big black bear was just wandering around Olympic National Park like people weren't there. We stopped with about five other hikers to watch the bear meander and look for food. It was a big, fluffy bear who didn't seem to mind at all that we were hanging around. We had some great views of the glaciers today and saw lots of ice climbers heading up to climb up there. At one point we passed through a cut log that was about twice as high as Ruby! These forests are phenomenal!

PNT Day #62

Today was another day of being mesmerized by the beauty of the Hoh Rain Forest. We stopped by the visitor center, awkwardly standing out from the other tourists, and learned a few things from the informational signs. "The Hoh Rainforest is one of four rainforests on the Olympic Peninsula . . . The most common types of trees that grow in the Hoh Rainforest are Sitka spruce and western hemlock (Washington's official state tree), which can reach over 300 feet high and seven feet in diameter." Ellery picked us up from the visitor center and brought us to a campground for the night.

PNT Day #63

We spent this Sunday relaxing, recovering, and touring around Forks, Washington. The girls may or may not have listened to the entire "Twilight" series together as we hiked this section.

PNT Day #64

We started our day at Third Beach, Olympic National Park. Because of permits and the tide, we needed to backtrack south along the beach to camp at Toleak Point Camp. We lucked out with perfect weather and conditions. Even though our group's ages range from 11 to 67, there was no obstacle too difficult. It was an amazing day of sunshine, climbing ropes and ladders, reading tide charts, building sandcastles, studying marine life, and setting up a fire with driftwood (the flames change colors!).

PNT Day #65

We left Toleak Point and hiked north towards our next reserved campsite at the Chilean Memorial. There were awesome tafoni formations (geology!) just north of Rialto Beach. All of us enjoyed the beach walking when the sand was compact and level. Other times we were on slippery rocks, and it was very slow-going. Occasionally we would see some interesting creature or something the tide brought in and would stop to check it out. It was a big push for us to get to camp that night, and we arrived after dark.

PNT Day #66

In the night, the noise of the tide had the girls convinced that the water was going to wash over them. We were safely away from high tide, but it is hard to convince a kid of that fact when they are exhausted. Nevertheless, we were safe, yet the rocky ground didn't help anyone get a good night's sleep.

Lots of buoys were found today, and some were carried for many miles by the kids who wanted to take them home. In the end, all but one was tied to the roots of a giant fallen tree at Yellow Banks Beach (giving it the look of a giant Christmas tree with round buoys for ornaments). We had an extra special last night on the trail with another driftwood fire (there were no fire bans in effect at that time).

PNT Day #67

"The act of driving your body, very occasionally, close to its limit of endurance is for some reason one of life's major satisfactions. And relaxing afterwards is one of life's most luxurious rewards." —Colin Fletcher, "The Thousand Mile Summer"

We woke up to very smoky air. Later we would learn that Washington was currently fighting many terrible wildfires. From Sand Point to Cape Alava, we had fun racing the tide. At Wedding Rocks we used the overland trail but never could find the petroglyphs other hikers had mentioned finding. From Cape Alava we had a great view of Ozette Island and Tskawahyah Island. We heard a lot of noises and figured it must have been coming from the hundreds of sea lions (at least we think that's what they were) out on the islands. We did get to see a family of beach bears!

Ellery, Adam's sister Ellynn, and her three sons met us at Cape Alava in the afternoon. There is no western terminus for the PNT (at least there wasn't in 2020), so we just took a few final pictures at the beach and started on the Ozette Loop boardwalk to the campground. There was much rejoicing to be reunited with our family. The last week of hiking in the Hoh Rain Forest and along the coast was some of the best backpacking we've ever enjoyed. We highly recommend it.

Part 3: Continental Divide Trail

April–September 2021

In late 2019, I applied for our family to be part of the Thru-Hiker Syndicate (an ambassador program for long-distance hikers). A few months later, we were ecstatic to hear that we were awarded the honor of being sponsored by Osprey, Vasque, NEMO Equipment, Darn Tough Vermont, and LEKI. Then COVID hit, and the sponsors could no longer endorse hikers for 2020. We were notified by our contact that we were going to stay on the list and would be given more information in early 2021. More sponsors joined the Syndicate: Sawyer, Peak Refuel, and Ledlenser. Everything seemed to be moving forward, with frequent encouraging emails. We had been getting updates from the Appalachian Trail Conservancy, but the vibe seemed to be "We are asking you to postpone your hike, but we know hikers are going to hike, so here are some tips we'd like you to follow to stay safe." We were good with that. But then we got the email saying the Thru-Hiker Syndicate cannot support hikers on the AT. My first reaction was "This is a blessing in disguise!" Adam said that we were okay on gear; there were just a few items that needed to get replaced between the six of us. It would be no problem if this was going to fall through on us. We decided we would call our contact at the Syndicate, Steph, just to see what was on the table and what other options there might be. I think she was worried we were calling because we were angry. When we wrapped up our conversation, she said, "Well, that went a lot better than I was expecting!"

Prior to the call with Steph, Adam and I talked about the possibility of switching to a trail on the list that wasn't asking hikers to postpone. The Continental Divide Trail was our plan for next year. We followed the Strawbridge family closely on their CDT thru-hike last year, and it looked fun. Plus, we have lots of supportive family in Colorado that would jump at the opportunity to help us if we needed it. The CDT suddenly looked better and better as our choice for 2021.

Aside from being "sell-outs" and doing all we could to keep our sponsorship, we also have another major concern. Our second oldest daughter, Kaia, has really been struggling with her asthma. She did great on the PCT until we hit the Sierras. We thought maybe it was just altitude-related. When we returned home to Washington, poor Kaia struggled more with her lungs. Our hike from July to September on the PNT went well for her, but she slid downhill fast when we returned home. We've taken her to multiple doctors, an allergy and asthma clinic, and even a vocal cord specialist, but there's no improvement; it's just getting worse. Maybe it is the wet climate of the PNW, we wondered. In November, Kaia moved to Colorado to live with my parents. She felt a little better but got COVID and was down for two weeks. Fortunately, many with asthma have found COVID doesn't have the effect on the lungs once predicted. Kaia doesn't like me to nag about this, but I think there is a direct correlation between her fitness level and her lung health. Hopefully, there will be sufficient time to train and ease back to hiking when we start in New Mexico. We had a lot of concerns about the heat and humidity on the AT for Kaia (and the rest of us too). We decided to switch to the CDT, and we get to keep our sponsors. It is a relief to know we will have family members within a few hours to lend a hand if asthma, COVID, or any other obstacles become too much for us.

To get our family of six plus our trail dog to the CDT's southern terminus, so many things had to fall into place. Thankfully, Adam is a logistical mastermind. On our flight, we only checked two bags, both under 50 pounds. One had our flattened Osprey packs, and the other was loaded with quilts, mats, and tents (plus a few other items stuffed in). Then each of us had a personal item, limited by Frontier's restrictions. I'm not sure how, but miraculously it all fit and fell into place! Adam's extra wonderful and helpful parents, Le Anne and Ellery, joined us on this adventure to drop us off at the trailhead (and are even hanging out for almost a week with some of their friends in Arizona, partly to make sure all is well for us at the start). We flew into Denver very late on Saturday, my brother came to pick us up, and we got to crash at my parents' house for the night. My grandparents joined us for breakfast the next morning (which included Gram's more-than-famous cinnamon rolls). Then they all dropped us off for our flight to Tucson. It was so wonderful to see them.

Last night we loaded our packs with the six days of food. Starting this trail is one of our "worst case scenario" moments. The first reliable water source is 13 miles away, and the next is 12 miles after that! Our food weighs about 10 pounds per day, plus a few liters of water! Base weight (only gear, not including food and water) for each of our packs is about 18 to 25 pounds. So, we are starting heavy (and Adam and

Tristan are carrying some of Ruby's share), but each day we will get a little lighter.

CDT Day #1

"Me thinks that the moment my legs begin to move, my thoughts begin to flow."
—*Henry David Thoreau*

Ellery and Le Anne dropped us off at the southern monument at 3:30 p.m. (2.5 hours of bad dirt roads southeast of Lordsburg, New Mexico). It was hard to say goodbye and not have Le Anne hiking with us! We stayed in the shade of the monument until 5:30 to let the desert heat die off a bit. There are lots of cows in this area, and it feels as though they are playing games with hikers by making a plethora of paths. Fortunately, the CDT has lots of signs for us to follow. The burden of six days' worth of food and four liters of water on our backs was intense (we had planned to start with more, but a trail angel assured us that the water caches were well-stocked and to only bring four). Some of our backpacking heroes, Buddy the Backpacker's parents, Dion and Andrea, run Crazy Cook Shuttle Service. We got to visit with them for a bit in Lordsburg. Tonight we were rewarded with a beautiful sunset, and after 4.5 miles we found a great spot to set up camp. The light pollution is so low, and the stars are so bright!

I love that the CDT southern monument says, "The trail unites us." It is a perfect motto for this trail and our family. We are out here to teach our kids that they can do hard things and encourage them to reach greater depths of gratitude for God, nature, family, and community. We've met so many wonderful trail angels and hikers thus far and look forward to more to come. It is awe-inspiring to realize how much there is to observe and learn in this amazing desert. But it is hard, and everything hurts—it wouldn't be Type 2 fun if it didn't!

CDT Day #2

"Walking: the most ancient exercise and still the best modern exercise." —*Carrie Latet*

We started waking kids at 5 a.m. and were on the trail by 6:15. The trail followed dirt roads and washes. During one rest break, we chatted with hikers named Lone Wolf, Mona Lisa (who both did the PCT in 2019 and are working on the Triple Crown too), and a newbie from Montana (no trail name yet). We arrived at the first water cache at 11:30 and set up our rain flys for shade (because there was no natural shade to be found). Some "new to us" plants we enjoyed seeing today: ocotillo, hedgehog cactus, and walking stick cactus. It was so very hot and windy during our siesta. Kaia wishes she was in the "green tunnel" (Appalachian Trail) instead of the desert. After a six-hour rest (don't judge us; it was hot!) we hiked for a few more miles down the road and camped in a safe pullout. Best quote of the day: "My lips feel like they are on salt fire." —Kaia

13.1–14.5 miles total for the day (depends on what device you believe is correct).

CDT Day #3

"Without new experiences, something inside us sleeps. The sleeper must awaken."
—Frank Herbert

We left camp at 6:15 and saw a plethora of vehicles bringing hikers to the monument, at least 30. We chatted with Long Bird and Crispy after our 3.5 hour siesta at a yucky cow pond (at mile 27, the first natural water source). A nice rancher drove up in his truck and asked us not to loiter around the water because then his cows won't drink when people are there, which is understandable. Behind us are the Big Hatchet Mountains, an awesome sight. We enjoyed seeing so many fishhook barrel cactus today. They are so cool looking. We are grateful that trail angels are stocking gallons of water about every 13 miles for the first 75 miles. We couldn't do this section without their help! Quote of the day: "Darn it! I just knelt on my crackers!" —Sierra

CDT Day #4

"Now I see the secret of making the best person, it is to grow in the open air and to eat and sleep with the earth." *—Walt Whitman*

We left camp at 6:30 to a beautiful sunrise. About 100 yards ahead we noticed a sleeping hiker, cowboy camping. It looked like we didn't wake him, but I don't know how because we were being so noisy. We chatted with him a few miles up the trail; his name is Vince, he's from Canada, and he hiked 200 miles of the PCT as a warmup so he can push 30-mile days on the CDT. Sierra helped out a hiker named Jess and threaded her two huge blisters (to prevent blisters from forming under blisters). We camped at mile 47.2. 16.5 miles. My watch said we did 19.4 miles and 42,861 steps.

Today's quote: "I've been hallucinating that I smell lasagna. I have no idea why." —Tristan

CDT Day #5

"They are able who think they are able." —Virgil

We left camp at 7:15 and headed two miles to the water source: a tire. I said it tasted like eggs, and Kaia shouted, "No water should ever taste like eggs!"

During a siesta we met OT (stands for Old Timer) and Jacobie. They are 67 and 62. They told us this is the best education we can give our kids and that this will shape the rest of their lives. They assured the kids that nothing will be too hard for them now; it's all mental. They were very nice guys!

Aaron Rogers, a newspaper reporter/fifth grade teacher from Silver City, New Mexico, reached out to me on Facebook. I called him for an interview while we were hiking. He also agreed that the trail is the best education for our kids.

Kaia got heat rash all over her legs, so we stopped short of our goal. During this afternoon's siesta she fell asleep, and her legs were exposed to the sun. She was in so much pain! We camped at 13.8 miles and watched another lovely desert sunset.

CDT Day #6

"Nature is the silent art that speaks to the soul." —Unknown

We got a late start today; it was about 40 degrees and so windy. Poor Kaia had a rough night but was feeling a bit better. OT and Jacobie had camped nearby, so I rushed over to tell them once again how much I appreciated their kind words. We got three liters each from a cow trough and headed out for nine miles at our fastest pace yet. Muir is limping sometimes; we are all very worried about him.

At high noon, we stopped for lunch and had a 4.5-hour siesta in a wonderful shady spot, cold and windy. We were excited to finally meet So Good and Cake, a few of the Strawbridge family friends on the trail right now. This area has beautiful lava rocks and bright white rocks together (we need to do more research to find out what kinds of rocks these are). We found a camp spot at mile 74.5 just after a nasty cow trough that had a faucet with clear flowing water! 13.5 miles; my watch says 17.23 miles, 37,747 steps.

CDT Day #7

"Like with any journey, it's not what you carry, but what you leave behind."
—*David Smart, "The Trail Provides"*

Town day! We made it the nine miles into Lordsburg at noon, picking up a lot of trash on our way in. We put Muir's little shoes on him, and that seems to be helping. He got a shower and an Epsom salt soak (he was not a fan). As I was brushing him in the parking lot, I heard someone say, "Hey, I recognize that dog!" Turns out it was our friend, Crazy Eyes, that we met several times on the PCT in 2019. It was so great to visit with him (for several hours!). We also had a nice chat with OT and Jacobie. Adam made us a very special dinner, a seven-layer dip in our ration cups. We got our food all sorted out and hope to hit the trail early tomorrow!

CDT Day #8

"If you can find a path with no obstacles, it probably doesn't lead anywhere."
—*Frank A. Clark*

Getting out of town proved to be more difficult than we hoped. I guess the hotel room was just way too big for us because we lost several important items therein. Finally, by 8:30 a.m. (two hours after I woke the children) all the bags were packed, lost items were found, and treasures were accumulated from the hiker box. It was a long road walk out of town past the train tracks, some dilapidated buildings, and lots of trash. We took a siesta at a windmill from 11:30 a.m. until 4:30 p.m.

to beat the heat. Poor Muir hates wearing his boots, but his pads must be sore. We got to eat our Peak Refuel dehydrated meals tonight—super delicious! We sang "Peaceful, Easy Feeling" as we went to bed: "I want to sleep with you in the desert tonight, a million stars all around . . ." Guthook says we made it 11 trail miles, and my watch says 34,191 steps and 15.4 miles.

CDT Day #9

"What we fear doing most is usually what we most need to do." —Ralph Waldo Emerson

We left camp at 6:30 a.m. to a lovely sunrise. The trail has been leading us mostly east, so we are walking right into the sunshine. It was so windy that I had on two jackets. Ruby was just wearing her long-sleeved hiking shirt. I complimented her on how tough she is, and she got a big smile. We crossed the 100-mile mark and finished the desert section! Unfortunately, Muir needs some time off the trail. He refused to move forward from mile 106.5, which is a water cache run by trail angels. Fortunately, the newspaper reporter who wrote up a story about our family put us in contact with a trail angel named Margie Grey. I told her about our situation, and within an hour she and her hubby drove two vehicles to come rescue us (and bring eight more gallons of water because the cache was out). While we waited for them to arrive, we chatted with a bunch of hikers, including Long Bird and Crispy (who now refer to our family as "The Croods"). We got pictures with Pax (a nice hiker from Seattle who is a PNT trail angel) and Longbird and Crispy too. The Greys brought us to their home in Silver City, fed us, got us set up with comfy beds, and are helping us come up with options to care for Muir.

CDT Day #10

"What the next generation will value most is not what we owned, but the evidence of who we were and the tales of how we lived. In the end, it's the family stories that are worth the storage." —Ellen Goodman

They say if you want to restore your faith in humanity, hike a long-distance trail! Our first zero was spent being spoiled by trail angels Margie and Owen Grey and their son, Zach. We had a feast for breakfast. Then Owen helped us get to Walmart, Morning Star Sports, and the UPS store (to return the kids' MP3 players that broke the first week on the trail). The kids played games, enjoyed the giant swing, and even got to operate heavy excavation machinery. Margie and her friends are section hiking the CDT and are very active trail angels in the Silver City area. Jennifer, John, and Kari came over for dinner and treated us all like superstars! Margie has offered to take in Muir for the next week or so while we hike the Gila alternate to Pie Town. Then Adam will hitch back to Silver City to get him. It is too much to ask, and these angels are going way beyond the extra mile (we hope to return the favor and/or pay it forward one day). We all want to be trail angels when we grow up!

CDT Day #11

"Remember that everything that is happening around you, good or bad, is in some way conspiring to help you." —Debasish Mridha

Margie started our day with super delicious omelets! Kaia got new inserts for her shoes, and I added metatarsal pads in hopes of helping with her foot pain. Ruby had a tearful goodbye with Muir. The Grays drove us to the Gila River alternate parking lot at about 10:45 a.m. We chatted with the trail angel named Cheshire Cat for a while and met a hiker named Cruise Control. We saw a lot of hikers on the road walk. Margie said it is too bad so many use this alternate because the official trail is so pretty. We are amazed to suddenly see so many giant pine trees! About 45 minutes after the Grey's dropped us off, Margie pulled up next to us on the dirt road. I had forgotten Ruby's umbrella in her car! She had gotten all the way home when she saw it. If Ruby hadn't stopped for a lengthy potty break, we would have started hiking up a dirt road that Margie couldn't drive on. She said she was praying the whole way she would catch us before that point, and she barely did! We are so grateful! We made it to mile 10.5 on the alternate and it was a beautiful hike (a handwritten note from a trail angel guided us to great water and camping). We are overlooking Devil's Garden and Moore Canyon from our camp tonight, and the view is so incredible.

CDT Day #12

"Research suggests that exposure to the natural world—including nearby nature in cities—helps improve human health, well-being, and intellectual capacity in ways that science is only recently beginning to understand." —Richard Louv

We left camp at 7:30 a.m. It was a cold morning, so we stayed in our tents an extra hour. We hiked through Sycamore Creek, an area damaged by fire and flood. It was a frustrating slog. I had hoped we'd make it 10 miles by lunch, but we only made it 5. After our one-hour siesta, we found the trail angel Cheshire Cat and his dog, Silvia, at a crossroads. He fed us fresh fruit! Mona Lisa and Lone Wolf showed up shortly thereafter. It was great to visit with all of them again. We made it to Sapillo Creek at 5:45 p.m. and stopped for a quick dinner before entering the Gila River. We passed by two brothers with four horses that were out hunting turkeys. They asked our trail names and then said, "Wait! Are you the family that was featured in the Silver City newspaper? We read that article, and it was so inspiring!" One of them said he had two young kids and would love to do something like this with them someday. He asked if Adam carried a cattle prod to get the kids up the trail. The kids said no, just candy. Entering the Gila River was exciting; it sure is beautiful here! We made it to camp before 7:30 p.m. The kids swam in the river—so fun!

CDT Day #13

"If it weren't for the rocks in its bed, the stream would have no song." —Carl Perkins

We woke to the sound of ducks and wild turkeys. I'd say this was our favorite day thus far. There were beautiful clear skies, nice cool water crossings (all day long), tadpoles and fish to watch, and we ended the day at Doc Campbell's (a general store run by an awesome family that is so helpful to hikers).

CDT Day #14

Quote from an informational sign we passed: "The mountains, the canyons, the valleys, the mesas, created the perfect home for the Chiricahua (Apache). Among these living spaces, our wikiups were hidden. The scattered valleys contained our fields, the boundless prairies stretching away on every side were our pastures, the rocky caverns were our burial places. Everything in our country was sweet." — *Apache Elder speaking of the Gila headwaters*

It took us until noon to organize our food and leave Doc Campbell's. One Amazon box didn't arrive on time, so hopefully it will get forwarded to the next town. A few hikers chipped in and donated food to us. Miraculously, with their generosity, we had everything we needed to eat for this next section. We met Catwater again (we met her on our first day on the PNT last year), and she told us to take the Little Bear Canyon to the Gila River. We missed the Gila Cliff dwellings because they were closed due to COVID, which was a bummer. Little Bear Canyon was extremely beautiful. I overheard Ruby say, "That was so fun!" after leaving the canyon and crossing the Gila again. We set up camp near Jordan Hot Springs, ate dinner, then soaked in the not-too-hot water. Unfortunately, we had to cross the cold Gila to get back to our tents. Tex, No Keys, and Moonshine are here too (we visited with them at Docs, and Adam and Tex talked about hunting wild boar for over two hours last night). Looks like the next three nights will be cold, below freezing even! We could be facing rain and/or snow for the next two days. We covered 10 trail miles today; my watch says 31,157 steps and 14.2 miles.

CDT Day #15

"First, I must explain my purpose in walking this strange path. Though I was quite willing to let my family think me insane, I would not leave the same as my cognomen upon the winds of history . . . Yes, I could have traveled quickly. But all men have the same ultimate destination . . . We are not creatures of destinations. It is the journey that shapes us. Our callused feet, our backs strong from carrying the weight of our travels, our eyes open with the fresh delight of experiences lived."
—*Brandon Sanderson, "The Way of Kings"*

I forgot to bring in my Sawyer filter last night; fortunately, it felt like 40 degrees when I woke and not the forecasted 33 (if our Sawyers freeze, they no longer filter water properly). I did wrap up my wet shoes and socks in a plastic bag and put them under the foot of my quilt in hopes of not having to put on frozen socks/shoes in the morning. It works! The barometric pressure alarm went off on Adam's watch at

5:30 a.m., signifying a storm is on its way. It sprinkled on us a bit while we were packing our tents. On and off through the day we'd get a little rain, big gusts of wind, and even hail, but it always stopped after a few minutes. It was another day with spectacular views in the canyon! We crossed the river many, many times (possibly a hundred times). It was rough on our knees, ankles, and feet with the water crossings, slippery rocks, and other obstacles. Nevertheless, we had a huge day: 19.6 Guthook miles and 22 miles on my watch!

CDT Day #16

"Heaven is under our feet as well as over our heads." —Henry David Thoreau

We woke the kids at 7 a.m. due to the rain and frost and finally got out of camp by 8:30. Because snow was in the forecast today, we opted to not walk the river for eight miles and took an alternate to the Aeroplane Mesa Campground. While passing through, we visited with Mona Lisa who is getting off trail due to injury (maybe a bone fracture in her foot?). She was teary, and we can imagine how hard it is to pull off trail to let an injury heal! Her husband's aunt and uncle live in Silver City but are out of town, so their neighbor was driving hours and hours to come pick her up! We saw him as he drove up the road, and he stopped to ask us for directions. I asked if he was here to pick up a hiker, and when he said he was, I said, "We call her Mona Lisa, that's her trail name." He said, "Oh, I just talked with some other hikers, and they asked me about Mona Lisa, and I had no idea what the hell they were talking about." The rest of the day was spent watching rain clouds roll in, getting rained and snowed on, brief moments of sun, then lots of snow. The kids talked us into stopping for dinner at 5:30 p.m. during a moment of sunshine. By the time we finished we could feel the snow hitting our faces. We were hoping to make it 20 miles today, but at 16.5 we saw a few big pine trees and ducked under to set up our tents. The snow was sticking to everything; it looked like a winter wonderland. Tristan said, "This is definitely not what I expected in New Mexico!" Fortunately, we all have our winter gear with us (some hikers wait until Colorado to get their warm stuff mailed out). Guthook says we did 16.5 miles; my watch said 19.8 miles.

CDT Day #17

"Live in each season as it passes; breath the air, drink the drink, taste the fruit, and resign yourself to the influence of the earth." —Henry David Thoreau

It snowed, then stopped, then got really windy during the night. I woke the kids at 7 a.m., and we struggled through the cold wind to get packed up. As I was helping Tristan pack his tent, I looked up to see a tall man in an English pea-coat standing a few feet away with a warm coffee in his hand. We were far from civilization, so my brain just couldn't compute what this guy was doing here. He said he was a trail angel and that he had pancakes! Then he walked away. We packed up as fast as we could, then followed a dirt road in the direction we thought the trail angel went. After five minutes, we couldn't find him, and I began to think he was a real angel and that we misunderstood his message. But then we saw a Sprinter van and smelled the pancakes (not just any pancakes—they were made from scratch with lots of ground flax and were so good!). We visited with Guru (turns out he hiked the PCT in 2018) and found out he's been a trail angel on the CDT for a few weeks, but today is his last day because he is starting a new job (we really lucked out!). We walked away with full tummies, a few apples, a few pops, and a whole new outlook on the cold day ahead.

It was so very windy! We got water at a cow trough (not too bad) and had lunch there because there was a bit of a wind block. A few miles after lunch, we crossed paths with Cheshire Cat again! He gave us pineapple and melon and helped loosen the laces on Sierra's shoes (hopefully that'll help with her blisters). Then we did more dirt road walking until we found a nice spot next to a cattle guard to camp (at mile 344.2). Today's miles: Guthook: 19.83 miles. My watch: 50,616 steps, 23 miles.

CDT Day #18

"Now these mountains are our Holy Land, and we ought to saunter though them reverently, not 'hike' through them." —John Muir

We woke to a clear, crisp morning! It was such a soft trail today. Dirt roads aren't too hard on the feet, but there is nothing like a bed of pine needles and soft dirt for sauntering on! We had brief moments of cell coverage as we hiked through the hills around Govina Canyon. It was so great to call and visit with our family.

At mile 349.1 we had a big decision to make: take a shortcut on the dirt road around John Kerr Peak (saving maybe 0.5-1 mile) or continue to the murky water at mile 349.5. (Some of the comments on this water per Guthook: "Nasty, but it'll work in a pinch" and "Collected two liters in the dark. Found a tent site . . . then found leeches. Three on the bottle, two inside, and one already eating my finger.") We decided we had enough water to take the shortcut and push on another 15 miles to Aragon Well. I found a muddy puddle and barely pulled out one liter with my scoop. At dinner, I filtered it through a bandana twice, then through my Sawyer filter. It tasted fine in my oatmeal, but it was a bit earthy when I just took a swig from my bottle. 22-mile water carry, 21-mile Guthook day, my watch says 54,842 steps and 25 miles.

CDT Day #19

"Nature is pleased with simplicity. And nature is no dummy." —Isaac Newton

We were moving slowly today and feeling the effects of the altitude gain/loss and the long water carry yesterday! We made it to the Valle Tio Vences campground at 1:30 p.m., and lo and behold, Cheshire Cat was there! He got us hooked up with bananas, apples, honeydew, and cantaloupe. We settled down for a lunch siesta and didn't get out of there until 4:30 p.m. As we were leaving, Catwater, OT, Jacobie, and Top'O were just walking up. We chatted for a bit while we filled up water at the water cache. A kind trail angel named Jetta drives 25 miles of bad roads to supply this cache. She left her number there so that hikers can let her know when the water gets low. There were less than two gallons by the time we and our friends wrapped up, so I texted her. I also mentioned that she needed to get a Venmo account going so that hikers could contribute for her time, gas, and water. She was excited about that idea.

I didn't take many pictures or videos today because my phone was low on charge, and my battery pack is dead! Hopefully we will get all charged up tomorrow at the Davila Ranch CDT rest stop. We camped at mile 16.7 on the Pie Town Alternate. Today's Guthook: 18 miles. My watch: 48,229 steps and 21.78 miles.

CDT Day #20

"For most of history, man has had to fight nature to survive; in this century he is beginning to realize that, in order to survive, he must protect it." —*Jacques-Yves Cousteau*

We left camp at 6:54 a.m. About a half mile before Davila Ranch, we got trail magic from JohnBoy. Kaia's face just lit up when he said he had Mountain Dew and oatmeal cream pies. When we got to the CDT rest stop, the guy who runs it for the Davila family was there. He was very nice and was just blown away that Ruby has logged so many miles. We cooked up eggs, potatoes, and baked beans they have stocked there for hikers, and he told Ruby to eat extra. We started a load of laundry and got quick showers (all in this three-sided shed with propane burners and a fridge). Then Aaron Rogers (the news reporter for Silver City) arrived with Muir, and there was a very happy reunion! Aaron stayed for about three hours, chatting with us and interviewing the kids for a possible future story. He's a great guy! We are so grateful he brought Muir to us so that Adam didn't have to hitch to and from Silver City. A week of rest did wonders for Muir; he says he's ready to walk to Canada. Lots of other hikers arrived while we were there: Catwater, So Good, Cake, OT, Jacobie, Fried Green Tomato, 13, Top O', Nope, and Ladybug from Quebec. It was a fun group of hikers! After making ourselves more eggs, potatoes, and beans, we hiked out another five miles and camped at mile 31.1 on the Pie Town Alternate). Total of 14.4 Guthook miles; my watch says 41,720 steps and 19.14 miles.

CDT Day #21

"Only a few find the way, some don't recognize it when they do—some don't ever want to." —*Lewis Carroll, "Alice's Adventures in Wonderland"*

We walked 9 miles into Pie Town with awesome views of Allegros Mountain, Castle Dome, and Capital Dome. Our parade of seven headed straight for the Pie Town Pies Bakery. It was packed with hikers! I guess after the Gila River section, lots of hikers take a zero or two here. We had planned to just grab lunch, pick up our resupply packages, and head back out to the trail. But we got sucked into the vortex. First, we had a delicious lunch and wanted more. Second, we realized a package hadn't arrived yet and thought it might be at the post office. Thus, we'd have to stay the night and check there at 8:30 a.m. tomorrow. Third, a storm hit with strong wind, cold temps, and rain and snow. Sarah (the owner of Pie Town Pies) invited us to sleep on the covered porch and even brought out a space heater! It was so wonderful! We bought more burritos and more pie and more muffins.

One of the packages we received was from a trail angel we met on the PCT, Sugar Mama. We met her on Easter Day, 2019, and she gifted all my kids Easter baskets. She asked if there was anything she could send us this year on the trail, and I mentioned that Ruby's birthday is in May. Sugar Mama mailed a birthday party in a box, complete with a cake Ruby got to frost herself, a birthday tiara, a stuffed animal, and party favors for the whole family (even dog bones for Muir!). She even sent plates, napkins, and forks! It was unbelievably awesome!

Total of 9 Guthook miles. My watch says 29,114 steps and 13.43 miles.

CDT Day #22

"We are now in the mountains and they are in us, kindling enthusiasm, making every nerve quiver, filling every pore and cell of us." —*John Muir*

Long water carries are not for the faint of heart! We left Pie Town with what we hoped was enough water to last 22 miles to the solar well at mile 436.1. While we were taking a siesta, we were passed by Lone Wolf, No Keys, and Doggone. Later, we saw Doggone resting in the shade on a lightweight camp chair he carries, and we chatted with him. He and his wife sold their home and furniture in Georgia and bought a teardrop trailer. She's running support for him and being a trail angel. He gave us her number (she goes by Taxi Lady) and insisted we call her if we need a ride to Walmart when we get to Grants (or anything else). It was so great!

We stopped for a second siesta because Sierra and Kaia are having trouble with hotspots and blisters. Kaia is breaking in a brand-new pair of Vasque shoes that were quickly mailed to Pie Town. I had sent an email at Doc Campbell's saying the pair she was wearing was too small. They immediately sent a different style with a bigger toe box that we really hope works. They are lighter, too, which she loved right away, but she's got a bit of a rub in the heel. We've all been super impressed with Vasque so far. The shoes held up well in the river crossings, the soles are sturdier than we are used to (which Adam thinks has nearly eliminated his foot pain), and the customer service has been awesome! Sierra is trying out Kaia's old shoes because she felt like she started with too small of a size (same with Ruby).

Then we were just walking along down this dirt road that is the trail for this section when a truck pulled over to chat with us. He said his wife was just at the Toaster House telling all the hikers that they can get water and camp on their property (16 miles outside of Pie Town). He told us to look for the flagpole, then drove off saying he was going to get started on making us dinner! His wife pulled up in a truck about thirty minutes later, so excited that she had found "the family." She assured us that there was indeed water ahead at the homestead, that we had about two more miles to walk, and that her husband was cooking up a storm for all of us. When we arrived, a nice hiker named Castanza (as in George), said, "I'm glad you made it! I saw you resting a few miles back, and I was worried you would stop there to camp. I almost started walking back to let you know this was here!" He's so nice! Turns out, he met the Strawbridge family on this trail last year while he was hiking Mt. Taylor. We set up our tents, then So Good, Cake, Tex, and Moonshine hiked in. We had an awesome spaghetti dinner feast and really enjoyed visiting together. The husband brought out some muffins, and the wife said, "Hikers call him the Muffin Man because last year he'd drive this section passing out his fresh baked muffins!" They are the nicest people! The Homestead is at Guthook mile 430.1. 16 miles today.

CDT Day #23

We rolled away from the TLC Ranch (aka The Homestead) at about 8:15 a.m. and walked a long, straight dirt road all day. We passed a cemetery, and later Moonshine told us she went in to look at the headstones. She said most of them seemed to be infants and children, which is so sad.

The first water source was a solar well that was pumping cold, clear water into a stock pond. Adam encouraged Muir to go swimming to cool off, and he loved it. We stopped for a three-hour siesta to rest in the shade. Then it was back to the road and the heat and the wind.

During our dinner break, a hiker named Happy walked up and visited with us for a while. We had met him our first week and haven't seen him since. It was fun to hear about his hike thus far and his life experiences.

We found a great camp hidden from the road with a water source that wasn't listed on Guthook! I went to check it out and failed to bring my camera! The sunset was phenomenal, so I grabbed three liters and rushed back to camp for my camera, but by the time I made it back the light had faded. Too bad! I did get to see a happy little bat skimming the surface of the water for a drink—magical. 15.2 Guthook miles; my watch says 40,815 steps and 18.5 miles. We camped at mile 445.3.

CDT Day #24

After about six miles of road walking, we got a delightful visit from Cheshire Cat! He jumped out of his car with a box of ice cream sandwiches, ran to deliver one to each of us, stopped to pet a barking Muir, then jumped back in his car and drove off! Just yesterday Adam and the kids were daydreaming about getting handed ice cream. About a mile after that, Tristan said to me, "I can still taste the ice cream!"

This is the fourth time we've received trail magic from Cheshire Cat. He always insists that just because there's six of us doesn't mean he's going to treat us any differently than the individual hikers. Previously he has had fresh fruit to offer, and if two want honeydew and three want pineapple and one wants cantaloupe, he doesn't insist that we all pick the same fruit to save cutting time! This is high on the top 10 list of things I hope my children learn from hiking this trail. We are all struggling on the trail of life, and a random act of kindness is a priceless gift and a huge boost.

We pushed until 12:40 p.m. to a picnic area with shaded picnic tables, trash cans, and pit toilets. From there, we opted for the Narrows

Rim Trail to avoid the road walk. It was amazing! The views were just WOW! We ended up having to follow a rough, steep "trail" (not a trail, mostly a scramble) back down to the La Ventana Arch trailhead, but it was worth it.

We had dinner at that trailhead at a picnic table again. At the table next to us were Catwater, TinMan, and Earl Grey Goose. We decided to press on another 2.5 miles to where we thought there would be water. Unfortunately, we couldn't find it in the dark; hopefully, we'll find it in the morning. We set up camp near the Zuni-Acoma Trailhead, Guthook mile 502.6. My watch says we covered 46,540 steps and 21.23 miles. We took an alternate to the alternate, so Guthook miles are hard to calculate.

CDT Day #25

Ruby's little feet have been giving her trouble (which is totally my fault; I didn't order her shoes a size up, but new shoes are being sent to Cuba), so she insisted she wanted to use her "hotel voucher" and hitch into Grants. Adam and I told the kids they would each get to choose one night on the trail to book the family at a hotel when they felt like they needed it. We left camp around 7 a.m. and hiked along Highway 117 to our water source: a spigot at a ranger's station that is closed for remodeling. For that entire six-mile stretch, the kids tried to get a hitch with no luck. After the water break, we hiked four more miles before a kind couple from Colorado pulled over. It had started to rain, so we quickly threw packs in the back of their truck (and a dog and half of our group), and three rode in the back seat. They dropped us off at Walmart and gave us their number. They are from Durango and said if we need help when we get near there to give them a call!

We attracted a lot of attention as we sat near the Walmart entrance, surrounded by all our gear, trying to come up with a resupply plan. One man stopped to look at us and said, "You look like travelers. Do you know anyone who wants some cute puppies?" We insisted that we did not. Another older gentleman insisted on buying us Gatorade and some desserts. He was so kind! While in Walmart, a woman stopped to chat with us and marveled about how many hikers she has seen walking into town recently. "There are a lot more coming; we are in a big bubble," I warned her. She seemed delighted to hear all about the trail and walked away with a determination to open a hiker hostel in Grants.

We got a quick lunch, then split up to get more tasks done. While Adam, Kaia, Ruby, and Muir were walking to check into the hotel, a man pulled over and handed them $20. Kaia said he didn't even ask if they were CDT hikers, and when Adam tried to say, "No, we're good!" the man just insisted they take it and drove off. Sierra, Tristan, and I had stopped in the shade at the gas station while I called my grandpa. Another kind soul just walked right up to Sierra and handed her two bags of chips, two bags of cookies, and a gas station sandwich. We are just blown away by people's generosity!

Hiking tip: Rinse all your socks in a sink or bathtub at the hotel or laundromat until the water is clear before putting them in the washing machine. It's the only way your socks are going to lose the dirt that makes them so stiff they can stand on their own!

CDT Day #26

We are having trouble with three of our resupply packages. One arrived at Doc Campbell's after we left that location, so Adam paid again to have it sent to Cuba. One should have arrived in Pie Town, but it still hasn't. And one should arrive in Grants on Monday, but by then we should be about 30 miles north. Hopefully, we can get it bounced to Cuba! We got a late checkout from the hotel and spent the morning buying and organizing our resupply. We road walked out of Grants for about seven miles before hitting the Mt. Taylor trailhead. It is so great to be back on soft trail! We knew there would be a trash can at the trailhead, so we packed out some heavier items for dinner. Adam cooked up some dehydrated refried beans, melted cheese sticks in there, added canned fajita meat, and put it on a tortilla. It was delicious! We rested for about two hours, then climbed to a viewpoint to camp. Guthook says we did 9 official miles, but my watch reads 35,784 steps, 16.1 miles.

CDT Day #27

Mother's Day! We left camp at 7 a.m. and started our climb to 11,300 feet, the summit of Mt. Taylor. We crossed paths with Cheshire Cat and Silvia Blue at about 10:40 and visited until noon. Muir and Silvia do not get along, but it is sure great to visit with Cheshire Cat (plus he gave us watermelon, pears, pineapple, and a Mother's Day sermon!). About a mile later there was a water cache left by Max the Knife, who we met yesterday while we were road walking. The climb up to the summit was so cold and windy, but we had a bit of cell service, so we made some happy Mother's Day calls. The view at the top was amazing but too windy to enjoy long. We set up camp at mile 8.9 on the Mt. Taylor Alternate, which is 17.3 Guthook miles for the day. My watch says 44,757 steps and 20.5 miles.

CDT Day #28

Today was a little bit of trail, a whole lot of dirt roads, and a whole lot of wind. We left camp at 7 a.m. and filled up with water at American Canyon Spring, then again at a cow trough at noon. We had a decent siesta under some giant pine trees. During our dinner break, OT and Jacobie came along and visited for a bit. They've taken more zeros than we have, but they consistently crush 20-mile days! The most geologically interesting spot today was Canon Del Dado, but we did not have to climb down there for water (thank goodness). 20 Guthook miles; my watch 46,747 steps and 23 miles.

CDT Day #29

We left camp at 7:25 a.m. and saw OT and Jacobie at the first water source (it was a .4 one-way hike to Los Indios Spring). It took so long to get and filter water that we just decided to have an early lunch. While we were there, Moonshine, No Keys, Lone Wolf, and Firehazard walked up. It was fun to visit with them and catch up on their hiking adventures. The trail seemed to follow a straight, flat path for about 10 miles, then it took a steep drop down a mesa. The view was fantastic! Ojo Frio Spring is where we stopped for dinner and to camp. We chatted with Moonshine and Firehazard a bit before they took off to log a few more miles. Tomorrow is Firehazard's 31st birthday, so they are trying for 31 miles. Ruby gave Firehazard her birthday tiara to wear tomorrow. Tristan climbed to the top of a nearby hill to get a picture of the sunset and our camp. We camped in a corral to try to hide from the wind, but it didn't work. The windiest night thus far! Guthook miles 18.1, my watch 50,465 steps and 23.16.

CDT Day #30

Beautiful day! The scenery was spectacular! We had a strange encounter with a horse. We don't know if was wild or just lost, playful or angry, but we hurried out of its way (it acted like it was going to charge us several times). We had a painfully long water carry today. One of our first water sources had a dead cow next to the trough, so we opted to fill up at the next source. Unfortunately, the most recent Guthook comment on that was that it was a working spigot, but it was not working. Thankfully there were a few liters left at a water cache. We got to visit with a nice hiker named Stormdasher. He was the one who went ahead from the cache and texted back to say the spigot wasn't working. We had barely enough water to get us the 15 miles to the next spring, so we pushed on. We set up camp at mile 603.3. Passing the 600-mile mark was exciting! 18.1 Guthook miles and 21.67 miles on my watch.

CDT Day #31

We left camp at 6:45 a.m. and made it to Jones Canyon Spring at noon. It was a long water carry and very hot. At the spring, we got to visit with No No, Cake, and So Good. Our long siesta included drinking as much water as we could, playing Uno Flip, and eating lunch and dinner. Muir happily takes the blame for lengthy siestas; it was just too hot for a dog to hike! When it cooled down, we logged a few more miles and set up camp in the dark. Tristan loves it when he can cowboy camp! 17 Guthook miles and 20.2 miles on my watch.

CDT Day #32

We made it into Cuba, New Mexico, by noon. First stop was "Food for the Soul," a yummy food truck where we each got a taco for $3 (but wished we could have eaten five more). Cake, So Good, Moonshine, Firehazard, and Earl Grey Goose were all there.

Ruby had two birthday packages waiting for her at the post office (thank you Gram, Pop, and Hana!). We loitered at McDonald's for a while, trying to figure out where four pairs of new shoes we ordered were. Fortunately, I opened the Facebook app and saw that Moonshine had posted about packages at the post office being rejected as general delivery if sent by UPS. Turns out, our shoes were across the street from the post office at a temporary UPS location. Unfortunately, we had to wait for a driver to return from his delivery route before we could ask about our shoes. So, we loitered at the grocery store. The kids all got a $21 budget to buy whatever food they wanted for the next three-day stretch. They were so excited! We also met a lot of very interesting locals.

It took a few hours, but we finally got packed and made it to UPS. A very kind driver gave us three pairs of shoes with no sign of the fourth pair we ordered. Bummer. I tried to get Sierra to take the new pair, but she said the toe box is too small, so she is going to stick with her original pair for now. Tristan was testing out a pair of shoes for Vasque that hasn't hit the market yet. We mailed back his old pair so they can see where the shoe wears out after 530 miles of rough use. He really likes the shoes and was excited to get another pair. Ruby also got new shoes, a whole size bigger (hopefully that'll help reduce the blisters on her poor little toes)!

We loitered around the library to charge battery packs in their outdoor outlets, then went back to McDonalds for dinner (we met a bike packer who told us to download the McD's app to get a bunch of free food, so we did that). Lots of going back and forth across town and strange interactions with people had us worn out and ready to get out of there! We made it about 3.5 miles outside of town and had some trouble with loose dogs, but we found a place to stealth camp in the trees. 12.5 Guthook miles and 17.9 miles on my watch.

CDT Day #33

We left camp at 7 a.m., packing out all our heavy town food. Pickles on the trail are my and Adam's new favorite! Bagels with cream cheese and cucumbers just don't fuel me as well as Gatorade bars and Cliff bars though. We are amazed with the beauty of the San Pedro Parks Wilderness Area. San Gregorio Reservoir had happy people swimming and fishing all around it. We got to chat with Doggone, Gravity, and Zig Zag and learned we have bus problems ahead of us (because of COVID, they only allow four people on the bus, no exceptions, but we will worry about that later). We saw a herd of elk and met fly fishing backpackers. All of us were post-holing in patches of snow and walking through very wet sections of trail. Guthook miles 15.2; my watch says 44,497 steps and 20.11 miles. We camped at mile 647.6, elevation 10,400 feet!

CDT Day #34

We left camp at 7:25 a.m. and loved hiking through beautiful meadows! The kids are getting along so well, quizzing each other on the periodic table and the capitals of all 50 states. At our lunch stop, we saw a trail magic sign! The kids rushed over to a parking lot while Adam, Muir, and I started filtering water at the stream. A sweet lady who had hiked the CDT in 2018 said hikers had almost cleared her out of goodies the day before, but she had a bag of spicy jerky and pork rinds to give them. Later she found us at the stream and gave the kids a bag of Skittles. "You have to have something sweet!" she said. She was so great!

It was a big elevation day for us, and we only made it 18 miles when we stopped for water and dinner (our goal was to hit 22 miles). Abandoner walked up to the water source having left from Cuba that morning—he hiked over 36 miles! We pushed on for another 3.6 and found a place to camp in the dark. 21.6 Guthook miles and 26.2 miles on my watch. Camped at mile 669.2.

CDT Day #35

As we packed up camp, Sierra pointed out that there were strange bugs all over. Turns out, they are the nymph exoskeletons of cicadas! We could hear the cicadas making clicking sounds as we walked through the forest. I thought Brood X was only on the east coast, but apparently New Mexico joins in the fun too.

We took Skull Bridge over the Rio Chama, and a note from Guthook informed us that it is the first major water source we've crossed in all of New Mexico! There was a river raft company there, just dropping in for a short trip. Adam and Sierra were delayed behind the rest of us when a rattlesnake refused to move from in front of the bridge. Eventually they made it past and chatted with the river guide and his guests.

A few miles down the road, the driver of the river raft company's van pulled over and asked if we wanted a ride (we were off the trail working our way to the bus stop for a resupply). He said he could only drive us about three miles, but he thought our family was very inspiring and wanted to chat with us! He has two young daughters and would love to do a long-distance trail with his whole family someday. He's even started making his own backpacking gear. After he dropped us off, we made it a few more miles, then stopped for lunch. It was a short break because it started to rain. We decided we'd rather be walking in the rain than sitting in it. Then the rain turned to hail and slush.

Just then, a big truck pulling an empty trailer pulled up and asked if we needed help. The driver was Brother John, a monk from the Monastery of Christ in the Desert just up the road. He was on his way to Española to pick up a tractor and was happy to give six stinky hikers and a trail dog a lift (he particularly liked Muir). It was so interesting to hear his life story, his conversion, and his view on fasting, prayer, and world religions. We drove past the beautiful Ghost Ranch, famous for the movies shot at that location and Georgia O'Keeffe's art gallery. Brother John dropped us at Walmart. We pigged out at Taco Bell, then took two different buses to Santa Fe (the bus system is tricky right now, so we're very grateful for that ride from Brother John). We did get to ride on a huge tour bus with giant windows into Santa Fe with a great view of the capitol, art galleries, and statues. It's a beautiful city! It was a 2.5 mile walk to Days Inn and so very cold! But we are showered, clean, and ready to rest. 5 Guthook miles and 15.23 miles on my watch.

CDT Days #36–37

We spent two zero days in Santa Fe! We ate a lot of food. All-you-can-eat soup and salad at Olive Garden was the moment we had all been waiting for. It did not disappoint! We learned how to use the public transportation system and toured around. Town chores included finding holes in air mats and collecting all the food everyone has been carrying (including some unloved items that had stuck around in food bags for way too long) and bought a fresh six-day resupply.

CDT Day #38

Just as we were realizing it was going to be very hard to get all seven of us back to the trail via the bus, I got a message on Instagram from a hiker who wanted to help us! Top has hiked the AT and PCT and plans to start the CDT SOBO in late June. He fit me and the kids into his small transit van and drove us to the trail while Adam and Muir took the bus to Ghost Ranch (about 1.5 hours later). Top gave out water and lemonade to us and two other hikers who came along, Powerhouse and Iron Will. Turns out, Powerhouse was hiking with our friend, Crazy Eyes, and told us he picked up giardia. That's so sad because he has had giardia before and was so determined to never get it again! In fact, he said he was going to filter all water (including hotel water and water caches). Poor guy!

We discovered that Muir will stop barking at approaching hikers if he is playing with his ball. The hikers get extra points if they play fetch with Muir for a while (but there's no guarantee that they won't be barked at in the future).

2 Guthook miles and 6.6 miles on my watch. We camped at mile 690.1.

CDT Day #39

We left camp at 6:45 a.m. and made it 11.5 miles by lunch (that's big mileage for us). We saw Iron Will at the water source, and he said when we hit Georgia (his home state) for the AT, he would be happy to provide trail magic. That is so sweet! I should have gotten a picture of him and Ruby together because they are both wearing baggy green pants and long-sleeved blue shirts. Iron Will (just like Ruby and I) believes the only way to keep the mosquitoes and sunburns away is full coverage clothing!

We also met Peanut from Nevada during our lunch break. She's a super nice lady. Kaia said she reminded her of her second grade teacher. It rained on us off and on all afternoon. We set up camp early to get out of the rain and cold wind! We were in bed by 7:30 p.m., what luxury! 19.3 Guthook miles, my watch 48,798 steps and 22.2 miles. We camped at 709.4.

CDT Day #40

We left camp at 6:45 a.m. again this morning and made it to Canjilon Lake by 9 a.m. There was a pit toilet and trash cans! After we filtered water from the creek feeding the lake, we had a few miles of patchy snow to deal with. Sometimes we postholed all the way to our hips (especially Ruby)! After lunch, we got pelted with rain and hail until we made it to the Rio Vallecitos. Some of the hail was thumbnail size! We found a great spot to camp, protected under four giant pine trees. 18.3 Guthook miles and 20.88 miles on my watch. We camped at mile 727.7.

CDT Day #41

We left camp at 7 a.m. and had a scary water crossing on an icy log over the swift-moving Rio Vallecitos. We arrived at a campground at lunchtime and met Ed and his wife. They've been helping CDT hikers for three years. They kindly invited us over to fill our water bottles, eat some yummy food, and visit with them. They were so nice! The wind was blowing strong and cold, so we found a shelter by Hopewell Lake to hunker down in for a few hours. It worked! The wind calmed down, and we hiked on until about 7:30 p.m. There was a beautiful sunset from camp tonight! 18.8 Guthook miles, 22.5 miles on my watch. We camped at mile 746.5.

CDT Day #42

I didn't take notes today; I was too tired. We did enjoy lunch at the Lagunitas Lake, which was so lovely. 18.7 Guthook miles and 23.15 miles on my watch. We camped at mile 765.2, 10,651 feet above sea level.

CDT Day #43

We left camp at 8 a.m. because it was too cold to wake up early! We were set up perfectly so that the morning sun hit our tents and melted the ice. We left the CDT at Guthook mile 767.3 to avoid over eight miles of deep snow, which still blankets the trail. We were on the fence about this decision until we met a group of three hikers and a dog headed south. They told Adam how miserable it was, and those words made up his mind. We took forest service roads, which still had a fair amount of snow and lots of mud, and we made great time. We crossed into Colorado with much celebration!

About two miles later, we had our first encounter with a bear! Tristan was up ahead of us and must have startled a bear that was in the trees to his left. Kaia just happened to be in the bear's path of escape, and she let out a yell when she realized what was running towards her (at first, she thought it was Muir running and panting heavily). The bear turned away from her just as Muir started chasing it. Adam called Muir back, and the bear ran off into the woods. It happened so quickly that I failed to catch anything on camera (I was so concerned that taking a video didn't even enter my mind). The bear was a beautiful color of chocolate brown, was very soft and fluffy looking, and was about ten times the size of Muir (none of us can agree on the actual size). It was small for a bear, I thought, and my first reaction was to worry the mama was nearby. Adam says it was a black bear and maybe young but not young enough to have a mama bear around.

We walked about three more miles to Cumbres Pass, and all of us got a hitch in a transit van with Heather (who is going SOBO on the CDT from Cumbres to Grants starting tomorrow) into Chama. We are camping at a nice RV park with laundry and clean showers!

CDT Day #44

I woke the kids up at 7 a.m. so we could start laundry and make sure all devices were charged before noon checkout. A very nice lady visited with us while she was doing laundry, too, and volunteered her husband to drive me and Adam to the post office (so that we didn't have to walk three miles with heavy packages). He was happy to do it, and he said he would drive all of us to the trail at 2 p.m. on his way to go fishing. It was perfect! We got to visit with several hikers while we did chores, learning about their various plans to deal with all the snow in Colorado. We've decided to take the low route because everyone on the high route is using snowshoes, crampons, and ice axes. A trail angel contacted me on Instagram and said she would meet us at Cumbres Pass at 2:30 p.m. with food! She brought us fried chicken and side dishes and even some treats for Muir! Her name is Michelle, and she is such a cool lady. There was another hiker at Cumbres Pass trying to hitch into Denver (to take some time off to let the snow melt). Michelle offered him food, too, then loaded all of us into her truck. She got us to Elk Creek Campground and handed everyone ice cream sandwiches! Ice cream is always a morale boost. We are now working our way to South Park on forest service roads with a six-day food supply.

CDT Day #45

We left camp at 8 a.m. The ice wasn't in a hurry to melt off our rain flys, so we packed them up wet. We tried to take a shortcut but ran into private property. To get around that, we had to do eight miles instead of four and ford the Conejoes River. Our first attempt at crossing the river was in an area too swift even for Adam. We went upriver about a half mile to try again. I was holding Ruby's hand, thinking I was keeping her safe. I lost my footing twice, and Ruby helped me regain my balance! She is amazing! My clothes and half of my pack got soaked, but fortunately everything inside my pack stayed dry. We took a long lunch to dry off, then had a beautiful walk down a dirt road for about 11 miles. My watch says 44,103 steps and 20.1 miles. We camped at mile 28.3 of the Great Divide Alternate route.

CDT Day #46

We left camp at exactly 8 a.m., and it was a very cold morning! We made it to the small town of Platoro by 11:30 a.m. and stopped in at the Gold Pan Cafe for lunch. The owner was very nice and gave us a plate of watermelon for free along with our three orders of cheeseburgers and fries (that we split between the six of us). He warned us not to filter water from the Alamosa River because of runoffs from the mines. Everything coming from the north side is bad, but the south side is fine. It is going to be a long water carry, but he filled up our water bottles from his tap (he promised that it was all state-tested and safe).

We ran into Cheshire Cat at the Stunning Campground. He fed us pineapple, watermelon, and oranges. We enjoyed visiting with him while we sat at the picnic table and ate our dinner of cold-soaked ramen and meat sticks. Then we logged another five miles until we finally found a spot to set up three tents (at a small pullout on a hairpin turn at 11,011 feet). We camped at mile 46.7 on the GDA; my watch says we did 49,647 steps and 22.7 miles.

CDT Day #47

This morning, we had a beautiful view of the Prospect Creek. We left camp at 7 a.m., hoping the anticipated snow would still be frozen solid. The Elwood Pass area was breathtaking, and we had great weather all day! We timed it just right and made it through the snowy sections with no trouble. Poor Kaia did have trouble though and started throwing up around 11 a.m. We took a four-hour siesta so she could rest. I melted snow with our stove and filtered it (it took me about three hours to get 13 liters!). We are still close to the mines, so I wanted to be safe (apparently there is a lake nearby so full of arsenic that it looks red in the satellite view). We think Kaia has altitude sickness and plan to take it easy tomorrow so she can recover! We camped at mile 9.8 on the Elwood Pass Alternate (elevation 9,491 feet); my watch says we did 35,529 steps and 16.3 miles.

CDT Day #48

It was a slow morning; we were just making sure Kaia was feeling better before we pressed on. We had a seven-mile dirt road walk, getting dusted by countless ATVs and side-by-sides. A very nice man from Texas gave us all a hitch into South Fork, then we had to split into two groups to get to Creede. Kaia, Tristan, and I got a ride with two guys who had just driven to Del Norte to pick up a puppy. He is the same breed as Muir (an Australian shepherd/heeler), and his new owner wants to hike the PCT with him someday! Our drivers, Josh and Ben, gave us a quick tour of Creede, including a drive past the fire station that is in an old mine. It's such a cool town! Then Josh and Ben went back to South Fork (twenty minutes one way) to see if they could pick up the rest of our family. Unfortunately, they don't have cell phones with reception in this area, so I couldn't call them when Adam texted five minutes later to say they got a ride. We were trying to get to Lake City that night, not realizing it was almost an hour and a half from Creede. It was getting late, but I put a message on the "Creede Helping Creede" Facebook page that we were looking for a ride to Spring Creek Pass, and almost immediately Ed said he could take us! He showed up in his truck, and as we were all loading up, Josh and Ben came back to check on us! They're so kind. Our friends, Betty and Grant (NoID and Grant-My-Wish), said they would meet us at Spring Creek Pass where Ed was going to drop us off. Ed is a super interesting guy who once tried to buy Red Mountain, our favorite ski resort in Canada (he had lots of great stories). It was 10 p.m. by the time we met Betty and Grant, way past hiker midnight. They had their truck and a Jeep they had borrowed from their campground and drove us back to Castle Lakes. It was a long day! No Guthook miles, my watch says 23,401 steps and 10.8 miles.

CDT Day #49

Zero day. We had so much fun at Castle Lakes Campground and Lake City with our friends, Grant-My-Wish and NoID. We met them on the PCT and had to do some reenactment photos. They spoiled us rotten, and we really enjoyed our time with them!

CDT Day #50

Today was also a zero. We made our way to Creede with the help of NoID and her friend, Michael Underwood (a phenomenal photographer, www.michaelunderwoodphotography.com). We were told by some locals that it was okay for us to camp at the baseball fields in town, so we did. Our friend, Doggone, came to see us from the RV park he's staying at and we worked on trail strategy. Again, we're searching for that safe NoSnowBo route.

CDT Day #51

We were waiting an extra day in Creede to see if our package (with new shoes for Honey Badger) would arrive. The UPS app had given me an error message late last night saying "Delay: Needs Attention." After much searching online and a call to UPS, I found out that UPS doesn't deliver to PO Boxes. I had called the Creede Post Office a few weeks ago and one employee said they do not accept General Delivery packages from UPS for hikers. A very kind employee named Kim gave me her personal PO Box number as a solution. Alas, it didn't work out. However, our friend Doggone saved the day when he said we could give the address of the RV park where his wife is staying in Creede. He also volunteered her to hold onto two days worth of food for us, so we only had to hike out of Del Norte with four days of food.

I accidentally left my battery pack plugged in by the ice machine at Castle Lakes Campground, so NoID is trying to find a local who is driving from Lake City to Creede that will drop it off with Taxi Lady. Whew! I sure hope that all comes together in the next few days.

Kaia, Tristan, and I were able to get a quick hitch out of Creede with Kathy and Eric (who have lived in Creede for 40 years!). They were fun to chat with and gave us two cinnamon rolls they were going to give their friends in South Fork (they said, "We can bake them more later.") Cinnamon rolls just so happen to be Kaia's favorite!

We got a second hitch into Del Norte with a police officer. He felt bad for us because it had started to rain (with lots of lightning and thunder), and no one was picking us up! He did run my driver's license before he started driving—lucky for me, it was all clear! His name is Anthony and hiking the CDT is a dream of his. So that was fun! Adam, Sierra, Ruby and Muir caught a hitch in an RV with a couple from France who have been touring the US for four months! We all met up at the grocery store, got our six-day supply, handed off two days' worth to Doggone and Taxi Lady, then started walking north. We really lucked out with a great camp spot and a phenomenal sunset! 13.5 miles on my watch. Camped at Elephant Rocks, an alternate to the Great Divide Alternate.

CDT Day #52

We left camp at 7 a.m. We road walked on mostly dirt roads. We were in the Penitente Canyon area, and the informational sign taught us this: "It is said that in the mid-20th century, a few men from the local community painted the image of the Virgin of Guadalupe (on the side of a cliff) that's still visible today. Local legend has it that they sat in tires and were lowered over the cliff on ropes to complete the painting." We didn't take a side trip to see it though.

We spent the afternoon and evening walking past private land on either side of the road. A highlight was crossing "hell's gate," where there were very cool rock formations! Finally, at 7:30 p.m. we entered the Rio Grande National Forest and found a spot to camp. There we saw a mama moose and her calf! We camped at mile 61.5 on the GDA. 20.4 Guthook miles, and my watch is dead.

CDT Day #53

Adam found us an awesome campsite last night, and we all slept great. I saw glimpses of the mama moose and her baby again this morning, but I didn't try to get closer. We took an alternate route to the alternate route and ended up bushwhacking for a mile or so, but it wasn't bad at all. Adam said, "Since we've survived the Lionshead bushwhack (on the Pacific Northwest Trail), stuff like this doesn't seem like such a big deal."

We made it to Luders Creek Campground and immediately, a neighbor camper came over. Her name is Dorothea Frohner, and she's originally from Switzerland. She's camping here for a few nights with her daughter. She was so kind and brought over some dark chocolate and pretzel snacks. She said if we make it to Denver, we should call her (she gave us her number), and she will give us real Swiss chocolate! Then the campers on the other side of us brought over some chocolate-covered strawberries! The kids started a fire in the firepit, and it felt so good to stand next to its warmth. We are at mile 93.4 on the GDA and did about 20 miles today.

CDT Day #54

We had a nice relaxing morning while we waited for Doggone to meet us at the Luders Creek Campground. He arrived around 10 a.m., and we visited while he ate his breakfast and rested (he did 10 miles before 10 a.m.!). He hiked with us the rest of the day, slowing down to our pace, and we made it to Taxi Lady at Highway 114 by 4 p.m. We picked up our two-day food supply that we had stored in her car and got a little charge on my phone while we visited. A guy in a Jeep pulled up to see if we needed help. Once he realized we were hikers, hiking to Canada at that, he teased us about how much better it is to drive. He was a nice guy though, and he wished us well after a quick visit. After saying goodbye to Taxi Lady, we made it about two miles before the rain and hail hit. We quickly found a bit of cover and set up camp near mile 1018.9. 12.1 Guthook miles, and my watch is still dead.

CDT Day #55

We left camp at 7:30 a.m. (we were supposed to leave with Doggone at 7, but I decided we needed to filter more water for the climb. Doggone was gracious and waited). We were passed by two fast hikers, Old Head and Ozark. We visited with them a bit while they dried their gear, and we filtered more water. There were only patches of snow on the trail, an unexpected relief! We had a huge elevation day with about 4,000 feet up and 4,000 feet down! We are beat! We camped at mile 1,040.1 near Tank Seven Creek. 21 Guthook miles and 25.9 miles on my watch (Adam has charge to spare, so I got to charge my watch last night!).

CDT Day #56

We started the day with a big climb. Sierra and I were lucky enough to be keeping pace with Doggone and listening to his stories. When he was a teacher, he would take groups of middle school and high school kids (anywhere from 30 to 100 of them!) on backpacking trips through Outward Bound. He also said the 8th graders would learn about Georgia history, and as part of that curriculum, he would have the kids build rafts in teams and float down the Chattahoochee River. The fire department would come out to help supervise. He got to do so many cool things that just wouldn't be allowed these days.

After lunch, we realized we needed to really step up our pace if Doggone was going to meet Taxi Lady at Monarch Pass by 6 p.m. Doggone, Adam, and Sierra took the lead. Kaia, Tristan, Ruby, Muir, and I fell behind because of foot trouble. While Kaia worked on hotspots and Ruby trimmed her toenails (something she should have done at lunch instead of watching "The Great British Baking Show" that Sierra had downloaded), I had enough coverage to contact our reps at Vasque. Kaia's shoes still haven't arrived at Taxi Lady's RV Park, so they are mailing a pair to my grandparents (who we get to see in about a week!). However, Kaia's feet are hurting, her shoes are falling apart, and we still have 180 miles to go before then. So, we will have to work that out when we get to Salida, Colorado.

Our group of five fell behind the fast group of three, and then the thunder, lightning, rain, and corn snow hit. Then there was snow on the trail, and that slowed us down even more. Ruby was in the lead, carefully tracking the footprints of the fast group, when I noticed we were on the wrong trail! The fast group had accidentally missed a turn on the Guthook red line at the Agate Creek Trail intersection. In their defense, there was a lot of snow, and the footprints they were following were leading to a clear trail. When I noticed we were off-trail,

I had my group of five hike uphill until we were on the red line. We looked around and found no footprints (except way off in the distance in the deep snow). I had the kids wait at the trail while I ran back to the intersection to see if the fast group left us a note that I'd missed, but there was nothing. I ran back to the kids, and we went through all our options. We had 7.8 miles ahead of us at high elevation (we were at 11,900 feet), the cold wind was blowing, it looked like more precipitation was headed our way, we were very exposed, and the red line trail appeared to be mostly covered in snow. However, the Agate Trail was snow-free, dropped quickly in elevation, followed a creek, was only 7.1 miles to the highway, and had our family's footprints on it. So, we took Agate.

About a half mile in, we heard Adam yelling for us. They had noticed about 1.5 miles in that they were on the wrong trail. He sent Doggone ahead, dropped his pack, left Sierra to guard it, and ran back to find us. He knew Ruby would be watching the footprints, and of course he was right. It was a huge relief to be back together, and the rest of the hike to the highway was beautiful. I had been sending messages to Doggone and Taxi Lady on my InReach with very little response (messages aren't getting in and out reliably, and it is so frustrating!). They weren't at the highway, so Adam stuck out his thumb, and a guy in a minivan immediately slammed on his brakes to pick him up. Adam guessed that Doggone was at a different pullout and left to go look for them. Less than five minutes later, Doggone and Taxi Lady pulled up. Long story short, we all found each other, and with the help of all our drivers, we made it to Monarch Pass to stealth camp. 14 Guthook miles then seven alternate miles down the Agate Creek Trail to Hwy 50; 25 miles on my watch.

CDT Day #57

We started hitching into Salida at 9 a.m. and were fortunate enough to have an easy time. A nice couple from Lake City picked up Muir, Kaia, and I first. They know our friends Betty and Grant, who work at Castle Lakes Campground! It was fun to visit with them. Adam, Sierra, Ruby, and Tristan caught a ride with a guy from Boulder, Colorado, who works for Honda. We all met at the Walmart, and my friend Renee and her husband Anthony came to get us. We went to their house and enjoyed a great visit, nice, hot showers, and laundry! Anthony took me and Adam to Walmart and Natural Grocers to get our resupply and solved Kaia's shoe problem by giving her a pair of his Altras! These two friends are unbelievably helpful and generous. Then they dropped us off at the trailhead for the Colorado Trail.

We've decided to take the low road for this section again to avoid the deep snow. We crossed paths with Freebird again, and he had some great advice for the safest route for us to take. 1 Guthook mile and 7.5 miles on my watch. We camped at CT mile 233.1.

CDT Day #58

We left our lovely camp near Cree Creek at 7 a. m. We got passed by a hiker named Solo shortly thereafter (we briefly met him outside of South Fork last week). He's a soft-spoken, gentle soul from Butte, Montana. We spent most of the day walking around the base of Mt. Shavano and Tabaguache Peak. Both are fourteeners, named after chiefs of the Tabaguache band of Utes. We passed through the Angel of Shavano campground (and got to throw away trash!), which is named after an angel-shaped snow formation on Mt. Shavano's eastern flank, visible each spring. The informational sign at the trailhead (from which I gleaned all this knowledge) said, "One legend claims that the snow represents an Indian princess who, during severe drought, knelt and prayed for rain. Her tears, in the form of melting snow, provide valuable moisture to the Arkansas Valley below." It reminds us of the legend of Mt. Timpanogos in Utah!

At lunch, Freebird entertained us with his bear encounters (he saw an all-white Spirit Bear near Stehekin, Washington). He's on his way to Twin Lakes to meet up with another legendary hiker named Billy Goat (who is training here in Colorado for a bit, then going to finish up a section of the PCT, which will complete his tenth PCT thru-hike and his fifth Triple Crown! He is 82!).

We are loving the views and wildflowers on the trail right now (and the lack of blowdowns and snow). The Colorado Trail is so well-maintained and beautiful! 20.8 Guthook miles and 22.5 miles on my watch. We camped in the free Bootleg campground (flat tent spots, privy, picnic tables, and a bear box!) at mile 253.9.

CDT Day #59

We didn't leave camp until 7:30 a.m. because I knew Kaia's feet were sore, and we only had a 15-ish mile day. We passed by the Mt. Princeton Hot Springs Resort and decided to get pizza from their convenience store. Unfortunately, it was an hour-and-a-half delay, but the pizza was delicious! We learned an important lesson about how some people will treat hikers at places like this. Our friend, Dirty Bird, tried to go into the resort and get a meal at their sit-down restaurant. True to his name, he wasn't looking super clean, and he said all the employees ignored him. He gave up and hiked on. Later we learned that Freebird went into the same restaurant, was seated immediately, had great conversations with the hostess and waiter, and was given a free dessert. Freebird's clothes (a button up shirt and khaki pants) are always looking like they've just been washed and ironed (we've seen him rinse his clothes often in streams. The ironing part is a mystery though). He also has very impressive people skills, so these things happen to him often.

It was a hot, exposed road walk from there, but we found a nice, cold creek to have lunch next to just after noon. There were great views today! We hiked around Mt. Antero. The informational sign at the trailhead said, "At an elevation of 14,269 feet, this mountain officially contains the highest concentration of gem specimens found in North America. This mineral-rich 'fourteener' has yielded an abundance of aquamarine, topaz, and quartz crystals." We didn't find any of those gems. Just when we needed it most, we found a perfect spot to camp at mile CT 269.7. 15.8 Guthook miles, 19.5 miles on my watch.

CDT Day #60

When we woke this morning next to Pine Creek, there was frost on our tents, and it was so cold. Our elevation was 10,400 feet. We started the day with a climb to 11,600 feet. When we were ready to stop for lunch, we found Freebird in a shady aspen grove and joined him. He talked to us about hiking the Te Arora in New Zealand (he was the first one to start that trail after it was completed and is friends with the trail planner).

There was a magical moment at lunch when a happy, curious, little hummingbird came to visit. Muir barked at it as it flew to each member of our party to check us out. The bird flew right behind Muir, as if to tease him, and we all laughed!

We made it to Twin Lakes by 4 p.m., and the kids and I soaked feet and swam. Adam pushed on because his feet are really hurting him. We met at the river ford. Tristan and Adam made it safely across, but it was sketchy. The rest of us tried and decided the three-mile walk to the bridge was a better idea. The owner of the Twin Lakes General Store gave Adam a hiker discount, but it was still $38 for a package of hotdogs, buns, chips, and a few drinks.

The mountain views from this area are incredible! We can see Quall Mountain, Mount Hope, Rinker Peak, Parry Peak, Mount Cosgriff, and Mount Elbert. It was an amazing sunset with the alpenglow all around! After dark, we stealth camped near the visitor center along with Powerhouse, Iron Will, Freebird, and Raven. 18.5 Guthook miles (on the CT and CDT) plus four miles into town (my watch died mid-day).

CDT Days #61–67

The bottoms of poor Adam's feet were killing him when we got into Twin Lakes, so we took Sunday and Monday off so he could rest. We had a great campsite right on Twin Lakes that we shared with two other CDT thru-hikers, Library and Overdue. The trail is beautiful, and the adventure is unparalleled, but the people we are meeting along the way are definitely the best part!

We stealth camped near Turquoise Lake and needed a ride into town Tuesday to meet up with my grandparents (we are taking a few days off in hopes that Adam's feet will heal up). Tyler, a local firefighter, had just finished up an early morning paddle boarding session when he saw our circus trying to get a hitch. He pulled over his sweet EuroVan, moved his paddle board from inside the van to the roof rack, and drove us into town. It was so cool to visit with him and hear about his job and his family's experiences living in Leadville.

The day before, Matt stopped as he was running through town to ask if he could be our trail angel and give us a ride. He shuttled all of us in his Subaru in two trips to the lake so we could camp for free!

That morning, Danny picked up all seven of us and drove us from Twin Lakes to Leadville (and told us about her experience on the Via Alpina thru-hike in Europe; now that is on our bucket list). The day before that, my daughter and I caught a ride to Safeway in a Transit van with an awesome couple, and then the sweetest 80-year-old lady named Hazel brought us back to the trail with our groceries.

A few hours before that, I was in line for food truck burritos, visiting with a couple about what my family was doing out here. While they were placing their order, I slipped out of line (deciding to get a less expensive breakfast at the grocery store instead). I passed by the woman a few minutes later, and she said, "Where did you go? My boyfriend was going to pay for your burritos!"

We receive so much kindness! We passed a hiker a few days ago, and after chatting for a bit she said, "Travel kind!" and hiked on. That phrase has stuck with me. We are meeting so many great people who really know how to be generous and kind as they travel through life!

CDT Day #68

After a blissful week off the trail, visiting family, eating all the things, and enjoying hot showers, temperature-controlled environments, and other luxuries, we were concerned about a loss of trail legs. We were not too concerned, though, because we decided to go ahead and attempt a summit of Mt. Elbert, Colorado's highest peak. While passing through Leadville, we stopped to visit with Doggone and Taxi Lady. We gave them two of Gram's famous cinnamon rolls. They offered to hold on to three days' worth of our food! We will just call Taxi Lady when we get to Turquoise Lake, and she will bring it to us. She's awesome! We hiked about 3.5 miles from where Gram and Pop dropped us off (where we left the trail at Twin Lakes last week) and found a spot to camp about 4.5 miles from the summit. Hopefully we can wake up early and make good time up and over Mt. Elbert.

CDT Day #69

If you ever attempt a summit of Mt. Elbert, we highly recommend the new south trail. It is so much nicer than the older northern approach trail. We climbed up the south trail and descended on the north. There were a lot of climbers; we felt badly for the ones scrambling up the north side! Poor Kaia worked up some big blisters on her heels from her new shoes. Fortunately, Leuko tape and lamb's wool helped a lot. 11.3 Guthook miles, 22 miles on my watch, and 139 flights climbed.

CDT Day #70

None of our pictures could do justice for how beautiful our views were today. We slept at high altitude, which we've found always makes it hard to recover overnight (especially after climbing Elbert the day before), so we were slow today. 15.4 Guthook miles, 20 miles on my watch, and 119 flights climbed.

CDT Day #71

We stopped to chat with a trail maintenance couple and they said, "We admire what you are doing a lot!" It was so great to hear that! 22.2 Guthook miles, 26.2 miles on my watch, and 104 flights climbed.

CDT Day #72

Our heroes, the Strawbridge family, just finished the Appalachian Trail and are on their way to California to finish 38 miles and wrap up their Triple Crown! We had been in contact on Instagram and had planned to meet for pizza in Frisco for dinner. I was supposed to keep it a secret, but I ruined that within two hours by blurting out some key information during dinner last night. It's okay, though, because then the kids were motivated to hike fast!

We only had 5.4 miles to Copper Mountain Resort where we could catch a bus into Frisco. While packing up our tents, Adam spotted Gillmore and Intro, two hikers we met on the PCT who are also wrapping up their Triple Crown. During the conversation, she said, "And you guys used to live in Colorado, but now you are in Washington, right? Wow, I sound like an Instagram stalker!" We laughed because we do the same and know the same about them! They hiked on ahead, but we visited with them for about an hour when we bumped into them at Copper Mountain. They're such a fun couple!

It was super easy to take the bus to the house of our friend in Breckenridge, and we quickly did laundry, showered, and hopped back on the bus to Greco's Pastaria. We put our names in for a thirty-minute wait, walked outside, and saw the six Strawbridges walking up the street. We gave hugs all around and enjoyed laughing and visiting with them for hours (and the pizza was exceedingly delicious). We all piled into their vehicle, and they crashed with us at the house (with permission; Shirley is the greatest). The poor Strawbridges are on east coast time and had driven all through the night to get to Denver to visit Vince's brother that morning. We should have let them just go to bed, but we kept them up visiting a bit longer. We just love them!

CDT Day #73

We reluctantly parted ways with the Strawbridges as they headed off to the California heat and we headed into high elevation storms. The bus was an easy ride again, and we stopped to have an early lunch outside a gas station next to our trail. A very nice grandpa was there with his three grandchildren and chatted with us. We learned that he is a ski instructor in Aspen, and his daughter and son-in-law are both retired pro cyclists (the son-in-law has competed in the Tour de France for many years and took fifth one year). He was a super nice guy and asked us lots of questions and kept telling our kids how proud he was of them!

The climb away from Copper was a big one, but it was beautiful! Everything was going fine until we were about 100 yards from the top of our second pass of the day, Eccles Pass (11,905 feet), and we got hit with hail, rain, and wind. We decided to press forward instead of turning back down to the treeline. We were soaked, but fortunately, the temperature never felt like it dipped below freezing. There wasn't enough shelter to camp where we first intended to, so we pushed on another 2.5 miles until Ruby spotted a flat spot big enough for us (all the while, it was getting dark, we had a plethora of fallen trees to maneuver over, and the rain continued intermittently). When we finally got all tucked in for the night, the sky opened, and it started to pour! 16.6 Guthook miles and 21.7 miles on my watch. We camped at 10,402 feet on the Silverthorn Alternate.

CDT Day #74

We are so wet; we're like drenched trail rats. I was so tired last night that I reminded the kids to keep their shoes tucked under the tent vestibule, but I failed to do that myself. One of my shoes was positioned just wrong and caught all the water dripping off the tent, and it rained all night long. We didn't get out of our tents until close to 8 a.m., when the rain finally stopped. At 10 a.m. the sun was just peeking out of the clouds, so Adam had us stop to lay out tents to dry. We made the five miles into town before noon and caught the free bus to Shirley's house.

On the walk to her house from the bus stop, a nice police officer pulled up next to us and asked if we were CDT hikers. He said he hiked the PCT in 2017, and he wanted to chat about hiking. He was a very nice guy! He asked if there was anything he could do for us. I asked if he had any popsicles in his car. He laughed and said he didn't, but he's going to start carrying stuff to hand out to hikers.

We grabbed our six-day resupply that we had stashed in Shirley's garage and headed back to the bus. Luckily for us, we needed something for dinner, and the trail goes right next to a Chipotle! We stuffed ourselves with burritos (we started out sharing three, but quickly thereafter, Adam went to buy three more). The sky was ominous looking as we left town on the Ptarmigan Peak trail. There was no camping two miles in, contrary to what the Guthook comment led us to believe. After searching for another one and a half miles, we made do with what looked like our best option. Immediately after getting the tents up, it started raining! I'm so grateful for that timing! 10 Guthook miles, 13.98 miles on my watch and 30 flights climbed. We camped at mile 26.4 (9,931 feet) on the Silverthorn Alternate.

CDT Day #75

We had a beautiful climb up to Ptarmigan Peak with a moment of sunshine to dry out our gear from the wet night. By 4 p.m. we were above 12,000 feet, the wind was whipping, and we got hit with rain and snow. We had a quick dinner; we were so cold.

We met a hiker going SOBO by the name of Cache 22 (he runs a water cache on the PCT that we stopped at in 2019). While chatting with him, Tristan passed out (then threw up shortly after coming to). It was so cold and wet that he wasn't making the effort to drink much water today, so we think he got dehydrated (and too cold). We quickly found a semi-flat spot to camp. Sierra got Tristan set up with some hot chocolate and made sure everyone was tucked in warm and dry. It was a difficult day! 14.3 Guthook miles, and Adam's watch said 19 miles.

CDT Day #76

No one was in a hurry to get out of their warm sleeping bags and put on wet shoes and socks (especially me), so we had a slow morning. The sun hit us at about 8:30 a.m., and we laid everything out to dry. We pressed on until about 10—when we laid stuff out again—but the sun was hidden behind thick clouds most of the time. We got to chat with a Denver water employee who lives in this area half of the year. He told us there are three tunnels here that very few people know about (they started building them in the 1930s). We would have loved to use the tunnel instead of the climb we had that day, but he wouldn't help us with that.

A mile or so into our climb, we met Lone Wolf (she started the CDT the same day we did, and we've bumped into her several times since). She went the red route out of Breckenridge and said the climb up Greys Peak was one of the scariest things she has ever done! She was so glad we didn't go that way, especially with the terrible weather lately. We told her we planned to go up and over the pass and drop down into the town of Empire. She warned us that a giant cornice was blocking the road and that it could be impassable. We decided to climb up and check it out.

Kaia's blisters have been hurting her for a week, and having wet socks and shoes is no help. We worked it out for my mom, Grandma

Shelli, and my brother, Jay, to meet us near Empire to come rescue Kaia so her feet could have a few days to heal. The cornice was a problem, but Adam figured out a way to get us all up and over (just as the wind was picking up and a storm was rolling in!). We made it down to the Big Bend Picnic area by 6 p.m., and Grandma Shelli and Jay arrived shortly thereafter with two giant Costco pizzas! Adam and I agreed all the kids could use some time off-trail to visit family and heal up, and Grandma Shelli agreed to take them. There was much rejoicing! Now Adam, Muir, and I have 2.5 days to make it from Berthoud Pass to Monarch Lake, where we hope to meet up with everyone again. 4.3 Guthook miles, 15.5 miles on my watch, and 109 flights climbed.

CDT Day #77

This morning's views were breathtaking all the way to the summit of Mt. Flora (13,123 feet), where we ran into Old Timer, Gravity, Top'O, and Wild Turkey! It was so great to visit with them and lay out our gear to dry in the sunshine! But it was a bummer to not have the kids with us for this reunion. There was a group of four ladies from Chicago at the summit at the same time. They watched in wonderment at this hiker trash reunion and "yard sale" as we spread out gear to dry. It was fun to chat with them and explain what we were doing. ("Five months of hiking?! What do you do for work?")

At noon we were lightly getting pelted with teardrop-shaped hail, so we found a spot under a cluster of trees and set up our tent. We are so glad we did because the hail increased in intensity, and thunder and lightning were so close. At 5 p.m. we ate our dinner, packed up the wet tent, and went three more miles to Fall River. We are saving the climb up James Peak for the early morning tomorrow (OT and Gravity told us we should not attempt a summit of James Peak today because of the weather, so we obeyed). 9.1 Guthook miles, 12.3 miles on my watch, and 111 flights climbed.

CDT Day #78

We successfully summited James Peak, and the view was awesome. However, we could see a storm was quickly heading our way. We had a two hour and twenty minute bushwhack in the Devil's Thumb area (to avoid the astronomical blowdowns from a microburst last year). We had heard another hiker, named Roger That, had made it through the bushwhack in thirty minutes (turns out he is superhuman and hikes at a 4-mph pace). 18.6 Guthook miles, 23.3 miles on my watch, and 265 flights climbed. We camped at 1315.1.

CDT Day #79

Adam, Muir, and I packed up early and headed off to Monarch Lake to meet up with my dad (Grandpa Don), Jay, and three out of four kids (Kaia was still taking care of blisters). We faced a few more blowdowns, but the majority had recently been cleared. It started to rain right at 2 p.m. when everyone arrived. We were waiting for the storm to pass when Earl Grey Goose and No Keys walked into the parking area. It was fun to visit with them, and Earl Grey Goose snapped a group photo for us. We were really happy to have the kids back and to have Grandpa Don and Jay joining us. The climb was steep, but the view of Lake Granby and the surrounding mountains was worth it! When we were looking for a campsite, Adam spotted an elk skull. That was such a distraction that we missed the turn for the best sites listed on Guthook and ended up settling for mediocre spots. (The next morning, during a potty break, Jay found awesome flat camping spots! Oh well!) 18.5 Guthook miles, 22.5 miles on my watch and 92 flights climbed. We camped at 1333.6.

Osprey asked us to write up a blog post for their fall catalog! I wrote the following: (It was too long, so I think only about half of it will be used by Osprey, but I thought I'd add the full version here.)

Pro parenting tip: take your kids on long-distance backpacking trips. Get them outdoors and away from screens as early and as often as possible. They will experience Type 1 fun (fun in the moment), Type 2 fun (fun to look back on when it is over), and Type 3 fun (not fun in the moment or even to think about until much later when you've forgotten some details). The best of humanity will be your associates when a kind soul (also called a "trail angel") feeds you fresh fruit at a trailhead. Your kids will meet people from all over the world: bright, vibrant, exciting people who have a passion for nature and exploration.

There are a lot of teachers on the trail, like professors of geology who teach your kids in just a few sentences things that textbooks cannot. They will meet people from all walks of life, from different social circles, and that will probably be their very favorite part.

Be sure to take pictures of wildflowers and look up their names. Observe the natural wonders of the forest and listen to your children's questions. You'll find the juxtaposition of life on trail versus that at home to be delightfully stark. You and your children will always remember witnessing the joy of curious hummingbirds, of scouting out the best campsite for the night, and of town food after too many days of trail food. Your kids will never take hot showers for granted again. They'll see trash that others have left behind and want to pack it out (bring disposable gloves). You'll walk through blown down trees cleared by handsaws, and they'll aspire to be a volunteer on a trail maintenance crew one day. Turning a corner of the trail, you'll be surprised to see a wild animal (hopefully from a safe distance), and everyone will scramble to get a picture but will just have to treasure the memory instead. You'll climb to a high peak—maybe the highest point in the state you are in—and your kids will decide they want to hit all the high pointers. (Maybe not Denali! You better have a serious chat about that one.)

Treasured memories will be formed when you stop for lunch and it turns into a several-hour siesta where everyone has their shoes and socks off, drying out in the sun. They'll be trading candy and snacks and belly laughing about funny things that happened that day or a joke someone told. You'll experience the "positive discomfort" of being way too hot or way too cold and wet or being pushed way out of your comfort zone, but the vistas and the memories will make it all worth it.

There will undoubtedly be some scary moments. You may find yourselves hiking at 13,000 feet and get hit by a storm. The wind might be blowing you sideways and the icy hail hurting your skin. Fingers will be too cold to reach back for the water bottles and unscrew the caps. Staying hydrated will be the last thing on everyone's mind when you are wet, cold, and walking a "knife's edge" path. As you rush to lower elevation to find a safe place to camp, you might see another hiker and stop to chat about conditions ahead. Your son might lock his knees while he stands there, shivering and cold, then suddenly fall over, passed out from dehydration (and maybe altitude sickness). When you get him to come to and pull him safely from the rocks and bushes, he'll say he couldn't have passed out because he didn't miss any of the book he was listening to. Later, you'll laugh together about that, but in the moment, you are thinking, "What if this had happened a few miles ago when we were near that cliff?" and you might tear up.

On very cold and wet nights, you'll worry that your kids aren't warm enough and go to check on them several times. If your gear is good and you've kept your sleep system dry, your fears will be unwarranted. You'll have discussions with your kids about food in ways you never would at home. Let them choose their own food for a day or a week, staying within your budget and caloric needs. Be sure to mention that protein and complex carbs are better fuel than sugary treats. They'll learn that on their own, though, if initially they don't want to take your word for it. Hearing one sibling ask another if they are okay when they catch their shoe on a root will be a testament that the trail is working wonders in developing empathy.

Organizational skills become survival skills when your children learn that misplacing essential items while on this journey could be life threatening. The back country is a great place to have heart to heart conversations with your children, away from their friends or "frienemies." You'll meet day hikers on the trail, and when you explain what you are doing, they will exclaim, "We're not worthy!" just like Wayne and Garth did in front of Alice Cooper. But weeks or months on the trail will also keep you all humble. Mother Nature is oh-so-powerful, and she'll remind you of that fact daily.

Your children will want to protect the beautiful places they've walked through for the next generation (and many after that) to enjoy. They will find the freedom of a minimalist lifestyle suits their needs and will be less interested in the burden of stuff.

Long-distance or thru-hiking will most certainly not solve all your family's problems, but like John Muir said, "Over-civilized people are beginning to find that going to the mountains is going home; that wilderness is a necessity." In that wilderness, you'll see characteristics and strengths in your children that will help them solve all problems. These tools just cannot be found in front of a screen, so invest in quality gear, hit the trails, and open a whole new vista of experiences for your family.

CDT Day #80

We hiked along the Colorado River, Shadow Mountain, and Grand Lake to get to the car Grandpa Don and Jay had left at the trailhead. It was a perfect day. We saw a female moose on the trail; she didn't care we were there and sauntered very close. We passed by the trail to the Shadow Mountain Fire Lookout but didn't take the detour to go up there (it is one of our favorite lookouts, and a great spot to watch fireworks over Grand Lake on the Fourth of July). Everyone was very excited that we'd made it out so quickly and were off to get Subway and McDonalds for lunch! This nero is the beginning of our 4th of July stay with my parents at their log house in Granby! 6.6 Guthook miles and 10.4 miles on my watch.

CDT Days #81–83

We did a little bit of work on the driveway at the log house and enjoyed Granby's Fourth of July parade and Kremmling's firework show, lots and lots of food, a complicated resupply made easy because Taxi Lady and Doggone let us store five days of food in their car, a double rainbow, Kaia's birthday picake (a pie inside a cake), watercolor painting with Grandma Shelli, and meeting Peanut from Sawyer Products and a fellow CDT hiker, 2 Taps, in town. It was so much fun!

CDT Day #84

My parents dropped us off at the trail this evening, and there were many tears. The Strawbridge family says there is a funk that lasts for several days after leaving family and returning to a thru-hike; this is very true. But the funk was counteracted a bit by a phenomenal Rocky Mountain National Park sunset, which included moose and elk sightings!

CDT Day #85

Bowen Pass was our first obstacle of the day. We saw two young male moose hanging out together from a safe distance. It was eerie to walk through the East Troublesome Fire area but so wonderful to see new life springing up! 18.6 Guthook miles and 23.5 miles on my watch. We camped at 1386.4.

CDT Day #86

Parkview Mountain was awesome! From the summit house we headed south and figured out about half a mile later that we were going the wrong way. We doubled back and eventually found our trail. We saw some lovely flowers and had enough cell phone coverage to look them up on iNaturalist. The app says they are slendertube skyrockets—what a cool name for such an awesome flower! We camped early because we got hit with a rain, thunder, and lightning storm. 12.8 Guthook miles, 16.8 miles on my watch, and 217 flights of stairs. We camped at 1399.2.

CDT Day #87

We got to hike more with Doggone today; it's always great to see him on the trail. We met Carrot and a few other hikers, and wow they are fast! We found an awesome aspen grove to camp in and really enjoyed all the wildflowers today. 19.6 Guthook miles, 22.6 miles on my watch, and 143 flights climbed.

CDT Day #88

Today we had a 5:30 a.m. wakeup call to beat the heat and to make it to Steamboat Springs, home of Big Agnes (one of our favorite gear companies)! The "meadow lettuce" is now taller than Ladybug! iNaturalist says it is called corn lily, but we prefer to call it meadow lettuce. As we walked the dirt road, we watched a few cowboys and their dogs herding a lot of cows (Muir was pondering his fate of being a trail dog instead of a cow dog).

We made it into Steamboat Springs via a hitch in time for McD's breakfast (after hiking 7.7 miles in record time for us)! A kind local stopped us to inform us of the Morgan Creek Fire. At the time, we didn't know if the fire would affect the Continental Divide Trail, but it seemed highly likely. We hung out at Walmart, gathering info from locals and forest service workers. They advised us to not continue north on the trail. We called a number for the local bishop of The Church of Jesus Christ of Latter-day Saints to see if we could spend the night on the church lawn. He told us we could and offered to come pick us up so we could take showers, do laundry, and have dinner with his family. We ended up spending the night at their awesome house instead, and we're so grateful! "The trail provides!" (And without a doubt, we've seen the hand of God daily in our lives.)

CDT Day #89

We woke up to news that the section of CDT ahead of us was closed due to the fire. Doggone and Taxi Lady said they would drive us around the fire closure (that's eight people and three dogs in their Highlander that was also pulling their tear-drop trailer). We had two boxes of food we had left with them to use from Encampment to Rawlins, so we divided that up. We made it four red line miles and camped at 1,524.3. It was a wildly beautiful sunset due to the smoke in the air!

CDT Day #90

Today was our earliest start and our latest night into camp thus far. A very kind trail-angel couple, the Hoovers, gave us trail magic. Vince (who we met on day two and is now going with the trail name of Snowballs) told them he was doing 45-mile days, and they thought he meant kilometers. He's so fast! We tried a new meal: freeze-dried hashbrowns, cheese, and bell peppers (success!). We ended up setting up tents twice because the first spot was too windy and too rocky to set stakes; we walked another few miles in the dark, which was not too fun. 20 Guthook miles + 4-ish on the alternate; Adam's watch says we've done 30.2 miles today.

CDT Day #91

Today is Kaia's birthday! Doggone and Taxi Lady bought a dozen donuts (really good ones, the kids said–definitely not grocery store quality) and found us along the road. Kaia loves donuts, so it was the most perfect trail magic treat!

There were lots of cows on the road today. When we were resting on the side of the road, trying to stay low out of the wind, the Hoovers found us and provided more trail magic! Oh, how refreshing that ice-cold Gatorade was! We camped near the Teton Reservoir with Hobo Toes (who we haven't seen since mile 106.5, when Muir was injured). The Great Basin is just ahead, and we are studying all the water sources and hiker comments. 19 road walk miles.

CDT Day #92

We walked 14.5 Guthook miles before lunch. That's a record for us! A kind older gentleman gave us ice water at the park in Rawlins. He has lived here his whole life and has watched many CDT hikers and bikers pass through. He said in the "old days" when they would ask him where to find water out in the Great Basin, he wouldn't tell them because he didn't want to be held responsible. Instead, he would tell them to get on a bus from Rawlins to Lander (which used to be the official route, but now we have Guthook).

Tristan used his hotel voucher because it was the day after Kaia's birthday (what a sweet brother he is!). We hit the hotel for showers and laundry, and then we went out to Country 6 (right next door to the saloon and laundromat) for steaks and cheeseburgers with Doggone and Taxi Lady. A big storm hit in the night with wind, rain, thunder, and lightning. We were so happy to be safe inside!

CDT Day #93

After a decent hotel breakfast, we walked to Walmart. A very kind lady stopped to chat with us, and with tear-filled eyes she told Ruby that she would treasure this experience one day! We hiked 11.2 miles to mile 1,628.4 and stopped two miles short of our goal (Bull

Springs) because poor Ruby has heat rash on both legs. 17.5 miles on my watch and 18 flights climbed.

CDT Day #94

We left camp at 5:30 a.m. to a beautiful sunrise. We pushed hard to make it to the A&M Reservoir by lunch for a siesta. It was so hot! Doggone and Taxi Lady were there. It took Taxi Lady three hours to find Doggone last night, and he ended up doing a 34-mile day! Freebird was also at the reservoir, having been slowed down by a foot injury. He washed his clothes and swam with us for a bit before pressing on. We siesta-ed until the rain drove us away at about 3:45 p.m. At our dinner stop, we met Savage. She is just finishing up a section she missed last year due to injury (then she is done with her Triple Crown!). Adam made us some awesome grilled cheese sandwiches with his new JetBoil frying pan! About four miles after dinner, we set up camp as quietly as we could because there was another tent nearby, and then we got hit with about ten minutes of heavy rain and wind. 25.5 Guthook miles, 28.6 miles on my watch and 13 flights climbed.

CDT Day #95

Just to keep myself entertained I logged our miles by the hour today:
5:40–6:40 = 2.6 miles
6:40–7:40 = 2.4 mile
7:40–8:40 = 1.3 miles
8:40–9:40 = 1.8 miles
9:40–10:40 = 2.4 miles
10:40–11:40 = 2.8 miles
11:40–2:40 = lunch/siesta/water filter
2:40–3:40 = 2.58 miles
3:40–4:40 = 2.1 miles
4:40–5:40 = 1.8 miles
5:40–7 = dinner and trail magic!
7–9 = 4.1 miles
The highlight of the day was that when we were feeling hot, thirsty, and exhausted, a truck pulled up offering us cold drinks! We

had our mats and packs spread out on the trail (which was a double-track jeep road) and were just getting ready to eat our Peak Refuel meals when the truck pulled up. We jumped up and tried to clear our stuff out of his way as fast as we could when we heard him shout, "No rush! I have cold drinks for you!" Oh, how fast those ice-cold drinks changed our attitudes! We learned that the driver's trail name is High Risk, and he did the PCT in '17 and the CDT in '19. It was awesome to visit with him, and he asked if he could take our picture, saying, "It is such a rarity to see a big family on the trail!"

We were hopped up on trail magic (with ice in our buffs to cool off our necks), and we pushed on another four miles after High Risk drove off. I'm so glad we did, too, because the sky was illuminated with a beautiful sunset, and we got to see our first glimpse of the Wind River Range (and even the Grand Tetons) off to the west! Looking like shark fins in the shadows of dusk, those jagged peaks boiled up excitement as we approached one of the most beautiful spots on the CDT. The Great Basin, while it is hot and dry, makes up for it in the amazing open vistas and sunrises/sunsets. 24.5 Guthook miles, 28.1 miles on my watch, and 19 flights climbed.

CDT Day #96

You are not going to believe this, but High Risk drove into town, got more ice and drinks, and came back the opposite direction to deliver them to hikers today! He said he'd seen about thirty hikers the day before, most of them behind us. We are guessing the fire near Steamboat Springs created a big bubble of northbound hikers because they all had to skip around it. We stopped at Weasel Springs for lunch and met a hiker named Hoover. It was the very same Hoover whose parents gave us trail magic two days in a row right before Rawlins!

We hiked to Mormon Springs (which had the very best water thus far: cold, clear, and so refreshing!), passing a plethora of cement posts marking the California/Oregon/Seminole Trail. Our ancestors (on both sides of the family tree) used this very trail on their way to Utah in the 1850s. We felt inspired by their sacrifice, humbled to be following in their footsteps, and very grateful to not be pushing a handcart or dealing with a team of oxen. These pioneers miraculously survived the trek without good shoes, ultralight equipment, dehydrated food, water filters, or an app giving them directions to camping and water. 20.3 Guthook miles, 22.9 miles on my watch, and 3 flights climbed (so flat!).

CDT Day #97

We made it to the Sweetwater River by 9 a.m. and enjoyed a quick swim. Then we hiked through the most barren, flat, forsaken landscape until we found a siesta spot by Willow Creek. (There was very little shade; our umbrellas are saving our lives out here!) The heat is tremendously oppressive!

After dinner, on a whim, we decided to take a 1.3 mile side trip to see the historic town of Atlantic City. We were too late to get cold pops at the mercantile store (we walked into town a little after 8 p.m.), but we had heard from a kind lady (who passed us early this morning in a truck) that the church had a hiker box. St. Andrews was built in 1913, and it is a beautiful log building. They had a few snacks for hikers and cyclists and a side building with bathrooms (with running water and soap!). It was getting late, so we asked a neighbor that was on his porch watching the sunset (another great one!) if they would let hikers camp in their parking lot. He said, "I've seen people camp there. I'm not going to tell you not to do it." So, we happily set up our tents and left some cash in their donation jar (I need to tell them about Venmo!). 16.1 Guthook miles, 21.5 miles on my watch, and 20 flights climbed.

CDT Day #98

Hiking from Atlantic City to South Pass City (there's some super interesting history in this area) to Highway 28 took us most of the morning. 1.5 hours and three hitches later, we made it to Lander. We hit Safeway first, replenishing our depleted calories (and getting an early birthday cake for Tristan). Our friend from Washington, Ryan Vinson, told us months ago that his parents live in Lander and would love to be our trail angels. The Vinsons treated us like their own family and were so good at spoiling us. They fed us pizza and salad, and it was very easy to accept their kind offer to stay the night in their wonderful home! 7.5 Guthook miles, 13.7 miles on my watch, and 11 flights of stairs.

CDT Day #99

Dennis and Susan Vinson cooked us up a delicious breakfast feast! A reporter from the Fremont County 10 News, Amanda Fehring, came to interview us about our time on the CDT thus far. It was an hour-long interview, and it felt like we laughed the whole time. Then the Vinsons let us borrow their truck, and Adam and I went to Safeway for a 10-day resupply. Our bear bags and bear spray are currently lost in the mail, so Adam had to buy new ones at the gear store (which was so expensive). Instead of bear cans (which are heavy and difficult to fit in a backpack), we've switched to Ursacks (which are bear-proof bags that you can tie to a tree and legal to use in most National Parks). We also bought ammonia to wipe on all our gear to deter bears (a little trick we learned from some outfitters in grizzly country last year).

Then we met up with the Vinsons and the kids at China Garden. The Vinsons are friends with the family who owns that restaurant, so we got the VIP treatment! The food was so good, and the family was so kind (we got hugs from the owner and got to go in the kitchen to meet her husband, the famous cook).

We spent the afternoon trying to organize our resupply. It is painful how long it took, but it was extra complicated because we had to pack a seven-day supply right now and set aside a three-day supply and extra gear that Taxi Lady is going to hold onto for us. At 5:45 p.m., we met up with Taxi Lady at the RV park, got a goodbye photo with the sweet Vinsons, loaded our gear, and were off for the trail again. We were so lucky to catch a ride with Taxi Lady because she just so happened to be picking up Doggone right where we needed to be dropped off.

We hiked in about a mile and stopped for dinner in the shade (there are trees in this section!). Doggone arrived not long after and we got to hear the report about the blowdowns ahead (not good). He told us about a spot to camp he saw a bit north of there, and we thanked him for scouting it out for us! 1.5 Guthook miles and 14.5 miles on my watch.

CDT Day #100

So. Many. Blowdowns. It slowed our pace some, but we pushed hard and still reached our mileage goal. Bridger-Teton National Forest is beautiful! 21.5 Guthook miles, 23.8 miles on my watch and 99 flights of stairs.

CDT Day #101

We saw wildflowers and butterflies, hiked near Cirque of Towers, and camped at Big Sandy Lake. There are so many elephant head flowers in the Winds! My favorites! 16.6 Guthook miles, 18.7 miles on my watch, and 167 flights climbed.

CDT Day #102

We met a nice family from Ohio with four kids: the youngest was six, and they were headed up Texas Pass (which is very challenging!). Today we hit Jackass and Texas Pass, swam in Texas Lake (which was so cold, but the water we filtered from there was delicious!), and saw the very beautiful Lonesome Lake. We had a lakeside dinner with Freebird, Raven, Side View, and Hush. 16.9 Guthook miles, 19.5 miles on my watch, and 198 flights climbed!

CDT Day #103

During our lunch stop, we got passed by our friends, Gilmore and Intro. She said she was so happy to see we were still on the trail and that we had to stay on the trail because we are her inspiration to keep going when it gets hard! I was so happy to hear that! I was having a hard time (it hadn't crossed my mind to get off trail, though), and I think it was in part because I wasn't eating enough (I'm worried about making our food stretch for seven days). Around 2 p.m., we ran into a hiker named Tim who said, "Do you guys need some food?" Those were exactly the words I wanted to hear! He gave us his extra food from his eleven-day food carry (he decided to only hike for nine days): a small jar of peanut butter, two Snickers, and two Nature valley bars.

It was just the calorie boost we needed! He also said he remembers seeing us on Second Chance Hiker's 2019 YouTube video!

When we stopped for dinner, Hush and Side View passed us. They were tucked off in the trees a few hours before and overheard the kids talking about Tristan's birthday tomorrow. He wants to hike for fifteen hours to celebrate turning fifteen. Hush suggested we take it easy and only hike 15 miles instead. 17.9 Guthook miles, 20.3 miles on my watch and 122 flights climbed.

CDT Day #104

Today is Tristan's birthday! We made it to a beautiful lake by 10:45 a.m. and swam and had lunch until 12:45. Then at 3 p.m., we stopped at Upper Jean Lake, which had a cave and more swimming. We got to camp tired and happy by 8:15 p.m. 20.4 Guthook miles, 22.8 miles on my watch and 140 flights climbed.

CDT Day #105

We left camp at 5:35 a.m.! We saw a porcupine next to the trail hiding in some blow downs, and it would not move. We made it 15 Guthook miles before noon for the first time ever! We met Second Chance and Feathers (and her dog, Lucy, and goat, Little Leaf), and they gave us trail magic (a birthday party surprise for Tristan!). Muir needed some New-Skin on his paws, so we decided to call it a day. We played chess and enjoyed visiting (and eating) and sharing a nice, big campsite at Green River Lake.

CDT Day #106

We are the luckiest thru-hikers you know! Second Chance made us an awesome breakfast, and we loitered around visiting with him, Feathers, Jazz Hands, and all the animals until 9 a.m. Then we rushed as fast as we could up and over Gunsight Pass to meet Doggone and Taxi Lady at Union Pass at 4 p.m. When we got there, they had pizza for us! We were soaked because it had poured rain and more was coming, so they let us pile in their car and brought us down to Dubois.

We camped under a pavilion at Pete's Pond and stayed nice and dry! 15.9 Guthook miles.

CDT Day #107

Today is Doggone's birthday! As they drove us back to the trail, we stopped to get treats and visit the "World's Largest Jackalope" exhibit. Then we hiked 21 miles and set a record by finishing by 6 p.m.! Well, we were "slack packing" (we left everything but food and water with Taxi Lady). Along the way we met up with Pogo and got to hear all his stories about the high route he took in the Winds. It rained heavily on us, but that probably helped us move faster. Taxi Lady had a big cake for everyone when she picked us up. (Coincidentally, it was Pogo's birthday yesterday too!) We came back to their RV park, and the very kind owners let us take free hot showers and do laundry!

CDT Day #108

Today was a zero day. Adam did some planning with Doggone and other hikers about the alternates ahead while I updated our blog and social media. Getting cell or WiFi connections in Dubois was a challenge, and I didn't get everything done I wanted to.

The Episcopal church lets hikers spend the night for a donation. They were full for the night, but we spent the day there taking advantage of their tables and visiting with hikers. We ran into several southbound hikers (the first we've encountered) and got to learn about trail conditions ahead of us. Blitz and Easy Money (both from Germany) entertained us with stories about their adventure so far. Blitz was so excited to hit a rodeo in Dubois that night, "What could be more American than that?!" We really missed running into foreign hikers last year due to COVID, but it was a fun gathering of hikers from many different countries here.

A sweet couple set it up for us to go to the Church of Christ to spend the night because more rain was forecasted. We had planned to hit the trail in the afternoon, but a few kids have blisters, and no one wanted another night in the rain. Instead, Doggone drove us to the grocery store and post office. When Ruby and I walked into the store, we saw Cheshire Cat! He was just checking out, and I was blocking the flow of traffic, so we only got to visit briefly. He pointed out that he was so happy to see us and to know that we were still on the trail. He had tears in his eyes, and so did I! He's such a sweet guy!

CDT Day #109

Doggone and Taxi Lady picked us up at 7:30 a.m. and dropped us on the trail on their way to set up their RV in Yellowstone. We saw No No and two other hikers hitching into Dubois. They looked like they've been very wet the past few days! I'm so grateful we stayed at the church and got a good night's sleep. It was a muddy mess the rest of our day and slow going. We had to ford two rivers, but fortunately they were no trouble.

Lunch was an experiment: mashed potatoes, freeze-dried cheese, and bell peppers. Kaia, in all her youthful wisdom, insisted we take the time to heat the water for this meal instead of cold soaking. She was right, and it turned out to be one of our very favorite on-trail meals.

Yoshi from Japan passed us as we were setting up camp. He is a much faster hiker than we are, but he takes more zero days. We camped at 1,903.7. 16.2 Guthook miles, 19.4 miles on my watch, and 88 flights climbed.

CDT Day #110

We left camp at 6:40 a.m. to a bright, warm morning. It got hot quick! We found a shady spot for lunch and were passed by a huge group of NOLES students going south and at least eight NOBOs that we had met in Dubois. We had to ford the North Buffalo Fork, but it was also no problem. As we were putting on our shoes on the other side, we visited with Blitz (he really enjoyed that rodeo!).

At about 7:30 p.m., we found a beautiful meadow to camp in, about 200 yards off trail. Ruby went off in the trees to use the restroom and found two camping chairs and a few supplies horse campers must have ditched. Unfortunately, the chairs were broken, and it was all too heavy for us to pack out for three days until we reach Grant Village!

We camped at 1,921.9. 18.2 Guthook miles, 20.9 miles on my watch, and 126 flights climbed.

CDT Day #111

A highlight for today was visiting Two Oceans Creek! From here, this little creek splits towards the Atlantic on the east and the Pacific on the west. It was very cool to see! We hit the Yellowstone boundary just in time to sit outside the Fox Park ranger cabin for dinner. It has a newer pit toilet—open air style like they have in Washington. It started to rain, but there wasn't room for the seven of us on the porch, so we pressed on three miles to where we had permits to camp (Crooked Creek Campground). Another tent was already set up in the best spot, but luckily, we found three other semi-flat spots and set up in the rain. 18 Guthook miles, 21.4 miles on my watch, and 103 flights climbed.

CDT Day #112

We hiked with our friend OT until lunchtime. Sierra spotted a giant elk skull and antlers on the side of the trail. Kaia and Tristan had passed it without noticing. The rest of us stopped to get lots of pictures and wished we could have packed it out! During one of our long breaks, I taught Tristan and Ruby how to make a duck/elk sound through a blade of grass. I quickly regretted that! We crossed the Snake River a few times and enjoyed a slower paced day. I had hoped to swim at Heart Lake because we heard the water was warm-ish due to thermal activity. By the time we got in the water, the sun had slipped behind the mountains, and I lost motivation to get all the way in. Adam did, though, then had four leeches on his feet and legs. We ate our last two Peak Refuel meals (that's the last of the 70 meals they sent us as sponsors. They are delicious, and we are so grateful!). We camped at Heart Lake. 15 Guthook miles, 17.6 miles on my watch, and 50 flights climbed.

CDT Day #113

We had a wakeup call at 5:40 a.m. so we could have a little extra time at the Witch Creek "hot tub." Here we met No No and OT and visited for a bit. No No had intended to hike 30 miles but decided to come back and soak in the hot pot with us instead. She hitched into Grant Village with us too (it took three different hitches).

The postal worker nearly gave Adam a heart attack when she told him she gave three packages to another hiker named Adam Bennett today. It was not funny! On short notice, my mom had mailed us a resupply here, and she got it just right. Thanks again, Mom! A family from France was camped next to us at the big group campground. They have been biking with their two pre-teenage children all over the world. They have an amazing story. We camped at the hiker/biker Grant Village campground. 9.5 Guthook miles, 17.4 miles on my watch, and 56 flights climbed (we had to walk around a lot in Grant Village to get food, to the PO, and to camp).

CDT Day #114

Yellowstone isn't an easy place to hitch unless you luck out and get picked up by hikers. The couple that stopped for Sierra, Kaia, and I had hiked in Olympic National Park last summer and got a few hitches while they were there. The guy that brought Ruby, Tristan, Muir, and Adam back to the trail also hiked the PCT in 2019! We met a lot of southbounders today, including Bop-it and Punisher; they started hiking in the Florida Keys in January with the intent to do the East Coast Trail, but since Canada is closed, they jumped on the CDT after they finished Maine. We camped at the lovely Moose Creek Meadow, mile 1,973.3. It was a low mileage day because we had to go with whatever backcountry permits were available. 9.4 Guthook miles, 14.9 miles on my watch and 49 flights climbed.

CDT Day #115

The geothermal magic of Yellowstone is blowing our minds! The hike through Geyser Basin was our favorite! On our way through this area, we got to cross paths with two hikers we follow on YouTube: Darwin (we watched a lot of his videos to get ready for this trail) and Smiles. Smiles is a thru-hike syndicate ambassador this year like us! It was so fun to visit with them!

We waited at Lone Star Geyser for over an hour to watch the eruption. It goes off about every three hours and isn't visited by tourists often because it requires a bit of a hike. Tristan took careful notes in the logbook about the timing and stages of the eruption. It lasted about twenty minutes and did not disappoint! We made it into Old Faithful Village, and the kids got to see that famous eruption at 5:58 p.m. while Adam and I rushed to the General Store to buy dinner before it closed at 6 (we got frozen burritos heated in a microwave!). 14.9 Guthook miles and 17 miles on my watch.

CDT Day #116

From here, we are rerouting due to fire closures on the trail. We have researched with other hikers and are doing what is known as the Big Sky Alternate. Our resupply in West Yellowstone started with a new kind of breakfast sandwich in McDonalds (two sausage patties, bacon, and cheese: they call it the McMuffin Triple, and it is a hit with hungry hikers). Eight other thru-hikers arrived. We resupplied at the grocery store, checked out the car show, got a few treats at the gas station, and then stood next to Highway 20 with our thumbs out. A guy filling up his Pontiac Vibe with gas called Adam over and said he was up to the challenge of getting us all to the trailhead! He even left us with a bag of popcorn he just bought at the car show.

As we were taking a picture of the "Welcome to Idaho" sign, a guy going the opposite direction quickly crossed the highway and offered us cold drinks from his cooler! Wow! My watch says we logged 10.8 miles today.

CDT Day #117

We left camp at 7 a.m. and walked eight miles to a ranch. Freebird had given us instructions on how to contact this ranch and arrange a boat ride. The owner was so very kind! After visiting with us and learning about our journey, she gave us six steak sandwiches with grilled onions and peppers, a bag of chips each, scones, and blueberry muffins! Then one of her employees drove us to the dock, and another gave us a free boat ride across Hebgen Lake. We just couldn't believe it! It was a four-mile road walk on Highway 287 to Beaver Creek Rd, which wasn't fun, but we took a break at a campground and picnic table area about three miles in. This area had an earthquake in 1959 that caused a massive landslide (turns out, Adam's dad was camping here with his family a week before the earthquake hit). This stopped the flow of the Madison River and created "Quake Lake." We made it up to the Lightning Lake Trailhead around 7 p.m. and decided to call it a day. Very cool thunder, lightning, and a heavy rainstorm hit us after we were all tucked safely in our tents. 22.2 miles on my watch and 100 flights climbed.

CDT Day #118

It is rough going out here without our Guthook app (we are on an alternate because of fire closures on the official CDT, and Guthook doesn't cover this area). We got a little lost, did some bushwhacking over crazy blow downs, had a sunny lunch to dry out gear, and found our trail. Tristan had a great time observing cool geological formations and explaining to me how he thinks they came to be. There were lots of "pokies" that got caught in our socks and gaiters. There is lots of evidence of grizzly activity in the area! We camped at the Meadow Creek Trailhead. Here we met two mountain bikers, and one said we would see a herd of buffaloes soon (we haven't, though). 21.7 miles on my watch and 165 flights climbed.

CDT Day #119

We saw seven bears today! In the late morning, Kaia and Tristan spotted a cub climbing up a tree. They stopped the train (what we look like all hiking in a line), and while we were all getting out our bear spray, the cub scurried down and ran off with its sibling and mama. We caught sight of them way off in the distance, fluffy and cinnamon colored. I only got a picture of a small bear print in the mud. During lunch, we heard a lot of side-by-sides passing in the distance. We walked through what felt like a racecourse that we thought belonged to a nearby ski resort. We got dusted by 4x4 vehicles passing us three times!

After dinner, near the end of a big climb to 9,000 feet, the kids all saw what they described as a teenage grizzly. They said the bear made eye contact with Muir, then took off up and over the mountain (so fast!). Adam and I missed it! Not even an hour later, a darker black bear mama and her two cubs crossed our path about 200 yards away.

We were on a trail owned by Yellowstone Club and could see lots of fancy homes and ski runs off in the distance. We found a spot to camp, and after we set up, Adam noted bear claw marks on several trees! All precautions were taken to hang our food properly! 21 miles on my watch and 207 flights climbed (that's 68 more flights than the day we climbed Mt. Elbert!).

CDT Day #120

It was not the most restful night's sleep! We think a curious deer was exploring around camp, maybe looking for salty trekking pole handles to chew on. Of course, our first thought to any sound in the night was that it was a bear. Today there were so many raspberries and then blueberries to snack on as we hiked along Jack Creek. We resupplied at the Family Dollar and grocery store in Ennis (which took us hours), visited with hikers, and got a one-mile hitch to the Ennis RV Park. We took our first showers in 13 days (a new record). We logged about 12 trail miles today.

CDT Day #121

We made our way to Upper Sureshot Lake and had lunch with Carrot. At our dinner stop, there was a heart carved into a tree. Kaia said, "What a sappy symbol of love!" (Lots of actual sap was involved.) It was very appropriate because today is my and Adam's 21st anniversary. We found a great camping spot where someone carved a double seat out of an old log. There is a meteor shower tonight, so we are all sleeping with no rain fly (no one was actually awake for the meteor shower; we sleep soundly out here).

CDT Day #122

We started our day with a big climb to the pass next to Horse Mountain and the Nicholson mines. We had lunch at an old cabin that was probably where the original miners lived. On the descent into Mammoth, we met Chop Chop and Not So Fast. As we passed a row of cabins, a nice man who was painting his porch stopped us and offered us water. He had a big jug set out and a sign that said, "Water for Continental Divide Trailers." (We decided we use the word "hikers," so he must say that people who hike long trails are "trailers.") We got a little lost twice today as we followed the Gaia app trail. We had a big climb after dinner, and we saw a dead badger draped over a big rock next to the trail (it was the first one we've ever seen on trail). 21.8 miles on my watch and 209 flights climbed.

CDT Day #123

At our first water source of the day, we crossed paths with Horsepower. He is attempting a calendar year Triple Crown, which is absolutely mind blowing. He started in January on the AT and hiked until the snow was too deep (he got to Vermont!), then went over to the PCT and completed that trail, then started SOBO on the CDT on July 31st. He's pushing about 30 miles a day! I just cannot believe it is possible. There are less than ten people that have succeeded at a CYTC (calendar year Triple Crown).

We had a hot afternoon, and we're so grateful to find the Bone Basin Spring, even though it was heavily trodden by cows. Muir got his fill of water, then took a nap in the cool mud. We took a side trip to the Renova Hot Springs on the Jefferson River. There was a big group of college-aged kids there setting up to camp and party, so we decided to not camp there. We made our way to Whitehall, where Carrot had told us he heard hikers could camp at the town hall. As we set up our tents, the mayor stopped by. Her name is Mayor Mary (her business card says "No Ordinary Mayor"), and she opened the town hall for us. She invited us to use the laundry, showers, bathroom, WiFi, electrical outlets, and hiker box all for free! She even provided all the soap and towels! We couldn't believe it! 19.9 miles on my watch and 92 flights climbed.

CDT Day #124

We were able to walk one mile from the Whitehall Town Hall to a church and enjoyed the Sunday meeting there. We had four new pairs of shoes and six new filters waiting for us in Butte. A man at Walgreens asked us if we were hikers, and when we told him we were, he handed us $20! I'm going to add it to our fundraiser for Lifting Hands International. Another man insisted on paying for our hotel room! It was unbelievable! We had a lot of number crunching to do… it looks like we need to finish the trail and hop on a train home before September 12, the day before Kaia starts college classes online. We're cutting it close! There are a lot of fires happening right now in Idaho and Montana, and all the smoke is hard on Kaia's asthma.

CDT Day #125

Kaia and Tristan saw a young grizzly, so they stopped to wait for the rest of us. There were no signs of any other bears around. The rain started in the afternoon, so we set up early, around 6 p.m. We were all tucked safely into our tents when a flash of lightning and a loud clap of thunder hit simultaneously right above our heads! 21.2 Guthook miles, 22 miles on my watch, and 73 flights climbed.

CDT Day #126

We couldn't tell if it was raining when we woke up or if the wind was just blowing drops of water down on us from the trees. We waited until 7 a.m. to get everyone going because it was just so cold! The temperature was probably in the high 30s, but when we stopped for lunch, it sure felt like it was getting close to the freezing point! It felt like we walked in a rain cloud all day, and oftentimes I could see the water droplets in the air like a thick mist. The trail was amazingly maintained in this area, and we came across an informative sign listing all the groups who contribute to trail maintenance. We are so very grateful for their efforts! 18.7 Guthook miles, 23.1 miles on my watch, and 105 flights climbed.

CDT Day #127

There was no rain when we woke up, so we broke camp quickly and hit the trail. We passed by a lot of slash piles and logging equipment and even got to chat with a logger about what they use all these trees for (posts and poles).

We made it to MacDonald Pass around 4:30 p.m., and Adam's dad's cousin, Susan, and her husband, Jim, came to get us in two cars! They are so very kind and dropped us off at the Costco in Helena (our hotel was right across the street from there) and promised it was no trouble to help us run errands or take us back to the trail tomorrow. 17 Guthook miles and 21.7 miles on my watch.

CDT Day #128

Stores we hit today to resupply: Costco, Home Depot, TJ Max, post office, Winco, Super 1 Foods, Sportsman's Warehouse, Lowe's, and back to Costco. Resupply locations for the duration of the trail are tricky and costly, so we decided to box up supplies and ship them. Then we went to dinner with Susan and Jim! We logged zero Guthook miles, but my watch says I did 9, and Adam's says he did 12!

CDT Day #129

Whew! Getting shipping boxes packed took way longer than I thought, but we finally got out the door at 10:30 a.m. Susan and Jim drove us to the UPS store, but it turns out it is cheaper to mail the packages from the post office, so we went there. We mailed eleven of the largest "if it fits it ships" boxes to four different locations; I didn't even ask Adam how much that cost. From there we drove 16 miles out of town to the trail.

We had to make some returns to Costco this morning, so we picked up six chicken bakes for lunch. It was fun eating those on our 2.5 mile uphill climb out of town, but we managed. Rain hit us hard around 1 p.m. We got passed by three other hikers, and Adam overheard them debating whether or not to set up their tents to get out of the lightning. That storm lasted less than an hour. We saw another one rolling towards us after dinner, so we quickly found camp around

7 p.m. We made it into our tents before the rain started! 13.3 Guthook miles and 17.5 miles on my watch.

CDT Day #130

It was so cold and windy that I didn't get out of the tent until 8 a.m. to wake everyone! These last few weeks are going to be a mental game. (I said, "I think I can," over and over.) We made it to a water source at lunch and again at 3 p.m. (both cow troughs with piped spring water flowing in). Ozark was at the second water source, so we hiked with him for a few hours. We listened to his stories from his time in the military. (He is one of many veterans we've met hiking on the trail. We had just heard the news that the US troops had pulled out of Afghanistan. It was interesting to hear his thoughts on the situation. It helped us understand a little bit better the sacrifices so many have made to serve this country. We are very grateful for their service.) It was windy throughout the day, so we were thankful to find a good spot to camp with trees blocking the wind. 18 Guthook miles, 21.5 miles on my watch and 213 flights climbed.

CDT Day #131

We left camp around 7:45 a.m. with a cold breeze pushing us up a big climb. Ozark caught up with us at a trail crossing, and we watched his pack while he ran about a quarter mile downhill to see if there was water in Nevada Creek. He came back with very little water, but he did catch a blue grouse! We tried to play a joke on Tristan and put the bird under his hat. He came back from the restroom, lifted up his hat, and said, "How did you get there?!" The bird flew away unharmed.

Around 3 p.m. we made it to High Divide Outfitters, a store right off the trail near Stemple Pass. There was a plethora of other hikers there, and we got sucked into the vortex. We bought treats and a few new umbrellas to replace broken ones. It is hard to imagine that this small store, miles outside of Lincoln, was so perfectly equipped for anything and everything hikers needed. The owner has really dialed in ultralight choices and has the best selection of any store we've been in (aside from 2 Foot Adventures on the PCT). We bought veggies and steaks at the Lincoln grocery store and walked one mile to our friends' cabin (they aren't there, but they gave us the code!). It was so fun to grill up dinner and eat meat that wasn't jerky. 19.6 miles on my watch.

CDT Day #132

It was a wonderful zero day! Also, I'm starting to get sick.

CDT Day #133

We got a hitch out of Lincoln from a nice grandma who loves to give CDT hikers rides and hear their stories! We arrived at the trail around 11 a.m. and hiked up, up, up. We were passed by six NOBO hikers during our lunch break (and we saw OT, No No, Firehazard, and Spidermonkey in town—they got a hitch much faster than we did). There was a cool yurt on the trail run by the Wildlife Research Institute out of Julian, California. They are observing golden eagles, but no one was there when we popped in for a rest stop. We hiked to the summit of Green Mountain and signed the logbook. We found a camp near mile 2,694.6. 8.2 Guthook miles, 12 miles on my watch, and 187 flights climbed.

CDT Day #134

We crossed through Lewis and Clark Pass, and I found this interesting info online: "The significance of Lewis and Clark Pass is that this is where part of the Corps of Discovery crossed over as they returned from the Pacific in July of 1806. On their way back, the expedition split up near present-day Missoula. Clark's group set out to explore what is now southern Montana, while Lewis took nine men to investigate this shortcut over the mountains and then explore north-central Montana. The Corps learned of the pass from tribes west of the divide who used it to travel east of the mountains to hunt buffalo. Nez Perce men guided the explorers to the pass but didn't venture any farther due to concerns about encountering the Blackfeet" (bigskywalker.com).

Right before we planned to stop for lunch, we met a hiker named Metric Ton. He was having lots of trouble with his gear and chatted with us for about 45 minutes. He was interested to hear what gear we have tested and what we recommend. He has a very heavy pack, 60 to 80 pounds, he said. 15 Guthook miles, 17.6 miles on my watch, and 249 flights climbed.

CDT Day #135

There was a lot less elevation today than yesterday. We are meeting our friends, the Fairhursts, on Sunday afternoon to get the food we mailed to their house. Thus, we've been able to hike fewer miles the past few days so we can time it right to meet up with them (great for me because I'm still feeling sick).

Highlight of the day: the Welcome Creek Cabin! This cabin was covered in thick foil by the forest service to protect it from fires. (Even though we had some good laughs coming up with theories for why the cabin is wrapped in foil, we acknowledge that it is a good idea the forest service has to protect these historic cabins!) We camped near mile 2,723.5. 14.5 Guthook miles, 16.9 miles on my watch, and 64 flights climbed.

CDT Day #136

Our morning was spent hiking through the leftover remains of the Canyon Creek Fire. The informational sign taught us that this fire started during the summer of 1988 and burned 247,600 acres. Some of the fireweed is starting to change to fall colors, and it is beautiful! We camped at South Fork Sun Campground, where we met Hat Trick's dad (who just happens to be from the same town in Georgia as Doggone and Taxi Lady, with an equally lovely accent), who is running support for his son and Rafiki. 9.1 Guthook miles + 7 miles on Straight Creek Trail, 18.4 miles on my watch, and 36 flights climbed.

CDT Day #137

A blissful zero day! We did some planning for Benchmark to East Glacier and into Glacier National Park (where we will be at the mercy of what backcountry permits are available). The Fairhursts (Kevin, Heidi, and their four awesome kids) brought us dinner, the four boxes of food we mailed them, the eight bags of mashed potatoes and thirty-six ramen packets we requested. (Heidi says there is a ramen shortage, and she had to go to three different stores to find them!) They had to drive for several hours to get to us in this remote location, and we are very grateful they did (otherwise resupply was going to be tricky). Kevin told us if they ever make a movie of our hiking adventures, he wants his role to be played by Kid Rock. We laughed and laughed. It was so great to rest, visit with friends, and eat greasy bratwursts!

CDT Day #138

The much anticipated 12-mile escarpment known as "The Wall" did not disappoint! We passed some hikers who had already chatted with our kids up ahead, and an older gentleman said, "Those kids are going to be well-primed to be wonderful adults." I thought that was very nice, and I'm certain he is right! 21.6 Guthook miles, 24.4 miles on my watch, and 115 flights climbed.

CDT Day #139

Our day started off great with a not-too-cold morning, a beautiful sunrise, and great views. Poor Tristan got an ocular migraine, and we stopped so he could rest. We were passed by Crazy Clubs, who we've seen four or five times along this trail. He's a nice guy. We passed a lake whose actual name is My Lake, and we laughed and laughed. ("Do you like My Lake?" "No, it's My Lake!") 18 Guthook miles.

CDT Day #140

The day started on a bad note when I told Kaia to go left at a trail intersection when I should have told her to stop and wait for Adam instead. Turns out, after the first river crossing, Adam lost sight of us and went straight. We went left when we really should have gone right. My Guthook app was frozen, and I gave bad directions. After a while, I got nervous that Adam wasn't in sight, told the kids to stop and stay, and went back to look for him. He realized he was off course and was retracing his steps when he heard me yelling his name. I then went back uphill to where the kids were and led them back to the intersection where we all should have gone right. We probably logged two miles just being lost.

Once we were on the right trail, it was a big climb up and over Switchback Pass! We camped at Gooseberry Guard Station with Rafiki, Hat Trick, Dusty, Hobo Toes, and Scout. We had beautiful views all day. 16 Guthook miles, 20.5 miles on my watch, and 251 flights climbed.

CDT Day #141

It was a super cold morning with ice on all the tents! There was a wild animal in camp last night that Muir scared off (but we didn't see it; we only heard it run past our tent). Normally Muir is in Tristan's tent at night, but Tristan wanted to cowboy camp on the porch of the ranger cabin. We had hung our bear bags on the hitching post and whatever animal it was came to investigate them. We also found one of Tristan's socks about 100 yards from the cabin—we're so grateful the curious creature dropped it where we could easily find it!

We hiked through a burned forest area for hours. It was so nice to get back to the green trees! We camped at mile 2837.5 under some big pines. 23.6 Guthook miles, 25.1 miles on my watch, and 93 flights climbed.

CDT Day #142

We lost track of Guthook miles because we took an alternate to avoid blow downs. We stumbled upon an old homestead, affectionately called "The Place" with an informational sign out front. We crossed the south fork of the Two Medicine River a plethora of times today! In the afternoon, we met two hunters on mountain bikes and two guys doing surveying with a dog that looked like Muir. We found a spot to camp in a lovely grove of aspens just as the sun was setting. 23.3 miles on my watch and 68 flights climbed.

CDT Day #143

We took forest service roads to a trailhead called False Summit, then road walked on Highway 2 into East Glacier. We had high hopes of catching the Mexican restaurant for lunch, but sadly it doesn't open until 5 p.m. Instead, we picked up tortillas, potato salad, macaroni salad, and carrots from the trading post and ate while sitting on the porch of the Mexican restaurant. We walked over to Luna's Looking Glass hostel, and Taxi Lady took me and Adam to the backcountry permit office.

At first, the employee acted like it was going to be impossible to get permits for the six of us so we could finish the trail! A few hours later, we had it all worked out (while waiting, we saw some bighorn sheep hanging out in the street). We will have to flip up to the Canadian border and hike backwards to East Glacier, and we will have to take a very circuitous route, but it was the best we could get. It also cost $210 in backcountry fees!

Then we had a scare when the four packages we mailed to Luna's couldn't be found. It was at least $350 of food (plus $85 in shipping costs), and it would cost so much more to replace it here in East Glacier. While I was doing laundry, I had the idea to ask a neighboring hostel if they had our packages. They did, and there was much rejoicing. 11.9 miles on my watch.

CDT Day #144

Adam and I rushed to the Amtrak station right when they opened at 9 a.m. and bought our tickets home for Saturday the 11th (a train runs directly from here to our home near Vancouver, Washington). Wonderful Taxi Lady said she would pick us up at 10 a.m. to drive us to the Chief Mountain trailhead. It was a winding road, and poor Ruby got carsick (that'll happen after five months of just walking). Luckily for us, a border patrol agent was sitting in his truck and gave us permission to cross the orange cones and take pictures at the monument! It was so exciting!

We had a quick lunch in the parking lot and were off as southbounders. This is such a well-maintained trail with phenomenal vistas! There is lots of bear activity out here. We are camped at Glenn Lake, a few miles out of our way, but it is worth it! Every backcountry site has a wilderness pit toilet (with walls and a door!). 14.7 miles on my watch and 67 flights climbed.

CDT Day #145

It was a super fun reunion today as we cheered on all the northbound CDT hikers! We saw Ricochet, Hummingbird, Red Stripe, Earl Grey Goose, Roadkill, OT, and Ozark on the trail. The climb to the Ptarmigan Tunnel was so beautiful! At Many Glacier campground, we saw Crazy Clubs, Carrot, .3, Samwise, and Hoover. The kids got to light a campfire, and we all loved visiting with everyone, enjoying being so close to the finish. Crazy Clubs talked about designing a house in his head while he hikes, even down to what he's going to grow in his garden. .3 and Samwise saw a grizzly on the trail today at Piegan Pass. It wouldn't get off the trail and was headed straight for them, so they had to use bear spray (then it got off trail, and they had no more trouble). Carrot filled an entire Gatorade bottle with huckleberries, brought it to the general store at Many Glacier, and poured it on his ice cream. There are a few late season berries, like raspberries, thimbleberries, and huckleberries (yum!). 16.8 Guthook miles, 18.3 on my watch, and 217 flights climbed.

CDT Day #146

We crossed paths with Old Head, Animal, Frisbee, Stubbs, Trigger, Tape Worm, Hush, Side View, Hot Lips, and Caveman while going up and over Piegan Pass. The first six hikers are all together and couldn't get permits, so they are just rushing through. We got a hitch from a nice couple from New York who had rented a van and are spending a week in Glacier National Park. They dropped us off at St. Mary's KOA, where Taxi Lady had reserved us a tent spot. It was

$150! If she hadn't already paid for it, we definitely would have backed out (later Adam asked around and found everyone around us paid a lot less, so he had a chat with Mr. Manager and got our bill dropped by $62). We enjoyed the hot tub though! Doggone, Caveman (the second by that name on the trail), and Stormdasher made it to the KOA at about 9:30. We haven't seen Stormdasher since Cuba, New Mexico. He said he's been asking other hikers if they knew the Bennett family, and he finally met Doggone, who had info on us. It was so fun to see him! 16 Guthook miles, 19.3 on my watch, and 180 flights climbed.

CDT Day #147

We got a pic with Doggone, Caveman, and Stormdasher, and then Doggone dropped us off at the trail headed to St. Mary's Lake. At Red Eagle Lake, we ran into Blitz. He is just two days away from finishing up his Triple Crown! I made him promise that before he flies back home to Germany, he will stop in at a Burger King and pick up a crown to wear. Then we saw Gillmore and Intro and had a great visit with them too! They said Luna's is packed with about thirty hikers who cannot get permits. What a mess!

We saw a family of mountain goats way up on a cliff next to a waterfall. The only animal on our wish list that we haven't seen yet is a wolf (well, we haven't seen a mountain lion either, but I'm certain at least one has seen us). 15.3 Guthook miles, 27.3 on my watch, and 124 flights climbed.

CDT Day #148

If you are looking for a backcountry permit in Glacier National Park, we highly recommend Morning Star Lake. We didn't camp here, just stopped in for our lunch break, but wow was it beautiful! Pitamakan Lake and Mount Morgan are so stunning. The Lake of the Seven Winds was really windy! Sierra spotted a moose when the rest of us hiked right past it. Favorite quote of the day, from Brown Streak (a thru-hiker we met for the first time on Triple Divide Pass): "Keep the legs pumping, and don't forget to look backwards!"

Today we got to congratulate the following hikers on being so close to their finish line: Moonshine, Chocolate Chip from Israel, Squishy, Brown Streak, Yoshi, Retune, Tokyo, and six guys hiking together (we didn't get their names, but they were excited to meet the family that they've been hearing about).

It was a big elevation day! A lot of hikers were pushing two passes and thirty-ish miles so they could hitch out to St. Mary's (because they couldn't get backcountry permits). I'm so glad we didn't have to do that! We were the only ones at the Two Medicine hiker/biker campground though, which was odd. It was a lovely sunset over Pray Lake. 19.5 Guthook miles, 22.5 on my watch, and 321 flights climbed (that's a record!).

CDT Day #149

Tristan insisted on cowboy camping last night. When it started to rain, he just put his rain fly over the top of him and went back to sleep. A man with a thick accent was taking pictures of us as we walked out of the campground. I told him we've been hiking for 150 days, and he said, "150 days! This is something to record! Let me take another picture of you!"

We saw our buddy, Crispi, at the backcountry permit office, and she ran up to give us hugs and congratulations! She said she was staying at Luna's also, so we parted ways, looking forward to seeing her again.

It seems like it shouldn't be a struggle to climb over a pass after 150 days of hiking, but the 2,500 feet of elevation gain out of Two Medicine was tough! It was also super smoky, so the big views were obscured. Bummer. We did see lots of bear poo and prints in the mud. Walking back into East Glacier was anticlimactic for our big finish. We ate three pizzas from Brownies, then headed over to Luna's. So many friends were there!

I had broken another crown, so a visit to a dentist was necessary. Lucky for us, our friend Kevin Fairhurst is a dentist (who also fixed a crown for me last year). Crispi let us borrow her car so that we could drive several hours to Westside Family Dental in Great Falls. We are so grateful for all their help! Everything fell into place, and we caught our train the next morning back to Vancouver, Washington!

Our second oldest daughter, trail name Honey Badger, is filling out college applications in between the CDT and AT and wrote some amazing essays. With her permission, I'm sharing this excerpt because it makes me so happy (and all the effort of getting her out on the trails worth it!).

The essay prompt is "Describe a topic, idea, or experience that you find so engaging that it makes you lose track of time. What have you done to learn more or engage further in the topic, idea or experience?"

"In my 17 years of life, I have only found one thing so engaging that I am able to lose myself completely in it, and that is backpacking. More specifically, long-distance backpacking. I have hiked three long-distance National Scenic Trails: the Pacific Crest Trail, the Pacific Northwest Trail, and the Continental Divide Trail. For most, the idea of spending months on end hiking across the country with only what you can carry on your back is almost revolting, but for me it is my passion. While on these hiking trips, I am accompanied by my parents, two sisters, brother, and dog. No two among us walk away with the same experiences or outlook on our journey. For me, these long-distance trails were more than just sport; they were a new way of life where I was able to grow physically, mentally, and spiritually.

"To have the strength to hike for days on end with your supplies on your back, you must have some physical strength. The funny thing about strength is you must build from the bottom up. I have been told time and time again, 'You must have been so strong to have hiked all that way' or 'You are much stronger than me; I could never do that.' I have never felt that I am a particularly strong person. I have never in my life been able to do more than 10 consecutive pushups, I was never good at sports, and I cannot lift heavy weights or run long distances—in fact, I have asthma, so I can't run much at all. When I began my first hike across the country, I was overweight, unconfident, and out of shape. One could say the odds were not in my favor, but at the same time, they were. I was forced to build myself up into the athlete I needed to be from the ground up. I took things one step at a time. Each day I hiked, I gained the strength I needed to hike another day. Before their journey, Thomas Jefferson gave Lewis and Clark some very valuable advice. He said, 'There is no habit you will value so much as that of walking far without fatigue.'

"Something I found much more difficult to gain than the physical strength I had to build was my mental strength. We have all felt at times like everything and everyone in the world is working against us. I definitely had days where I didn't feel like I would be able to walk a single step more, much less another mile. Quitting, giving up, and going home were the only thoughts on my mind. Then I had days where the amount of joy I felt just being out in nature was so ineffable I can't express it in words. The Pacific Crest Trail tested my mental strength unlike any test in school ever could. In fact, it was more like the high school bully than the paper test that waited lifeless on the wooden desk to be filled out. The trail jumped out at you and tried to trip you at every turn. The first couple of weeks of my first backpacking adventure, I was constantly tormented by this new bully. It was a relentless enemy. But then something changed. I cannot describe what changed or when exactly this change took place, but seemingly all at once, this trail was my best friend. I began to appreciate the high mountain peaks she made me climb and the way she snaked through beautiful forests and deserts. She gave me front row seats to the best sunsets in the whole world and backstage passes to the concerts performed by the birds each morning. She made every day a reverent veneration.

"This leads to my spiritual growth while on the trail. Backpacking is a simplified version of life. There are no deadlines or no distractions; it is only you and your thoughts. It gives you time to really dig deep and find what it is exactly you believe. I think for the first time in my life, I understood that there was a higher power out there. It started with recognizing miracles and incredible events to be the work of God, and soon I was seeing God's hand in everything. I finally understood the vastness of God, how He was all that was good in this world, and this world as well as innumerable others were created under His direction. I had always visualized Heavenly Father as this faceless entity that sat on a throne high in the clouds and watched over us from a distance. I never felt a close connection to this image of Heavenly Father. I never got to experience the boundless love that many talk about when they describe Heavenly Father. This was not God's fault; it was my own ignorance and lack of spiritual balance. Overcoming that was difficult for me. It took wrestling with the Lord to find answers to prayers that I thought were going unanswered.

"I learned so much about the world and myself during my long journeys. I found an irrepressible love for the outdoors and a new outlet to help me live life to the fullest capacity. Having hiked these trails at such a young age, I have had the opportunity to be raised by Mother Nature, in a sense. I am filled with so much gratitude for the knowledge I have acquired at her hands. Most people will sadly never experience backpacking in the way I have. For me, it was an eye-opening new way of life; for others, it will merely be a fun weekend getaway into the woods. I can write about my walks in the woods all day, but that does nothing to teach one how to adventure; it merely teaches them how I adventure. However, I think it is important to be inspired to take that jump into the unknown, to find an interest, and to be willing to pursue it with unwavering dedication to succeed. Even if you fall short, there is growth that comes from stretching yourself."

Part 4: Appalachian Trail

April–September 2022

We jumped on a flight in Portland, Oregon, which was running an hour behind. Luckily our connecting flight in Denver was running late too. We maneuvered through the Atlanta airport and waited for over an hour at baggage claim only to learn that our one checked item was back in Denver. Among the items in this checked bag were all the poles and stakes for our tents. Poor Doggone (our trail angel that we met last year on the CDT) was waiting for us for over 1.5 hours. We finally left the airport with the promise that they'd get our bag to us somehow/sometime soon. We didn't get to the campground until 1:30 a.m.! Doggone loaned us poles and tent stakes because he and Taxi Lady were staying in their teardrop trailer. Also, our daughter Sierra was called to serve an 18-month church mission in Alabama and would not be joining us for the AT. We invited our cousin Madi, and she agreed! Turns out, our first night camping at Amicalola was Madi's first night in a tent. She is tenacious and committed to hiking the entire trail with us, and we are so grateful to have her along. We also are sponsored by Topo Athletic shoes for this trail!

AT Day #1

"Running more than 2,100 miles along America's eastern seaboard, through the serene and beckoning Appalachian Mountains, the AT is the granddaddy of long hikes. From Georgia to Maine, it wanders across fourteen states, through plump, comely hills whose very names—Blue Ridge, Smokies, Cumberlands, Green Mountains, White Mountains—seem an invitation to amble." —Bill Bryson, "A Walk in the Woods"

East Coast birds start singing loudly at 6 a.m. (3 a.m. PST). Adam contacted the airport and convinced them of the urgency of our situation. Without our poles and stakes, our tents are useless in the upcoming rainstorm. Plus, we only have food for 3.5 days and can't be waiting around. Instead of trying to get it to us tomorrow through UPS, they said they would have a driver bring us our package.

Doggone drove us to the Amicalola Falls Visitor Center, and we got our Appalachian Trail tags (#2,800–2,805) and listened to the Leave No Trace presentation. We got our picture taken at the famous arch. Doggone helped us identify dogwood trees and mountain laurels. Then we drove to see Amicalola Falls and the Lodge.

At the Lodge, we decided we were hungry and wanted the buffet. We drove back to get Taxi Lady and had a feast. Our lost package was delivered to the lodge by 1:30 p.m. We loaded up the resupply that Doggone picked up for us, and he drove us to the Springer Mountain parking lot. Doggone brought his drone and hiked to the top of Springer with us. What a fun moment; it's one we've been anticipating for so long!

We stopped at the Stover Creek Shelter for some foot care, dinner, and potty breaks. An awesome ridge runner was there. (A ridge runner is someone who has an 11-week contract with the AT to keep an eye on the trail and educate hikers.) Her name is Chelsea, and she told us about some hemlock trees that we will see soon. I need to make note of what she said so the kids can share it with their science teachers. The hemlocks have been struggling with a bug infestation that is killing them. When the hemlocks die, the ecosystem around them changes for the worse (water temperatures rise, there's less shade, etc.). We will see some of the trees marked with a silver tag, indicating that some medicine has been injected into their roots that provides 10 years' worth of protection from the bugs. She said it was such a beautiful hemlock forest, a real sight to see.

We left the shelter to get a few more miles in (plus there were about twenty people there). We stopped .5 miles short of the Three Forks parking area at a great spot near Stover Creek. Mile 3.9; 4.8 miles total for us today.

AT Day #2

"[The Trail] leads not merely north and south, but up to the body, mind and soul of man." —Myron Avery, "In the Maine Woods"

"God be willin' and the creek don't rise" is a Southern saying we came to appreciate today. Buckets of rain started at 4 a.m. My hiking clothes that I keep warm at night in my quilt (in a mesh bag) fell out when I adjusted it to not get wet and were completely soaked when I woke up this morning—rookie mistake. When we passed the Three Forks campsites, we were grateful we hadn't slept there. Most of the tent spots were giant puddles from last night's rain. The ridge runner told us to take the detour to Long Falls. I'm glad we did. We grabbed water from a stream and filtered it at Hawk Mountain Shelter. A group of four guys visited with us for a bit. They are out for a four-day section hike, and it looks like they are moving fast. We enjoyed a nice, long siesta in the shelter, hiding from the wind and misty weather.

At 2 p.m. we took another break in the shade at Horse Gap. There we met SOBO (her actual trail name, not just the direction she's hiking. She also hiked the PCT in 2019, but we never crossed paths) and Boony (who packs a ukulele in a UL pack and wears a tacocat shirt). Just before getting to Justus Creek, we met another very nice ridge runner. She said if the Devil's Kitchen campsite was too full, we could camp on an old road. It was too full, so we did. After a lackluster dinner of protein bars and cold soaked mashed potatoes (spiced up with the Tony's Creole Seasoning Adam packed out), we crawled in bed. We camped at mile 14.4, and we did 10.5 miles today.

AT Day #3
"The woods are lovely, dark and deep / But I have promises to keep, / And miles to go before I sleep, / And miles to go before I sleep." —Robert Frost

We left camp at 8:45 a.m. with temperatures in the low 40s. We visited Gooch Mountain Shelter, Muir got called a corgi (he's an Australian Shepherd/Red Heeler), and we stopped at a very crowded Woody Gap to use pit toilets and throw away trash. We made it to Lance Creek at 4 p.m., but there was no room for us. We hiked another .2 miles and set up on another old road. We had lots of time to organize food for tomorrow's resupply and sit around and laugh. We camped at mile 24; 9.6 miles today.

AT Day #4
"People wish to be settled; only as far as they are unsettled is there any hope for them." —Ralph Waldo Emerson

The "sweet Southern rain" started about 3 a.m. When we broke camp at 7:30, it was no longer raining, but a thick mist was all around us. When Tristan opened his tent flap, he said it looked like the reflection off a lake, as if he were in the middle of the water.

Trilliums are in bloom everywhere! There are red and yellow varieties that I've never seen before and beautiful white ones by the thousands.

Blood Mountain was quite the climb! Tristan tried to do the last mile to the summit in twenty minutes, but it took him thirty. Luckily for us, the rain had stopped, but there was a stiff breeze. We ate a quick lunch, asked "just Tim" to take pictures for us, and rushed down in the slippery mud to Neel Gap.

Earlier in the day, Kaia met a hiker who offered us a hitch to the Walmart. She found us at Neel Gap just as Adam was saying, "Okay, I need to start hitching now." So immediately Tristan and Adam had a ride into town with Whisper (she hiked the AT in 2019). I noticed her teeth were a bit discolored, and as she walked to her car, I heard her say to Adam, "Sorry about my teeth. I ate a dandelion today."

Another "the trail provides" moment was at the hiker box outside the Walasi-yi Center. There was a mostly used bottle of Sawyer Permethrin, just enough to apply to Muir (I forgot to do that before we left home!), and some almond butter, beef jerky, Trader Joe's mangos, tiny shampoo, and sunblock. Adam and Tristan returned safely from the Walmart in Dahlonega.

There are trees here that have used hiking shoes hanging from the branches. Either hikers give up at this point and throw their shoes up there, or their shoes are causing pain and they swap them out. We hiked up the hill from the Neel Gap and camped at mile 31.8; 7.8 miles today.

AT Day #5

"On life and peaks it is the same. With strength we win the grail, but courage is the thing we need to face the downward trail."
—*Jacob Clifford Moomaw*

Tristan: [as the sun clears the fog] "Beautiful! I don't think there's been a single day on this trail that I haven't been enchanted with it."

Our "up and down" day looked like this: up Levelland Mountain, down to Swaim Gap, up Turkeypen Mountain, down to Rock Spring, up to Wolf Laurel Top to Green Cliff Top to Cowrock Mountain, down to Tesnatee Gap (where we missed trail magic by five minutes), up towards Wildcat Mountain, down to Hog Pen Gap (where there was trail magic but no trail angels, just a nice note wishing us a happy Easter), then up Poor Mountain and Sheep Rock Top, and finally down to Low Gap.

There are at least thirty other hikers here; it's so crowded! Spring in northern Georgia is blowing our minds! There are so many beautiful wildflowers, and the trees are just starting to bud. We camped at mile 42.8; 11-mile day.

AT Day #6

"Hiking is not escapism; it's realism. The people who choose to spend time outdoors are not running away from anything; we are returning to where we belong."
—*Jennifer Pharr Davis*

We got buckets of rain again last night. I made another rookie mistake, and now my shoes are soaked! I thought I could put my shoes under my backpack to prop it up (hoping it would get less wet and muddy during the night). Instead, I woke up to a tipped-over muddy pack and shoes with puddles inside. I'll blame Muir for moving things around in the vestibule last night so he could get comfy.

Lyrics I am singing today: "Mama told me there would be days like this," and "The sun will come out tomorrow." Turns out it wasn't a problem that my shoes got wet in the night because a monsoon-type rain hit us as we were packing up. Adam let out a defiant Viking-type yell as he got soaked, like "bring it on!" The trail was a muddy slog all day. We were lucky that the rain was pretty much done by the time we stopped for lunch, but the wind was blowing (so we still got wet).

Some fellow thru-hikers were planning on camping at the Blue Mountain Shelter, but when they got there and it was so cold, they decided to call a shuttle to Unicoi Gap and get a ride to the Holiday Inn. I can't say I wasn't a tad envious. We are due for some laundry and showers, especially after today! But I've heard the climb up Rocky Mountain is a beast, so I'm happy we've got a head start on it. We camped at mile 53.4, three-quarters of the way up Rocky Mountain (we will be singing John Denver tomorrow for sure!); 10.6 miles today.

AT Day #7

"When we strive to become better than we are, everything around us becomes better too." —Paulo Coelho

It got below freezing last night. Tristan shared his tent with Muir so they could both stay warm. It was a one-dog night, as my grandpa would say. The wind sounded like a freight train rushing through camp for most of the night. We let the sunshine warm us until 8:30 a.m. before we started breaking camp.

We met some section hikers at Indian Grave Gap and visited with them for a while. One was having knee pain, so Adam told him about using trekking poles to massage the IT band from the knee to the hip. Hopefully that'll do the trick.

We stopped at Trey Mountain Shelter for a long lunch in the sunshine. It was so great to get gear dry, filter water, and visit with a few thru-hikers. We passed "Swag of the Blue Ridge" and learned that a swag is just slightly different from a gap. We got water from John's Spring, where the water is literally flowing right from a giant tree's roots. We camped earlier than planned because Kaia's feet are really hurting her. We stopped at Sassafras Gap at mile 62.8, 9.4 AT miles (13.7 today according to my phone).

AT Day #8

"Sunshine is delicious, rain is refreshing, wind braces us up, snow is exhilarating; there is really no such thing as bad weather, only different kinds of good weather." —John Ruskin

A strong, cold wind was whipping through our camp this morning while we were packing up. Our first obstacle was Kelly's Knob, the last climb over 4,000 feet in all of Georgia. In no time at all we were at Dick's Creek Gap and caught a ride all together into Hiawassee. The first item of business was lunch at the grocery store. We're so grateful they had a nice outdoor eating area where we could consume our chicken strips, baked beans, yogurt, and peanut butter. A few locals stopped to chat with us; everyone is so kind! One couple had a lot of questions, said a prayer with us, and left us with their number in case we needed anything. (I noticed too late that while typing, I missed a number, so we never got to text them, bummer!) We walked over to the Holiday Inn and enjoyed hot showers and laundry. Dinner at the buffet was disappointing, but we all left full. 6.4 trail miles today.

AT Day #9

"Before you criticize a man, walk a mile in his shoes. That way, when you do criticize him, you'll be a mile away and have his shoes." —*Steve Martin*

It's hard to pull away from the hotel breakfast and get packed up fast on town days! We hit a few gear shops and the post office. Our first hitch picked us up because he liked our dog but could only drive us two miles (it felt a bit like the opening scene of the movie *The Jerk* (the tv-edited version) where he gets a hitch to the end of the fence). It took a while for another car to stop, but a very kind mother of five in a minivan got us all back to the trail.

It started to rain during our lunch stop, but it was short-lived. We had a great conversation with a ridge runner. She was excited to hear about the other trails we've hiked and chat about backcountry "leave no trace" principles. Right after meeting the ridge runner, we crossed from Georgia into North Carolina! We camped at Bly Gap at mile 78.2; 9 miles today.

AT Day #10

"There is an intense but simple thrill in setting off in the morning on a mountain trail knowing that everything you need is on your back. It is a confidence in having left all inessentials behind, and of entering a world of natural beauty which has not been violated, where money has no value, and possessions are a deadweight." —*Paul Theroux, "The Happy Isles of Oceana: Paddling the Pacific"*

After we left camp, we had some big climbs to deal with. During a rest stop, we visited with John and Susan from Scotland. They discouraged us from doing the John Muir Trail in their country, unless on bike, because it's on concrete and through the cities. Instead, they recommended the coast-to-coast trail in England or Scotland. Susan noted that they were "not dedicated trekkers," and if they have injuries or get bored, they plan to rent a car and tour around. They are here for three months, then must get home for a wedding. On the back of Susan's pack hangs a Scottish flag, and they each have cups attached to their packs. John says it is because in their country, they can just scoop up water and drink it without a filter.

We had a sunny, relaxing lunch spot at Deep Gap. We arrived at Coleman Gap at 7 p.m., hoping to camp, but it was too full. We pushed on another 1.5 miles to Carter Gap Shelter, and there were so many people! Luckily, we found three semi-flat tent spots and quickly claimed them. A guy next to us was already tucked in bed for the night, laying on a heavy-looking cot under a small tarp. He asked if the girls had ear plugs because he snores. And boy did he ever! Mile 93.5; 15.3 miles today. ("Now we are cooking with peanut oil!" is another favorite Southern saying of ours.)

AT Day #11

"But a radical new body of evidence shows that people are at their best—physically harder, mentally tougher, and spiritually sounder—after experiencing the same discomforts our early ancestors were exposed to every day. Scientists are finding that certain discomforts protect us from physical and psychological problems like obesity, heart disease, cancers, diabetes, depression, and anxiety, and even more fundamental issues like feeling a lack of meaning and purpose." —Michael Easter, "The Comfort Crisis: Embrace Discomfort To Reclaim Your Wild, Happy, Healthy Self"

Our neighbors at Carter Gap started packing up at about 5:30 a.m., way before the sunrise. We rolled out of camp at 8:30, and by noon we had summited Albert Mountain. That climb was no joke! There is an old fire lookout there, and we had lunch in its shade. A lot of hikers congregated there to rest, and it was fun to visit with them. A hiker named Coach asked us a lot of questions about hiking as a family (he is hiking with his adult-age son).

We crossed the 100-mile marker! Yippie! We made it to Rock Gap Shelter (mile 105.6) at 4 p.m. and enjoyed a relaxing afternoon. Gumby and Jillian were also there early, and we visited for hours. Gumby told us about some hikers she met at Beech Gap who came into camp with no backpacks and said, "They were returning to the scene of the crime." Turns out, one of them had hung his food bag with his wallet in it, and a bear stole it! They searched for hours and found the bag and wallet about 300 yards from the shelter. The bear took all the food but kindly left the wallet.

Rock Gap Shelter has a display of artwork and short essays titled "Dangers on the Trail" by a 3rd grade class. Some brilliant teacher came up with the idea to display them there to entertain hikers. My favorite one was about avoiding tripping on roots and logs while hiking.

We saw a lovely sunset through the trees that are just starting to bud leaves. 12.1 miles today. (At 9 p.m., Fire Lord surprised us all and brought a full pizza from the road .1 miles away and said our family could have it. There was much rejoicing as we all hopped out of our quilts to feast. There is even a bear-proof trash can, and he threw away the box for us!)

AT Day #12

"In normal life, we hardly realize how much more we receive than we give, and life cannot be rich without such gratitude. It is so easy to overestimate the importance of our own achievements compared with what we owe to the help of others." — Dietrich Bonhoeffer

We left Rock Gap at about 8:30 a.m. and got to Winding Stair Gap before 11. There were two different types of trail magic going on there! Dead Eye served up hamburgers with all the fixings and chips. The other group had a bunch of candy that the kids really enjoyed.

A kind couple from Mexico and their 11-year-old daughter picked us all up in their truck and dropped us off at Walmart in Franklin, North Carolina. We did the fastest resupply ever, and just when we were getting ready to hitch, a man walked up and said he had a van and would drive us back to the trail! His trail name is Steppenwolf, and he hiked the PCT in 2018. He said he was just out looking for hikers to help when he spotted us! He was so great!

We were back on the trail by 2 p.m. and had a big climb to the top of Siler Bald. It was hot and the air was smoky because of a fire nearby. Poor Kaia and her asthma! We camped near the Wayah Gap Picnic Area at mile 115.2. 9.6 miles today.

AT Day #13

"When my kids ask why we have to do some uncomfortable thing or another, like ice fishing or taking a long hike in hot weather, I've found myself answering their

questions with this glib-sounding but entirely truthful answer: we're doing it so you'll be able to hang out with the cool people when you grow up." —Steven Rinella, "Outdoor Kids in an Inside World"

Another hefty elevation day! To our delight, a couple was doing trail magic from their van at Wayah Bald. He had hiked the AT last year, and she met him with support every six days. They were a delightful couple to chat with, and they were serving up Dunkin' Donuts, fruit snacks, oranges, tiny bags of cashews, and hot chocolate! What a treat!

A man stopped to chat with us while we were eating our lunch near the lookout tower and said he had gotten his Triple Crown twenty years ago ("before phones, ultra-light gear, etc."). He was a funny guy, and he is right; we have it much easier these days.

We took a rest stop from about 2 to 3 p.m. and got passed by so many hikers! When we reached Cold Spring Shelter, most were there enjoying the shade and cold water. We pressed on, determined to get in 13 to 15 miles today. When we got to Tellico Gap, we didn't see any flat campsites. Kaia and Madi's feet are hurting, but they gave the okay to climb Wesser Bald in hopes of finding campsites. There is an awesome observation tower at the top, but we decided against cowboy camping because the weather report predicted a 70% chance of rain. We did get to catch an awesome sunset and found semi-flat tent sites nearby. We made it to mile 130.2; 15 miles today.

Madi has us "honk laughing" so often. I really need to remember to write down her quotes immediately. This one I did get: "If I don't get in bed right now, I'm going to cartwheel party launch myself off this cliff."

AT Day #14

"Better than a thousand days of diligent study is one day with a great teacher." —Japanese Proverb

Mrs. Marvin Day! Ruby and Tristan have had Mrs. Marvin as a teacher or counselor since 2019. She is one of those off-the-charts, extraordinary, award-winning teachers every kid should have in their life. She flew from Washington to Tennessee to visit her family and made the Herculean effort of tracking us down on the trail. She and four of her grandkids hiked southbound on the AT from the Nantahala

Outdoor Center and met us at about noon. Then she bought four giant pizzas at the restaurant, and we all happily stuffed ourselves. She patiently waited while we charged devices and got our permits printed for the Great Smoky National Park. Then the five of them joined us for a bit as we hiked northbound. It was a huge moral boost to have them come visit (Ruby has had an extra pep in her step for days in anticipation). These are treasured memories! We camped at 139.4 and made it 9.2 miles today.

AT Day #15

"The ultimate purpose? There are three things: to walk, to see, to see what you see." —Benton MacKaye

The elevation gain and loss took its toll today! Our app says we did 4,300 feet up and 3,500 feet down. Adam looked up what ascent/descent we hiked in the Sierras in 2019, and it is very similar to what we are doing now (except the Sierras had bigger food carries, longer water carries, and more than double the elevation).

In addition to sore feet and screaming calf muscles, we haven't found a level tent spot all week! Adam said, "If there is going to be a reason to quit this trail, it's because the tent sites are all so awful!" Muscle recovery at night seems to not be happening because we are tossing and turning and rolling downhill. Now it makes sense why hikers seem to rush from shelter to shelter; the floors seem pretty level inside (we haven't slept inside a shelter yet).

An informational sign at Stecoah Gap read, "The Appalachian Trail was created as a simple footpath to connect people with the restorative power of nature, to protect the region's natural beauty and cultural heritage and to ensure enjoyment today, tomorrow, and for centuries to come. The trail was originally proposed in 1921 by Benton MacKaye, whose idea was taken to end-to-end connected reality in 1937 by Myron Avery. In 1968, with the passage of the National Trails System Act, the A.T. was designated the first National Scenic Trail. The 2,193-mile trail, stretching from Maine to Georgia, passes through 14 states, 8 National Forests, 7 National Parks, and more than 60 federal, state, and local parks and forests. Its terrain ranges from flat woodland paths to near vertical rock scrambles." We camped near Brown Fork Gap Shelter at mile 152.9. 13.5 miles today.

AT Day #16

"When we try to pick out anything by itself, we find it hitched to everything else in the Universe." —John Muir

Today we met with Dawn, my grandpa's cousin's daughter, and her husband Mike. They brought dessert to share and drove me and Adam to get our three big resupply boxes from the Lodge. Three weeks ago, Mike (a former paramedic) witnessed a car accident and was able to save the driver's life. In the process, he hurt his leg in such a way that his doctor is going to amputate it on Monday! He has such a positive attitude, and it was very enlightening to hear his story. We camped at the Fontana Crossing at mile 164.3. 11.4 miles today.

AT Day #17

"Nature is one of the most underutilized treasures in life. It has the power to unburden hearts and reconnect to that inner place of peace." —Janice Anderson

Today was our first day in the Great Smoky Mountains National Park! We started the day at 6 a.m. so we could leave camp at 7. Our first stop was the "Fontana Hilton" (a shelter that also has a restroom with flushing toilets and free showers). It took a very long time to get us all showered and ready to hit the trail again, but oh, did it feel so good! It had been nine days since our last shower.

Immediately after entering the National Park, we dropped our paper permits in the "iron ranger," then started the big climb to Shuckstack Lookout. There are the remains of an old warden's cabin and a very tall fire lookout tower with an awesome view! From here forward, we follow the North Carolina/Tennessee border through the park. We noticed lots of upturned soil as we hiked along and overheard another hiker saying the wild boars do that. We set up our tents near Mollies Ridge Shelter, and there are a lot of people here! Mile 177.7; 13.4 miles today.

AT Day #18

"The sum of the whole is this: walk and be happy; walk and be healthy. The best way to lengthen out our days is to walk steadily and with a purpose." —*Charles Dickens*

It got very windy during the night! We woke up the team at 6:20 a.m. and were packed and on the trail by 7:30. We stopped at Spence Field Shelter to eat lunch, filter water, and use the very nice privy. We ended up visiting with other hikers and stayed way too long—an hour and a half!

The afternoon miles came slowly; there was a lot of uphill. At the summit of Rocky Top, we visited with a trail runner who is preparing for a big race in Utah this summer. We met a ridge runner named Amelia, trail name Treeline. She hiked the AT in 2017 with her dad, and it brought tears to my eyes to hear about her awesome experience. She asked if we were going for our Triple Crown and said she had heard of our family through a friend of Crazy Eyes (we met him on the PCT, saw him twice on the CDT, and we are about 250 miles behind him on this trail). She had a quote from her dad tattooed on her arm in his handwriting. It really touched me how much she loved her dad.

After a wild uphill scramble, we made it to Derrick Knob Shelter at about 4 p.m. We had a nice, relaxing dinner in the sunshine on the grass by our tents. Adam found the first tick of the trail on Muir; it must have just gotten there because it was super easy to pull out. Everyone is doing tick checks. Mile 189.8; 12.1 miles today.

AT Day #19

"What makes aerobic exercise so powerful is that it's our evolutionary method of generating that spark. It lights a fire on every level of your brain, from stoking up the neurons' metabolic furnaces to forging the very structures that transmit information from one synapse to the next." —*John J. Ratey, "Spark: the Revolutionary New Science of Exercise and the Brain"*

There were twenty-two tents around us when we woke up this morning. It didn't rain in the night like we expected, so that was great! We rolled out of camp at 7:15 a.m. and did a quick six miles to Double Springs Gap Shelter. We got poured on for about an hour before the shelter, so we hunkered down there for a long siesta. As we were getting ready to leave, a group of hikers showed up, and one started a fire in the shelter's fireplace. We've never seen anyone so enthusiastically start a fire. (We don't know his trail name, but we now call him Fireguy. Madi said, "I think he was trying to impress us. And it worked!") It was hard to walk away from that fire! But the weather was starting to clear, and we needed to make miles.

The climb up to Clingmans Dome was beautiful! Suddenly, we were in a pine forest with lots of bright green moss. It felt like home because it looked like our trails in Washington! We decided to take the side detour to the tourist tower, and I'm so glad we did. Just as we were walking out of the woods, a lady started taking a video of us and asking questions about our hike. We felt like superstars!

We're so happy to hit the 200-mile mark; only 2,000 more to go! There was no view from the top of Clingmans Dome because we were surrounded by thick fog, but it was fun to walk to the top of the lookout. It was a quick hike down to the Mt. Collins Shelter. Even though the elevation was similar yesterday and today, for some reason today's miles seemed so much easier. Maybe it's because the weather was cooler, and the trail was more maintained. We camped at mile 202.8; 13 miles today (Adam's watch says we did 15.1).

AT Day #20

"I learned this, at least, by my experiment: that if one advances confidently in the direction of his dreams, and endeavors to live the life which he has imagined, he will meet with a success unexpected in common hours." —Henry David Thoreau, "Walden: Or, Life in the Woods"

We hiked 4.9 miles from the Mt. Collins Shelter to Newfound Gap. Within a half hour, Butch and Diane from Cherokee, North Carolina, picked us all up in their big truck. They had passed us, felt badly, said to each other, "What would Jesus do?" then turned around and came back.

Our first stop was the awesome NOC, where we checked the hiker box and gathered intelligence. Then we went to Cici's pizza buffet, where they may or may not have lost money on us. The kids stayed at the pizza place while Adam and I walked a few miles to what we thought was our hotel. We had booked on Priceline and a free breakfast was promised, and when we arrived the sign out front also promised breakfast, but inside we learned breakfast was not available. So we canceled that reservation and rode the free trolley around the wild tourist town of Gatlinburg. The trolley got us to the post office 10 minutes after it closed, which was a big bummer, but we did get to Food City to do our resupply. We finally ended up at the Days Inn with free breakfast but no laundry. I had to walk to three other hotels carrying two giant trash compactor bags full of smelly hiker laundry before I found a washer and dryer I could use. One couple asked me, "What's in the bags?" then explained they were listening to a podcast about murderers and that I looked suspicious. Hiker chores were completed, and nice soft beds were enjoyed.

AT Day #21

"Let children walk with nature, let them see the beautiful blendings and communions of death and life, their joyous inseparable unity, as taught in woods and meadows, plains and mountains and streams of our blessed star, and they will learn that death is stingless indeed, and as beautiful as life, and that the grave has no victory, for it never fights." —John Muir

We had a late start today because Adam had to take the trolley to the post office (where he learned that his package was sent to Nashville, and UPS told him he should just go there to get it. Nope!). It took about two hours to hitch out of Gatlinburg with three different hitches. We had a quick lunch at Newfound Gap and pressed onward and upward. We had hoped to go farther, but it was either stop at Icewater Spring Shelter (three miles in) or push eight more miles to a shelter with negative comments about the tent spots. ("A very sloped area without many good tenting spots… some of the flatter spots are very close to the privy and don't smell very nice.") So we found three spots, ate a quick dinner, and were happily in our beds by 7 p.m. We stopped at mile 210.8; 3.1 miles today.

AT Day #22

"The trail will only provide if you accept its offer. All of it. You must leave home. You must be broken. It will cost you your entire life as you know it. And then, and only then, can you receive. What you receive will be far greater than anything you had or anything you lost. It will change you. It might even heal you."
—Ben Crawford, *"2,000 Miles Together: The Story of the Largest Family to Hike the Appalachian Trail"*

We got a good amount of rain in the night with a little bit of thunder and lightning in the distance. The trail mostly followed the ridge line, past monuments named "Charlie's Bunion" and "The Sawteeth." We stopped for water and lunch at Pecks Corner, but the stream was just a tiny trickle. We went up and over Mount Sequoyah and Mount Chapman with no views because of the fog and trees.

A group of people on seven horses were out doing trail maintenance. We're very grateful for that! We wandered around Tri-Corner Knob Shelter for a bit until we found camping 500 feet away next to the horse camp. Mile 223.4, 12.6 miles today.

AT Day #23

We met a ridge runner named Rick who hiked the CDT southbound last year. He knew some of the hikers we had crossed paths with, but we don't remember seeing each other. Adam asked him which trail he prefers, the CDT or the AT. Without hesitation he said the CDT, which surprised us because he is from the East. It was fun to chat with him about thru-hiking. He hopes to do the PCT next year and the PNT someday. Also, he has a prosthetic leg just below the knee. He's a very cool guy.

We decided against visiting Cosby Knob or Mt. Cammerer Shelters and just had lunch on the side of the trail while we filtered water. We hit a big milestone today of doing 10 miles before lunch! It was a big downhill kind of day as we walked our way out of the Great Smoky Mountains (6,500 feet of descent and 2,000 feet of ascent). We camped at mile 240.4; 17 miles today.

AT Day #24

"Doesn't it feel like we are walking through a giant garden?" —Tristan Bennett

We made a quick visit to the Standing Bear Hostel to pick up a few snacks and charge devices. It was a cool place! As we were hiking along in formation today, we heard Madi making terrible gagging sounds. Turns out, a bug had dive-bombed into her mouth, and she swallowed it. With fear in her eyes, she asked Kaia, "Am I going to die?!" She said the bug was spiky, and it was the worst thing that has ever happened to her. It was so hilarious; I wish I had a video.

The summit of Snowbird Peak has an unusual communications tower. I thought it looked like a bowling alley. Unfortunately, we couldn't take shelter from the rain under the roof; warning signs told us to stay away. We didn't go across the famous Max Patch as planned because the wind, rain, lightning (our biggest fear on trail), and thunder were so intense. Instead, we decided to stealth camp at mile 254.5; 14.1 miles today.

AT Day #25

There are so many new wildflowers in this section! We left camp later than usual; it was pouring rain. Max Patch summit was so windy that Kaia's umbrella got blown inside-out and broke! We stopped for lunch at Walnut Mountain Shelter, and we were delighted to be the only ones there. That only lasted for ten minutes or so. At first it was "just Bob" who showed up, and we enjoyed visiting with him for twenty minutes. Then ten more hikers arrived, some of whom intended to sleep at the shelter. We were quickly crowded out of the six-person shelter and rushed to pack up.

The kids were really hoping to set up camp early today because they are so sick of hiking in the rain (and sore, pruned feet hurt!). At 5 p.m., Ruby spotted some tent sites that were so flat and mud-free that we couldn't refuse (plus the rain had stopped, and a slight breeze promised to dry out our tents). We even had dinner and got all tucked in before it started raining again! We camped at mile 267.4; 12.9 miles today.

AT Day #26

We were off like a herd of turtles at about 8:45 a.m. There was a puddle at the bottom of Tristan's tent, we all had wet, muddy clothes to put on, and even though the rain had stopped, the trees were still dripping on us. It was mostly downhill, so we made it into town by noon. Our first stop was Laughing Heart Hostel, right off the trail. We gathered intelligence, chatted with hiker friends, paid $5 for a load of laundry, and loitered at the picnic table. Adam, Madi, and Kaia walked to the Dollar General and picked up a feast of bratwursts, buns, chips, salsa, canned yams, and baked beans. Later, Adam, Ruby, and I walked to the Bluff Mountain Outfitters to pick up shoes that Topo mailed us, but they weren't there. So, we will have to hit the post office in the morning for Adam's package and wait around until the afternoon UPS delivery for the shoes (hopefully). After all our devices were charged and our bellies full, we hiked to an abandoned forest service road to stealth camp. Mile 274.5; 7.1 miles on the trail today.

AT Day #27

We started our day with eating some cereal and milk from the Dollar General and gathering information at the Hot Spring's Welcome Center. We checked the post office and the outfitter to see if packages arrived, but no luck. We decided to hit Spring Mountain restaurant for an early birthday lunch for Ruby. The waitress had the sweetest southern accent, and the food was delicious. The package with two pairs of shoes (for Kaia and Madi) never arrived, so we decided to hike on.

A big climb out of town on a hot, humid afternoon (with bellies full of town food) was a butt kicker, but we made it. At one point we stopped to catch our breath, and I didn't notice when the team started hiking on. I heard Ruby's voice up ahead say, "Mom, do you need help?" I thought that was very sweet of her to be looking out for me! The Rich Mountain fire lookout was full, but we found a great campsite not too far away. We camped at mile 283.3; 8.7 miles today.

AT Day #28

We had a 5:50 a.m. wake-up call to a lovely sunrise. We stopped at Spring Mountain Shelter to filter water, use the privy, and visit with other hikers. Cowboy and Toothpick were there. He let Kaia use his phone to call his friend that was still at Happy Heart Hostel, and he found her raincoat that she forgot on the clothesline! The manager there will keep it safe until we can come get it on Saturday (and our two packages that arrived the day after we left town). The plan is to rent a car, retrieve those things from Hot Springs, drive to Damascus to catch AT Trail Days, and then return the car early Sunday morning. We had a fantastic view for dinner at the summit of Big Firescald Knob and a fun rock scramble down. We camped at mile 300.4; 17 miles today.

AT Day #29

We were on the trail by 7 a.m., and the first obstacle of the day was Butt Mountain (many jokes were made). We took a short side trip to visit the graves of three men killed during the Civil War. We found conflicting stories about their deaths in our trail app, but it sounds like two of them were Union soldiers coming home to visit family and were ambushed by Confederate soldiers. The third was a spy, just 13 years old.

Coincidentally, today is Ruby's 13th birthday. When we stopped for lunch, I told all the other hikers (nine of them), and they wished her a happy birthday. We rested by a waterfall around 3 p.m. and had enough cell coverage to make a few phone calls so that family could visit with Ruby. About a mile before Hogback Ridge Shelter, we stopped for dinner. It was a beautiful, breezy evening, and we found three flat campsites before the trail to the shelter! We camped at mile 317.3; 16.9 miles today.

AT Day #30

We had a big climb today to summit Big Bald. There was trail magic at mile 325 from a local hiking club. I overheard one hiker say, "I was so excited to see that trail magic. I almost started crying!" We felt the same! We took a long lunch and had breaks at 3 p.m. and for dinner. We camped at mile 333 with Gumby, Big Daddy, Galaxy, Tin Man, Gator, and Lisa. 15.7 miles today.

AT Day #31

We woke up, packed up, and headed off with a pep in our step because today is a town day! We arrived at Uncle Johnny's Nolichucky Hostel and Outfitters (mile 344.2) at about noon. A birthday package had arrived for Ruby from friends in Washington, and it was so fun (they included gifts for everyone, which was so thoughtful!). We had to split into two groups to hitch into Johnson City, but it all worked out (and we got all cleaned up in a hotel). 11.2 trail miles.

AT Day #32

Today was our first zero day! Adam walked about two miles from the hotel to Enterprise Rent-a-Car, dropped me off at Walmart, then drove to Hot Springs to get the package of shoes and the raincoat Kaia accidentally left there. I grabbed a twelve-day resupply, and the kids helped me organize it into three-day, four-day, and five-day boxes. Adam returned from his two-hour backroads drive and picked us all up, and we took off in the other direction for Damascus, Virginia.

We arrived at Trail Days just in time for the Hiker Parade! It was so much fun to see hikers we've met on this and other trails and see all the vendors! Tristan won a big prize in a raffle (a $300 Gossomer Gear backpack, wool socks, Goodr sunglasses, and a book by Julianna Chauncey). A local church was feeding hikers, so we joined in and got some nachos and dessert for dinner. We dropped off our three-day food box at the Broken Fiddle hostel and our five-day food box at Mountain Harbor B&B (it isn't typical that one could stash food at these places, but our friend Walmart—a four-time AT hiker—helped us get special permission). Then it was back to Johnson City for another night in a cheap hotel!

AT Day #33

We enjoyed the hotel waffles, made a quick stop at a church, then went back to Uncle Johnny's. Adam left to return the rental car and was back way faster than we expected. A man just out for a Sunday drive took him from Johnson City to Erwin, then a local mountain biker picked him up and dropped him at Uncle Johnny's.

Meanwhile, the kids and I mailed extra gear, swag from Trail Days, and Tristan's prize winnings back home. It was nice to visit with hikers (Cowboy, Toothpick, Walmart, and Breathe Right were there) and eat some salads we had picked up at the store. It started to rain, so we loitered even longer. Finally, at about 1:30 p.m. we ventured off to start the climb out of town. We stopped for a rest at Curley Maple Gap Shelter and saw our first rattlesnake!

Someone had made a bow and arrow set out of a stick and string, and Tristan was playing with it. He accidentally broke the bow, and Madi said, "Great, Tristan! That was our only weapon!" Pancho was nearby and laughed with us, saying, "Did you think you were going to kill a bear with that?!" We made it to mile 352.5; 8.3 miles today.

AT Day #34

We left camp later than usual, and it seemed to derail our whole morning. It had rained through the night, and I didn't wake the kids until about 7:45 a.m., when the rain lightened up. There was a trail magic group that called themselves the "Billville," and they were set up near Beauty Spot. We stopped and visited with them for about thirty minutes. They go to AT Trail Days every year, then come to this spot for "after days trail magic." They're awesome people! We climbed up and over Unaka Mountain and tried to identify the difference between fir and spruce trees, per some instructions on Far Out. There was a big group of trail maintenance folks at a spot called Apple Orchard. We are so grateful for their hard work! We camped at mile 368.5; 16 miles today.

AT Day #35

We hit the trail about 7:15 a.m. and did six miles in about 2.5 hours. We stopped to filter water before the big climb up Roan Mountain and visited with our friend Walmart. When we stopped for lunch, we saw our friend Gumby, and she was slack packing. She said she really hurt her ankle two days ago and hiked to a hostel. The people that run it are so very kind and took her to two different doctors so she could get it looked at. Her ankle isn't broken, so she decided to slack pack for two days, then get back to the heavy hiking. We sure hope she heals up quickly!

Entering the Roan Highlands with perfect weather is a highlight of this hike, for sure! We met a big group of women who stopped us to chat. They took our picture and treated us like super stars. It was so fun! We made it to the Overmountain Shelter area around 7:30 p.m. The shelter is closed to hikers because the Forest Service has deemed it unsafe, but it sure is a cool, old barn-like structure. Cowboy and Toothpick were camped nearby, and Cowboy challenged Tristan to another game of chess. Tristan returned to his tent at about 8:30 p.m., saying that Cowboy had won again. We are at mile 386.1; 17.8 miles today.

AT Day #36

It was a beautiful sunrise at our camp this morning! We rolled out of camp before 7:30 a.m. and passed by Cowboy and Toothpick. She said she had hoped to be on the trail before us, but Cowboy moves really slow in the mornings. Kaia challenged him to pack up before us next time we run into them, and he said, "Challenge not accepted!" We made it to the Mountain Harbor B&B, where we had stashed our five-day supply of food, by noon. They are famous for their delicious breakfast, but we knew we wouldn't make it in time. Instead, we ate ramen, peanut butter, and some pretzels from the hiker box while we loitered. They are very hiker friendly and didn't mind that we charged our devices, took 2.5 hours to pack up our resupply, and made several trips to their General Store. They have a beautiful covered picnic area and a waterfall feature. It looks like a wedding venue! Kanook took our photo, and then we were finally on our way at 3 p.m.

It was a big climb away from Bear Branch Road, the heat and humidity were oppressive, and we were loaded down with more than six days of food. It was a struggle! We stopped at Jones Falls, hoping to camp there based on a comment on Far Out. The waterfall is beautiful! Tristan and Ruby scrambled up the sketchy trail to the top of the waterfall (with the assistance of a rope someone had tied there). Another hiker named Freebird (not the same Freebird we met last year) was up there with his dog, Mogley, but there were no good, flat tent spots. We filtered water, then pressed on another 1.6 miles and finally found camping at 8:15 p.m. We passed the 400-mile mark! We camped at 402.3; 16.2 miles today.

AT Day #37

I woke to the sound of someone throwing up at 5:45 a.m—not a great way to start the day. It was a hot night, and poor Kaia had been nauseous in her tent for hours before barely making it out in time. She thinks it was something she ate; I think it was at least partly caused by the heat and overexertion yesterday. Madi is also not feeling well. They do not seem to have Norovirus symptoms, so we're hopeful! We let them sleep in and left camp at 10:30. We made it two miles before stopping again, and staying the rest of the day and night to rest. We camped at mile 404.1; 1.8 miles today.

AT Day #38

No one threw up in the night! Madi said her water bottle lid looks like a mouse chewed on it! We made it to the "Hardcore Cascades" for lunch and enjoyed soaking our feet in the cold water. Poor Tristan started feeling sick this morning, and it hit him hard by lunch. We took lots of breaks in the afternoon and stopped for water and dinner at Moreland Gap Shelter. Tristan wanted to press on, but we could tell he just wasn't up for it. While he was off using the "restroom," we set up his tent and declared that we were staying put. Our friend, Gumby, arrived at about 7:45 p.m.; her ankle is really hurting her. She has also had to cut back on miles the past few days. Mile 413.7; 9.6 miles today.

AT Day #39

Today we entered the Pond Mountain Wilderness and stopped at the lovely Laurel Fork Falls for lunch. Gumby hiked with us most of the morning. She told us another hiker had warned her about baby rattlesnakes being in trees to sun themselves. He showed her a picture of the trunk of a tree and said, "Look really closely." In between the cracks of the bark were tiny rattlesnakes! We haven't seen them yet, but I've been on the lookout ever since she told us that story.

After Laurel Fork there is a big three-mile climb, and it was crazy humid and hot. Just when we were about to reach the top, a rain, thunder, and lightning storm hit and cooled everyone down quickly. We made it to the Boots Off Hostel at about 5 p.m. A nice trail angel handed us some ice cream sandwiches from the window of his camper trailer. It would have cost us $114 to spend the night in our own tents on the lawn of Boots Off ($19 per person), so we decided to move on. But first we bought three frozen pizzas, cooked them up in their toaster oven, and hit the jackpot with the hiker box. Some section hikers had just dropped some dried berries, nuts, Nutella, and my favorite Costco nut butter (all unopened) in there!

We found some nice, flat, free camping near Watauga Lake. A super nice guy was camped nearby and offered to charge our battery packs overnight for us, which was awesome! We camped at mile 429.2; 15.5 miles today.

AT Day #40

We left camp around 7:30 a.m. and enjoyed the flat walk around the lovely Watauga Lake. We crossed the dam at the same time as our friends, Gumby and Franz. What a view! We entered the Big Laurel Branch Wilderness, which is part of the Cherokee National Forest. It was another wildly hot and humid day! One local hiker told us it'll take us at least two weeks to get used to hiking in this heat and humidity.

At lunch, Adam and I hiked .6 miles off trail to find water. It was a steep descent to the spring, and we seriously regretted not reading the warning comments on Far Out earlier. The afternoon cooled down quickly as another storm rolled through. Luckily, we had time to eat dinner and set up tents before it really started to pour! We camped at 444.3; 15.1 miles today.

AT Day #41

It is hard to motivate this team to quickly pack up in the rain. We didn't leave camp until 8:15 a.m. There was a break in the rain for about an hour, but then the sky opened and didn't stop (the forecast says it'll continue dumping on us like this until tomorrow afternoon).

We stopped at Double Spring Shelter for lunch. Gumby and Franz were there, and we got to visit with them briefly. Gumby said she heard what she thought sounded like a wounded dog while she was hiking yesterday afternoon. She was so worried that it was Muir, and when we didn't show up to camp near the Iron Mountain Shelter (we camped .3 miles before there), she was even more concerned. So she was greatly relieved to see all was well with our trail dog. After they left, ten more hikers arrived at the shelter to take cover. We quickly ate lunch and pressed on, knowing we were in a hiking bubble and were all racing for the Abingdon Gap Shelter, just 8.3 miles away. We can sure hike fast in the rain!

We found a spot to set up our three tents at about 5 p.m. I don't think we could be more drenched if we had been sprayed by a firehose! The shelter nearby was so packed with hikers, they looked like wet rats stuffed in a cave (it was a shelter for 6 people and there were probably 14 in there!). I think Adam was hoping we would keep hiking, but even he had to concede that the misery level was pretty high, and a semi-dry tent was alluring. We camped at 460.5; 16.2 miles today.

AT Day #42

The rain stopped around 5 a.m., which felt like a miracle because it was forecasted to last until 1 p.m. There was sunshine while we packed up our wet tents and gear! We made the eleven miles into town in record time! Our first stop was the post office, where we were delighted to discover that all five of our packages had arrived! We got new shoes for Adam, Tristan, Ruby, and I (the Topo Ultraventure Pros held up great for 500 miles!), new higher temperature quilts for me and

Adam, our Big Agnes double-wide sleeping mat, and calf sleeves for me. We mailed home my and Adam's twenty-degree quilt (too hot!). Then we set up under the city park pavilion, charged electronics, and laid out gear to dry. Adam and I walked to the Broken Fiddle Hostel with our laundry (it was $15 for three loads) and picked up the food we stashed there. Our friend, Ryan Vinson, spoiled us with some money for dinner, so we took the family to the Damascus Diner. It was delicious! By the time we finished all our errands, it was 8 p.m.! I foolishly thought we could get in and out of town in four hours, but it took 8.5 hours instead. We got back on the trail and hiked 1.2 miles up to a great campsite. We camped at mile 472.1; 12.1 miles today.

AT Day #43

I woke up the team, and everyone cooperated to break camp in 60 minutes! We had a bit of a climb (5,700 feet ascent for the day's total), but it was cool and misty instead of hot and humid. We met up with some new and old friends at the Lost Mountain Shelter and decided to take an early dinner so we could visit. Gumby and Franz were there, and we met Farmgirl and Opa. We decided to push on another four miles to get up and over Whitetop Mountain, and it was a white-out (with strong winds to boot!). We camped at mile 492.4; 20.3 miles today!

AT Day #44

We were up and rolling early, in hopes of getting in some miles before the rain picked up in intensity. We had a great lunch at the Thomas Knob Shelter with a hiker named Margaritaville. We opted not to summit Mount Rodgers (the highest peak in Virginia) because of the storm (and not wanting to walk non-AT miles). We entered the famous Grayson Highlands and saw two wild ponies. Right as we sat down for dinner, I asked Madi what has surprised her most while on the trail. "Well, everything, really. I had no idea what I was getting into!" We laughed, then it started to rain really hard, and everything got muddy (including mud splashing into our dinner). I wanted to cry, but

Kaia and Madi kept me laughing. We set up tents in the pouring rain and camped at mile 515; 22.6 miles today.

AT Day #45

So much rain hit us in the night! The girls' tent was in a mud puddle, and their quilts and jammies were wet. All of us were ready to get dry, and luckily for us, the sun was out most of the day. We made our way to the Hurricane Campground where we heard it cost $2 per shower (which was so great!). We laid out all our stuff to dry! A sweet trail angel named Goat was camped nearby, and she brought us cookies and offered us a ride to the Dollar General. Adam and Tristan went with her husband to get our resupply (we had planned to hitch tomorrow, but this would save time), and we girls packed up our dry gear. We almost had everything put away when it started pouring rain again! This awesome couple let us stand under their pavilion and sort out our resupply. Luckily, the rain didn't last long, and we were back on the trail by 3:30 p.m. We hiked until 8 p.m., only taking a quick dinner stop, and set up camp in a wonderful spot with three flat tent sites. We camped at 527.4; 12.4 miles today.

AT Day #46

Yesterday I tried to send a message to Adam to pick up dog food when he was at Dollar General (I had accidentally left it off the shopping list), but he never got it. Muir is down to one day's worth of food, so we hustled 6.7 miles this morning to get to the Mt. Rogers Visitor Center, where Adam hitched into a Walmart in Marion, Virginia. While he was gone, the kids played card games, and I visited with an injured hiker named Strider. Adam returned with lunch and all the groceries we needed. He said it was super easy to hitch in and out of town. Unfortunately, it is not so easy for us to pack up quickly. 3.5 hours later, we were back on the trail.

Poor Tristan was not feeling so good, so the four-mile uphill slog went slowly. We made it to the "Settlers' Museum" around 7 p.m. Adam and Tristan went on a guided tour of the farmhouse, and the girls and I walked ahead to the schoolhouse. We found a bit of trail magic (some food and a bottle of Sawyer permethrin!) but decided against sleeping in the one-room school. Instead, we set up our tents in a freshly mowed field and saw fireflies and stars when the sun went down! It was a magical night! We camped at mile 543; 15.6 miles today.

AT Day #47

We knew it was going to be a hot day, so we did our best to leave camp early. We're so very grateful that the museum let us use their electrical outlets, flushing toilets, and picnic tables! After walking about three miles, we crossed a road and got lured into a gas station. Many snacks were purchased, and there was much rejoicing.

We had a peaceful stop near a stream for lunch and listened to Freebird sing and play his ukulele during our 3 o'clock snack stop. At dinnertime, we came upon another road with signs directing us to the Bear Garden Hiker Hostel (the sign said, "ice cream," so we went). We loitered, bought and ate more snacks, and then ate our dinner of cold mashed potatoes and summer sausage. We finally got out of that vortex by 6:45 p.m. and headed back to the trail. There were ten other tents set up at Lynn Camp Creek when we arrived at 8 p.m. Luckily, we found room to squeeze in three more! We camped at mile 561.6; 18.5 miles today.

AT Day #48

It was dark when I woke everyone at 6 a.m. because we were in a deep hollow. It was a hot, muggy night! Our challenge of the morning was to ford Lick Creek because the bridge was washed out in 2020. Then we had a five-mile climb in the heat and humidity! But we did it and made it to the top to Chestnut Knob Shelter around 1 p.m. We took several breaks to rest in the shade and met a few new-to-us thru-hikers. There was a big bubble headed for the Jenkins Shelter, and we found semi-flat tent spots next to each other there (I counted 18 other tents tonight). We camped at mile 580.5; 18.9 miles today.

AT Day #49

We made it 11.7 miles in a hurry this morning to get a hitch into Bland for a resupply. It was so hot! A very kind man in his seventies pulled over his truck and told us all to jump in. He said he likes to give hikers a ride. The grocery store had the coldest air conditioning I've ever felt, and we loitered as long as we could. Tristan went to the library to download some books, and he said they were very kind to him. They had him put a pin in the map of where he is from and offered him snacks and bottled water. A wonderful lady stopped to give us a ride back to the trail. She only had room for three at a time, so she made two trips!

We had intended to hike five miles when we got back on the trail but were more than willing to stop sooner if we found a spot to camp. Every time we passed a campsite, it was full! Finally, at about 8:45 p.m. when it was getting pretty dark, we squeezed in by two other tents (a lady asked that if anyone snores they set up their tent as far from her as possible, so we complied, and Adam and I set up on the biggest slope yet). Tristan, who is normally a very strong hiker, was really struggling tonight (and for the last several days). When I felt his forehead, it was apparent he was burning with a fever. He had a lot of bug bites and had symptoms of Lyme disease, so I immediately started him on antibiotics (which my doctor prescribed before we started the trail for just such an occasion). He was back to himself within 24 hours. We camped at mile 596.3; 15.7 miles today.

AT Day #50

We packed up and scurried out of camp before any of the other tents around us. It was a bad, bad night's sleep. We had a water carry of about nine miles, and once we got to water, we didn't want to leave. We ended up taking a 3.5-hour siesta to beat the mid-day heat, and it was wonderful!

Finally, we pulled ourselves together and did 5.7 miles to Kimberling Creek in less than three hours. We walked up the road to "Trent's Grocery," a gas station where we ordered cheeseburgers and fries and picked up a few snacks. We had heard there were showers and laundry nearby, so we asked the owner if he could give us the "family deal." Instead of charging us $6 per person, he said we could shower, do laundry, and camp for $20. Sold! It wasn't the nicest set up, but we are clean! We camped near mile 610.2; 13.9 miles today.

AT Day #51

The rhododendrons, azaleas, and mountain laurels are in full bloom right now, and it is heavenly! The weather called for rain and 80 degrees. We took a lunch siesta and got to visit with a hiker named Pathfinder. She started the trail almost a month before us but got COVID and had to take two weeks off. Now she is going slow with a hurt ankle. Poor girl!

We dodged the rain until we got into Pearisburg, and then it started to pour. Adam, Tristan, Ruby, and Muir went to look for lodging for the night, and Madi, Kaia, and I hit the Food Lion grocery store to grab dinner. The "hiker friendly" hotel was all booked up, so they tried the one next door. This hotel manager said they were also booked but had one room where the people hadn't checked in yet (at 7:30 p.m.). So he gave that room to us! Hopefully some rained-on hikers didn't show up later only to be told their room was no longer available. Pearisburg, mile 636.1; over 20 miles today.

AT Day #52

We hit Food Lion again to grab a four-day supply. The same girl who checked us out the night before was our checker again, and she asked where we ended up staying last night. When we told her she said, "Oh no! The bedbug hotel?! That place is awful!" Adam assured her that he did check for bedbugs, but it really was a run-down, dirty room.

As we were packing up our resupply and eating lunch, a trail angel named Twig stopped to chat with us. He said he would be happy to drive us back to trail, so we loaded up in his truck! It was a beautiful evening, and the climb out of town ended with some great views. We camped at mile 645.6; 8.5 miles today.

AT Day #53

We started the day with a 10.5-mile water carry. Luckily for us, it was fast going with only one big climb. We made it to the Pine Swamp Branch water source by 11:30 a.m. and enjoyed soaking our sore feet and eating lunch. The trail after that point was tricky because it was all loose rock (some big ones moved when you stepped on them)! My feet were screaming by the time we got to a water source at 6 p.m. We saw an unmarked tent site that would fit three tents, so we went for it. We camped (on flat tent spots) at mile 663.1; 17.5 miles today.

AT Day #54

It was a beautiful, cool morning with an awesome, orange sunrise! We stopped at John's Creek to filter water, and I was rushing everyone so we could start the big climb up Kelly Knob before it got too hot. We made it to an unofficial campsite just after noon and took a nice, long siesta there.

At about four, we stopped again to filter water and enjoy the picnic table at Laurel Creek Shelter. There, we got to visit with Poison Puff, Hoops, and Outlaw Pete. The latter are a couple who also have four kids (three girls and a boy too), but they waited until their kids were grown up and moved out before they started the AT.

We toyed with the idea of doing the three-mile climb to Sarver Hollow Shelter tonight, but we had taken too long of breaks today. Plus, that shelter is .3 miles off trail, and no one wanted to add extra miles. So we set up in the "very sloped tenting area," according to Far Out, right before the climb. Tristan is in his hammock, happy as a clam. The rest of us have our backpacks under our legs to try and balance us out. We camped at mile 678.6; 15.5 miles today.

AT Day #55

Our first monument of the morning was Keffer Oak, the largest oak tree along the AT in the south (estimated to be over 300 years old!). A kind section hiker was handing out trail magic before the 2.5-mile climb to the Audie Murphy monument. We had cell coverage, and Adam looked up info on Audie Murphy. (He's a WWII veteran, the most decorated American in that war, and movies have been made about him.) He was only 47 when his plane crashed in this area in 1971, leaving behind a wife and two sons. We camped at mile 698.2; 19.6 miles today!

AT Day #56

Virginia has its own version of the "Triple Crown": a high-use area that features awesome rock formations named Dragon's Tooth, McAfee Knob, and Tinker Cliffs. We hit the first two today, and they are awesome! The informational sign taught us, "This part of Virginia was a large basin collecting sand, mud, and calcium rich materials eroded from mountains to the east. As these different deposits were buried deeper and deeper, time and pressure turned them into different types of sedimentary rock: sandstone, shale, and limestone … Erosion has since continually cut into the uplifted layers. The easy-to-erode rocks, such as shale and limestone, weathered deeply and formed valleys. The hard-to-erode rocks, such as sandstone, formed ridges and rock outcrops such as the giant tooth shaped spire now known as Dragon's Tooth." We camped at mile 714.8; 16.6 miles today.

AT Day #57

The trail closely followed the Blue Ridge Parkway today with awesome views. We made it to Jennings Creek at about 4:30 p.m. and took a refreshing swim in the swimming hole. About ten other hikers showed up while we were there—another bubble! About half of them got a shuttle to get cheeseburgers at a restaurant, but we pressed on another four miles to a tent spot about .7 from the Bryant Ridge Shelter. We camped at mile 762.1; 19.7 miles today.

AT Day #58

We started the day with a pit stop at Bryant Ridge Shelter. (Wow, is that a nice one! Far Out says it can sleep 20!) Gumby signed the logbook, noting she was the only one there last night. She saw lots of fireflies and a bat.

The nine-mile climb to the top of Apple Orchard Mountain was just as hard as it looked. At the summit is an old FAA long range air traffic station. Posted signs say that the radio waves in the area exceed the FCC public exposure limit. That doesn't sound good, so we didn't hang around long. One hiker commented that they camped up here, and their compass was forever 180 degrees off after that.

The next highlight of the day was a cool rock formation called the Guillotine. We stopped a little early for camp, around 6:30 p.m., because no other spots looked promising between here and Glasgow. It was a beautiful evening! We camped at mile 779.6; 17.5 miles today.

AT Day #59

We made it to the James River by 11 a.m. and went for a swim. The kids tried to get a rope swing untangled, but they didn't succeed. Kaia, Madi, and I swam the width of the river and walked back on the footbridge to our packs.

It was an easy hitch into Glasgow. A kind man named Gordon drove me and the girls into town. He had his kayak and was hoping to float for a few miles, then catch a hitch for himself. In town, we hit the Dollar General for lunch and our resupply. Then we loitered at Glasgow's free hiker shelter, took a free outdoor shower (and did some hiker laundry), and charged devices. Tristan, Ruby, and I enjoyed the air conditioning in the library and the WiFi for a few hours. It was 91 degrees with more humidity than we thought possible. At 6 p.m., we joined more than thirty other hikers at the Presbyterian church for a free hiker dinner! It was so delicious!

A very nice museum curator picked up me and the girls when we were hitching back to the trail. She had just brought another hiker to town and was so nice to load up four more smelly hikers in her tiny car! Adam, Tristan, and Muir made it to the trail about twenty minutes later. We hiked 1.5 miles and decided to stop at 9 p.m. and set up tents. It was the hottest, most humid night I can ever remember experiencing while backpacking! We camped at mile 788.8; 9.2 miles today.

AT Day #60

It was a rough night! A loud "alarm" bird was squawking until after 10 p.m., and the oppressive heat and humidity didn't let up until around 2 a.m.! I woke up the team at 4:45 a.m., and we were out of camp by 5:50. We did nine miles before 10 a.m. with a big climb up Bluff Mountain. It was surprising to see a monument up there for an almost five-year-old boy who supposedly wandered away from school and died at this summit in 1891!

We had lunch at the Punchbowl Shelter and made the decision to push all the way to Buena Vista tonight. At 6 p.m. we made it to the highway, and it took about thirty minutes until a kind man in a big truck pulled over to help us. He drove us all the way to the Glen Maury campground, where hikers can camp and shower for $5 and get a free ice cream cone! We made it to mile 809.1; 20.3 miles today.

AT Day #61

The amazing Kyle Chandler, son of my grandma's best friend, picked us up at the campground at 7:15 a.m. and brought us to his house! His wonderful wife, Jamie, had a delicious breakfast cooked up for us: bacon, eggs, pancakes, and juice! We were dumbfounded by their generosity. They let us do a load of laundry, and the kids got to relax at their house while Kyle drove us to the post office and grocery store (and gave us a tour of Southern Virginia University, where he is a professor and track coach).

After we had sorted our resupply and packed up (which always takes longer than I think it should), Kyle drove us back to the trail! It was so great! Hoops and Outlaw were at the trailhead. It was fun to chat with them while we all mentally prepared to do the big climb in the heat! We found camp at Hog Camp Gap with a spring .3 miles away. Not long after we arrived, about twenty army guys came marching in and set up camp. Adam chatted with a few of them; turns out they plan to do the same 19 miles we plan to do tomorrow. We camped at mile 815.5.

AT Day #62

We heard the army guys say they were leaving camp at 0600, so we planned to do the same. They left right on time; we rolled out twenty minutes later. We eventually caught up to a small group of them, and I mustered up the courage to say, "On behalf of my family, I just want to tell you how grateful we are for your service." They were all very kind, and we played leapfrog with them throughout the day.

At lunch we had a nice long chat with a southbound section hiker from New York named T-bone. Adam took a dirt road and walked four miles to the Montebello post office. There he picked up Kaia and Madi's new shoes and a package with a "no-see-um" proof mesh interior net to help me and Adam sleep cooler on these hot nights. He got a quick hitch back to the trail by a couple from Louisiana.

At the Priest Shelter, we were attacked by swarms of biting black flies while we filtered water; it was awful. We quickly moved on and hustled down three miles to the Tye River (where we met up with Adam, safely crossed the bridge without getting stung by wasps, and swam in the river to cool off).

Adam had already picked a great campsite for us. He took Kaia and Madi's old shoes back to the parking lot to see if anyone would be willing to throw them away for us. The army guys were all there, and one was getting an IV because he was dehydrated. Adam said at least five guys came up to shake his hand and tell him how impressed they were with our family! We camped at mile 834.5; 19 miles today.

AT Day #63

Our morning was spent hiking next to waterfalls and perfect swimming holes while we were wishing we could stop and spend the day swimming! Instead, we pressed on and enjoyed some trail magic from a hiker named Papa Smurf around noon. We caught a few views of the Blue Ridge Parkway and Waynesboro Valley, and then a thunderstorm hit. We hunkered down in some picnic area bathrooms with a few other hikers for an hour or so. The storm passed, and it turned out to be a lovely, cool evening.

A note Papa Smurf left on our Facebook page: "It was my pleasure to meet the Bennett Family Friday at Reid's Gap while serving some drinks and snacks. They had just climbed and descended the Priest and summited Three Ridges, which is no easy task by any means. The teens, looking none the worse for wear, took a short break while waiting for Mom and Pops to appear with their dog. Letting mom and dad take a break with drinks, they loaded up and were on their way. Thanks for dropping in to say hello with your awesome family. I hope the shade break from the heat of the day and drinks helped you on your way. Godspeed my friends. —Papa Smurf."

We camped at 856.8; 22.3 miles today.

AT Day #64

We had an easy, mostly downhill hike to the highway this morning. We passed a couple doing trail maintenance, which was very awesome. It took about 20 minutes to get a hitch. A couple on their second date drove past us, then flipped around to offer their help. They were headed to hike a tunnel nearby but happily drove out of their way to drop us at the grocery store in Waynesboro. His name is T.J., and he even offered to help us again in a few days when we are closer to his house! We picked up lunch and ate in a gazebo next to the store. Then we hit the YMCA for free showers (towel, shampoo, conditioner, and soap were included, too!). From there, we picked up our free permit to camp at a designated AT hiker spot. Adam and I walked to the laundromat, then picked up food to grill up some pre-Father's Day cheeseburgers at the park. We ended up having extra food, so five other hikers joined us for a memorable feast! Mile 864.3; 7.5 miles today.

AT Day #65

We packed up, grabbed our resupply, and were walking through town when a guy pulled over and asked if we needed a ride back to the trail. We didn't even have our thumbs up! His name is Frank, and he volunteers a lot for the Wounded Warrior Project. When he dropped us off at the trail, there was a big table with trail magic (and even a tomahawk throwing station!). We stayed too long, eating and visiting, and finally hit the trail at 10.

Shenandoah National Forest is quite lovely; it's mostly a green tunnel though. We stopped to get water near the Calf Mountain Shelter and again stayed too long visiting with other hikers. At dinner time, we sat on a rock wall at a pullout with a view and again stayed too long visiting with other hikers. At 7:30, the girls at the front found three wonderfully flat stealth tent spots, so we decided not to pass them by. We didn't hit our mileage goal (for the day or the week) but feel confident we can make it up later. We camped at mile 875.4; 11.1 miles today.

AT Day #66

It was a green tunnel kind of day… until we walked a few miles on Skyline Drive so we could get some views at the overlooks. We stopped in at the Loft Mountain camp store to get some refreshments, charge devices, use the fancy flush toilets, and loiter at picnic tables. We pressed on for a few more miles, and then took a dinner break at an overlook. After we finally got packed up and moving, a truck pulled up and said he had trail magic. We walked about 100 feet back to the parking lot and enjoyed visiting with trail angel Nutz and drinking ice-cold Gatorade. We finally made it to the shelter at 8:30 p.m. It was so crowded, but we found two tent spots, and Tristan was able to hammock. We camped at mile 898.2; 22.8 miles today.

AT Day #67

We left Pinefield Hut Shelter at 8 a.m., which is very late for us! I guess we were feeling leisurely because we knew we only needed to do 11 miles before 3 p.m. Our trail angel from Waynesboro, T.J., had agreed to pick us up at 3 and bring us to his home near Elkton. We had no idea we were in for such a big treat! T.J. had a huge variety of fruit and drinks for us in the car. He drove us about 20 miles to his beautiful house and told us to make ourselves feel at home. We showered, did laundry, swam in his pool, and even borrowed his car to pick up our food resupply. Meanwhile, he was cooking up a pasta feast for us and six friends he invited over! His friend, Renee, owns a cupcake shop and brought over two dozen awesome cupcakes. It was so much fun to visit and enjoy "normal" life. Mile 909.8; 11.6 miles today.

AT Day #68

We were up early because T.J. said he had enough tubes for all of us to do a short float on the South Fork Shenandoah River! We put our tubes in the water at about 8:30 and were out by 9:15. It was beautiful and relaxing. It was not quite an "aqua blaze," but we will always refer to it that way. (An "aqua blaze" is a term for hikers floating a river near the trail instead of hiking on the blazed trail.)

Before we left, T.J. had put a breakfast casserole in the oven, and it was perfectly done when we returned! We had a feast with berries, buttery toast, casserole, and cupcakes from the night before. We packed up our gear and food and were on the way back to the trail when I decided to call the post office in the next town, Luray, to see if they had our shipment of four pairs of shoes. They did not. I ran the tracking number, and it said that package was in Waynesboro. T.J. didn't skip a beat and said it was only 30 minutes away and he would be happy to drive us there (even though it meant he would be late for a work meeting). What a relief! We got the shoes and were dropped off at the trail around 12:30. Money cannot buy the service T.J. did for our family; we are just in awe!

We tried to do 10 miles this afternoon, but it started raining around 5, so we took cover at the Poccsin Cabin. It was an impressive amount of rain with lots of fun thunder and lightning. After the storm, the girls set up their tent, Tristan set up his hammock in the shelter, and Adam, Muir, and I slept on the stone floor of the covered porch. Halfshell and his dog Indy were there and got a great fire going in the fireplace. It was so dark, but as the lightning struck, we could see the silhouettes of the dogs as they looked over the valley. Mile 916.1; 6.3 miles today.

AT Day #69

It was a surprisingly good night's sleep, even though another wave of rain, lightning, and thunder hit at 9 p.m., lasting for about

30 minutes. The bottom of our quilt got a bit wet, so we thought we'd stop by the Lewis Mountain Campground (only two miles from where we had camped). Turns out, their power got knocked out by last night's storm, so we couldn't use the dryer. Instead, we enjoyed the clean restroom, filled our water bottles, and met a family section-hiking with their five kids. We got some sunshine when we stopped for lunch at Big Meadow Wayside. We laid our gear to dry and chatted with other hikers who were doing the same. A highlight of the day was standing at the Little Stoney Man Cliffs and looking down on a bride and groom all dressed up for photos.

It was an awesome sunset, and we found a great spot in the trees to set up our tents. I took Tristan's picture as he was looking into the misty trees with sunlight filtering through. He said that the sunset tonight was his favorite color! We camped at 937.3; 21.2 miles today.

AT Day #70

About a mile and a half after leaving camp this morning, we arrived at a "comfort station" (bathrooms and drinking fountains). It was very convenient. At 2 p.m., we arrived at the Elkwallow Wayside and treated ourselves to sandwiches, fries, and blackberry milkshakes. We've been so spoiled by the amenities in the Shenandoah National Park! In fact, we've been able to supplement our two-day supply and stretch it to a 3.5-day (thus enabling us to skip a resupply trip into the town of Luray).

We saw our friend Galaxy today, and she told us about her adventurous aqua blaze on the Shenandoah River. It was supposed to be a three-day trip, but it got cut short by a series of problems (including the big storm that hit the night before last). Galaxy said a tree was blown over during the storm and landed about five feet from her—very scary!

We were hoping to visit with her more tonight at the Gravel Springs Hut, but when we arrived, it was overflowing with people! Our app said it would have room for four tents, but we saw 11 tents set up! We hiked on and finally found three semi-flat spots right next to a lady who is section hiking. She was very kind to let us squeeze in. We ate our dinner while we watched the sunset from some rocky cliffs. It was just magical! We camped at 959.7; 22.4 miles today.

AT Day #71

I received a message on Instagram in early June from Candace, a friend of my brother-in-law and sister-in-law, Geof and Darla. She said her family has been following our adventures and would love to meet up with us near Shenandoah National Park. After changing the date and location on them several times, we finally worked out meeting for dinner today.

We hitched into Front Royal in three different vehicles (Adam and Tristan got picked up first by a local; a guy named David was at the parking area to get other hikers but was early, so he offered to take three of us and Muir; and Kaia rode with Yahtzee's mom and another hiker). We met at the grocery store, got lunch and a three-day supply as fast as we could (which isn't very fast), and hopped on a free trolley to the heart of the town. We were walking down Main Street when a minivan pulled up and Candace's husband, Tim, yelled out the window, "That looks like some Bennetts!"

We had a great visit with them and their four awesome kids. They fed us a taco feast, including two different types of meat and beans warmed up on their propane stove, Cafe Rio sauce, and guacamole made right before our eyes by their 10-year-old son. After dinner and dessert (they gifted each kid a bag of gummy bears and gummy worms!), Candace unloaded her minivan so all the hikers could comfortably fit and returned us to the trail. She offered help if we needed anything on our journey forward, which always makes me tear up because it is such a comfort to know we have help if needed! We hiked about a mile from the road and set up our tents near Bear Hollow. We camped at 972.8; 13.1 miles today.

AT Day #72

We had big goals of making it 18 to 20 miles today, but it just wasn't meant to be. Four miles into the day, we came across the Jim and Molly Denton Shelter (named for trail maintenance volunteers who had been working on the AT since the '40s). Not only was there a shelter but there was also a solar shower, a privy, a picnic table and pavilion, a horseshoes game, and lovely flowers. We showered and loitered, visiting with other hikers.

At noon we were about to stop by a brook for lunch, but Adam said, "There is a parking lot up ahead; we should see if there is trail magic there." And there was! Thru-hikers we had met a few days ago—a couple named Bed and Breakfast (because he carries the bedding and she carries the food)—and their local friend, Greg, had been cooking up a feast for hikers since 8 a.m.! We caught the tail end but still got cheeseburgers, hotdogs, scrambled eggs, croissants, and meat sticks. Oh, and there was ice—a desirable commodity on a hot day! We started the 2.5 mile climb, but the heat and humidity were killing us. Fortunately, we found a shady spot to rest and had enough cell coverage to listen to Madi's sister, Chloe, speak in church for her mission farewell. Madi's name was mentioned several times; everyone at home loves and misses this sweet girl! We are so grateful to have her with us on this adventure, though!

At 3:30 we arrived at the Manassas Gap Shelter. The sky was dark and ominous, the weather forecast called for a lot of rain tonight, and three out of the six of us are feeling under the weather with cold symptoms. We decided to call it a night and stay here. We set up our tents just as the rain began with lots of thunder and lightning in all directions. We camped at 982.8; 10 miles today.

AT Day #73

It was a nice cool morning with about an hour of rain, and we pushed hard to do 13.5 miles before lunch! At the Rod Hollow Shelter picnic pavilion, we ate and visited with other hikers. Everyone was excited about crossing the 1,000-mile mark today! We also entered "the rollercoaster" section, and the kids humored me by posing for the photos I've been imagining for months (pretending to be seated on a roller-coaster in front of the sign). We camped at mile 1,003.1; 20.3 miles today.

AT Day #74

The highlight of the morning was stopping at the Bear's Den hostel, a stone mansion built in the 1930s, now owned by the ATC. The kids bought $1 drinks, and we met a former thru-hiker named Blackbear who gave us cookies! We crossed into West Virginia right before our lunch stop, a much-anticipated event! We made it to Keys Gap at 6:30 p.m., and a thru-hiker's dad was handing out trail magic. Adam called the Stoneybrook Farms hiker hostel, and they sent up a nice guy in a truck to pick us and a hiker named Hollywood up! We ate at their delicious Yellow Deli, toured the facilities, did laundry, and took showers. We jumped off the trail at mile 1,019.8; 16.7 miles today.

AT Day #75

We joined our hosts for their 7 a.m. religious gathering, then helped them pick beets from their garden. Ruby and I worked alongside 9- and 12-year-old girls, and they told us about their year-round homeschooling schedule. Then we had an awesome breakfast at the big house with eggs, brown rice, and fruit. At 9:30 am., Luke drove us back to the trail. Adam chatted with him on the drive about different facets of their religion (the Stoneybrook Farms is part of the Twelve Tribes).

Back on the trail, we hustled five miles into Harpers Ferry to the Appalachian Trail Conservancy headquarters. There we got our picture taken for their yearbook and were given new numbers. (We started with 2800 to 2805, and now we are 1246 to 1252. Muir was awarded a halfway number too.) We had to choose between catching the 2 p.m. bus ($30 roundtrip for all of us to get to Walmart) or getting to the post office before it closed. We chose to walk to the post office, but unfortunately, they didn't have Madi's new leggings. (Here, if a UPS general delivery arrives and isn't picked up within 24 hours, it gets sent back. No other post office we've encountered does this!) We walked through Harpers Ferry, in awe of the history (reading informational signs and admiring the architecture). We got a hitch to Walmart in two separate rides. It took a long time to resupply because it was 2:30, we hadn't had lunch yet, and we were hangry. Adam suggested that we just grab lunch/early dinner foods, go outside in the shade to eat, and then try our resupply again. By that time, we had missed the bus back to the ATC, so Adam booked us a hotel. No one complained (did I mention it was a hot and humid day?). We stopped at mile 1,025.4; 5.6 miles today.

AT Day #76

Getting out of town is always problematic, but especially when we pass a Wendy's that has new strawberry frosties. We met a man there with a Blood Mountain AT hat on. He said he helped build the next two shelters we would come to on the trail. He also offered us a ride, but we would have to wait for his wife to arrive, and they had to drop a vehicle off at a repair shop first. We thanked him but decided to push on. It was only a one-mile walk to Walmart, where we expected to catch a 10:45 a.m. bus. It never arrived. We bought some lunch and caught the 11:45 bus instead.

Back at the ATC, we visited with hiker friends and got to meet two members of the "nut family" (another family on the trail with two parents and four kids, ages 6 to 12, whose trail names all involve nuts). We walked through the historic district of Harpers Ferry and decided to stop in at some museums.

At 2 p.m., we finally hit the trail, walking along the Potomac River for two miles until we decided it was just too hot and jumped in. We swam, cooled off, enjoyed dinner, then started the two-mile climb. We finally stumbled into camp near the Crampton Gap Shelter at 9:30 p.m. and set up in the dark. We camped at mile 1,036.8; 11.4 today.

AT Day #77

We left camp at 6:45 and hustled to the Dahlgreen Backpack campground 5.2 miles to the north. Too bad we didn't make it here last night because they have free showers, but we quickly enjoyed the other features (running water and flush toilets). Our next stop was the informational signs and Civil War monuments at Fox Gap and the original Washington monument (first built in 1827). We made it to the Pine Knob Shelter for lunch just before a big rainstorm! We all slept in the Ensign Cowell Shelter with a very nice hiker named Lego. He is a retired general contractor from Boston with a great accent. We camped at 1,057.6; 20.8 miles today.

AT Day #78

Mid-morning, we stopped for a "comfort station" break at the Raven Rock Shelter. A hiker approached Kaia and Madi to ask if they had a working cell phone. This poor guy had fallen, landed right on his phone, and broken it. He texted his wife to tell her he wasn't going to continue his section hike to Harpers Ferry and was headed home. He gave Kaia a bag of jerky for letting him use her phone, which she kindly shared with the rest of us!

Our lunch stop at Pen Mar Park was so fun! There was an awesome zip line that hikers of all ages took turns riding; it was a blast. We crossed the Mason-Dixon Line and walked into Pennsylvania (state #7). Just before the rainstorm hit, we sat under the picnic pavilion at Old Forge Park. The temperatures dropped a speck, and there was a cool breeze occasionally as we did the final climb for the night up to Chimney Rock. Surprisingly, we had the campsite to ourselves, and we could hear fireworks off in the distance as we fell asleep. We camped at 1,076.8; 19.2 today.

AT Day #79

We had a big push to get nine miles done as fast as we could so that we could shower at Caledonia State Park before hitching into Chambersburg. Unfortunately, the showers weren't free, so we hitched and went to church all smelly. Everyone was very nice to us though, and a nice guy named Eric dropped us off at the Grocery Outlet and said he would drive us back to the trail when we were ready.

It took a few hours to buy and organize our resupply. Plus Adam and the kids decided to do the "half gallon ice cream challenge" using Walmart ice cream (instead of Pine Grove Furnace State Park's more expensive ice cream with a limited variety of flavors). Only Adam completed the challenge; the rest nearly made themselves sick trying.

Eric drove us back to the trail and even walked us to his favorite picnic table, where he does trail magic sometimes. We had our dinner, and Galaxy walked by as we were packing up. We visited with her and a few other hikers at the beautiful Quarry Gap Shelters. It was tempting to stay there, but we pressed on another two miles. We camped at 1,089.5; 12.7 today.

AT Day #80

The Fourth of July! It would have been cool to hitch into Gettysburg for the holiday, but we couldn't pull it off. Instead, we paraded through the very crowded Pine Grove Furnace State Park amongst all the swimmers and park goers. We stopped for an afternoon snack of loaded French fries, and they were delicious! The AT museum was a cool stop. We met Dragonfly, a two-time AT thru-hiker and the oldest woman to hike the trail (she's 74). Ruby was excited that we crossed mile 1,111.1 today! We found the greatest flat campsites right after Madi and Adam got stung by evil hornets, so we quickly decided to call it a night. We camped at 1,112.3; 22.8 miles today.

AT Day #81

I woke the team up at 4:30 a.m., and we pushed hard to get into Boiling Springs quickly. We visited with a few locals and some other hikers and swapped out Darn Tough socks with holes for new ones. By noon, we were at PA Route 641, where Adam's awesome sister, Brooke, picked us up in two shifts and brought us to their beautiful home! They live at the Army War College where her husband is a Colonel. It was delightful to spend the rest of the day getting cleaned up, eating, playing games, and visiting! We left the trail at mile 1,128.5; 16.2 miles today.

AT Day #82

We were up early so that Brooke could drop us off at the trail at 6:30. She needed to have her truck to the repair shop by 7. Kaia forgot her hat in Brooke's garage, so luckily her truck was finished early at the shop, and she met us along the trail at 10:45. We stopped for lunch next to a lovely stream, and there is an old car wreck there (Adam estimates it is from the 1950s).

After lunch, our day really took a terrible twist. Adam and Ruby left about five minutes before Tristan to start the climb and stop at the privy at the top. I thought Tristan knew to stop and that he was also going to use the privy. All Tristan heard was that there was a hiker spaghetti dinner at a church in Duncannon and that we were rushing to get there between 5 and 7 p.m. So, while Adam and Ruby were off-trail at the Darlington Shelter, Tristan hiked right past them.

For the next 10 miles, Tristan was thinking that he was rushing to catch up to Adam and Ruby. He said he stopped for about 30 minutes to wait for those behind him, then got worried he would miss the dinner, so he pressed on. Meanwhile, I was convinced Tristan had taken a wrong turn, realized he was lost, and was sitting waiting to be found. We checked for his footprints on side trails and went off-trail to check each shelter. Luckily, Adam chatted with a southbound ridge runner named Jon, and he verified that he saw Tristan in front of us. Jon and I exchanged numbers, and he went to his car, drove way out of his way, and parked at the parking lot where he thought Tristan would leave the trail.

When we got to Duncannon, Adam and Ruby went to the spaghetti dinner at the Lutheran church, but Tristan wasn't there. Turns out, he had gotten lost in town (he had taken a glance at the map earlier in the day but was surprised to find a plethora of churches in town). Adam and Jon drove through town looking for him to no avail.

Back on the trail, Kaia, Madi, and I came across a thru-hiker who had fallen and broken his ankle. The ridge runner had a splint, so he ran about a mile up to the injured hiker, where Kaia and Madi were also waiting to see if they could help. Kaia ended up carrying the hiker's pack to the parking lot and giving him her gloves (and water and ibuprofen because he had none). I was rushing down the trail when I got a call from our friend, Gumby, who reported that Tristan had safely arrived at the spaghetti dinner. What a relief!

Adam and I walked there together and listened to Tristan's side of the story while we ate spaghetti, meatballs, a delicious salad, rolls, and dessert. They even made to-go boxes for Kaia and Madi! We all met up at another church, Duncannon Assembly of God, where they let hikers sleep in the pastor's basement (with an awesome shower, kitchen, and hiker box). Our friends Gumby, Maverick, Bear Slayer, and Aldo were there. It was a fun evening after a stressful afternoon! Mile 1,150, 21.5 miles today.

AT Day #83

I didn't take good notes today—too hot and humid, I guess. We camped at mile 1,167.7; 17.7 miles today.

Some thoughts about thru-hiking life: we have missed out on a few big family events these past four summers (a wedding—sorry Jackson and Liv—and family reunions), which has been difficult. A thru-hike attempt means you are placing a higher priority on escaping into the woods over civilized responsibilities, extended family, and all other priorities and wants. We have been so fortunate that there were no major life events that required us to leave the trail thus far. As parents, we wondered if we were doing the right thing concerning our kids' development (physically, socially, intellectually, and spiritually) by pulling them away from the structure we had at home. It was a big unknown how the hiking community would affect all of us. A seasoned thru-hiker friend told us that aside from some aspects of trail life (sleeping in a pit toilet occasionally, maybe eating out of a dumpster, getting rides from strangers, being at the mercy of the natural elements, not showering for long stretches of time, etc.), the trail is a beautiful place to grow. While we haven't eaten out of a dumpster and have managed to not spend the night in a pit toilet yet, we have found that these experiences have benefited our lives. By stretching and strengthening our abilities in ways we never thought possible, we have seen our family draw closer and have a greater perspective on what is important in life. A profound appreciation for provident living now runs through our veins. We've developed a stronger faith in God, ourselves, and those around us.

AT Day #84

The highlight of today was that Adam and Ruby got an easy hitch into Pine Grove, where they picked up Wendy's for our dinner! The guy who picked them up waited for them at Wendy's, then immediately drove them back to the trail. Our friend Newfound put in an order before Adam left and visited with the rest of us while they were gone. Then we all sat on benches and ate our delicious fast food dinner, just like normal Americans! But unlike most Americans, we still had to hike a few miles uphill before we could go to sleep. We camped at mile 1,186.2; 18.5 miles today.

AT Day #85

Again, it was a hot and humid day, and I failed to take notes before falling asleep. But my pictures show that we crossed the "1,000 miles to go" mark, saw a few vistas, got trail magic in the 501 Shelter, passed the 1,200-mile mark, and saw a monument dedicated to a fort from 1755! We camped at mile 1,205.1; 18.9 miles today.

AT Day #86

We maneuvered through a rough spot out here in "rocksylvania" as quickly as we could and made it to Hamburg by noon. We had an early birthday meal for Kaia at the Chinese buffet (where we really got our money's worth!). Adam, Madi, and Kaia walked to Cabelas to get Kaia a new pair of shoes (her sole came unglued). Tristan, Ruby, and I hit Walmart to resupply and charge devices. There was a free shuttle from Cabelas to the trail at 5 p.m., and we rushed from Walmart and made it just as the shuttle was leaving. Luckily Adam had made friends with the driver, and he said he would come back for us.

A very kind lady stopped and asked Adam if we were all hiking the trail. She then handed him some money and said, "Get some nourishment!" Our shuttle dropped us off, and we walked down to the Schuylkill River, hoping to get in a refreshing swim. We didn't find a spot to camp, so we quickly swam and then started a big climb. It was just getting dark when we set up camp in almost-level tent spots. We camped at mile 1,221.2; 16.1 miles today.

AT Day #87

Poor Tristan's hammock ripped in the night, so he cowboy camped instead. We had a nice long siesta and cold showers at the Eckville Shelter. We passed the 1,234.5-mile marker and stumbled our way through more Pennsylvania rocks! We camped at the Allentown Hiking Club Shelter at mile 1,242.5; 21.3 miles today.

AT Day #88

We left camp at 6:15 a.m., hoping to push big miles before it got hot. At 11 a.m., we entered a wonderful trail magic vortex. Oak and his brother, Twin Oak (because they are twins), were serving up hot dogs and all kinds of treats. We stayed and visited and ate and ate. It was wonderful!

There were more rocks today. Three out of six pairs of shoes are having trouble with the soles coming unglued. Good thing we have superglue and Leukotape!

We camped at the Outerbridge Shelter at mile 1,260; 17.5 miles today.

There was a southbound thru-hiker that we got to visit with here, first one we've met on trail thus far. While we were getting settled for the night, a hiker came up to the shelter with bags of leftover pasta salad from a party he was at during the day. The party host had asked him if he knew of anyone who needed all that food, and he said, "I know how to find some hungry hikers." We visited with him for a while and helped lighten his load. Then, after we were tucked in our quilts and almost asleep, a hiker arrived with a headlamp on. He had packed several pizzas and beers a mile up from the parking lot to share with hikers here. We took out his pizzas for him, but he was on his own with the beer. It was so fun to visit with him and go to bed unusually full.

AT Day #89

Today is a special day: it's Kaia's birthday! Kaia has been lucky enough to celebrate her birthday on long-distance trails the past four years. Adam and Tristan left the shelter early on a top-secret mission to get some birthday donuts in Palmerton. We decided to take the blue line for a big climb, and we are sure glad we did (we chatted with Poison Puff later, and he said it was a straight-up rock scramble on the official trail). Later, we crossed paths with our friend Stretcher, and she made Kaia's birthday extra special by packing a small box of chocolates to gift to her. It was so sweet! We had long gaps without water, and all the water in this section is at least a half mile off trail. There are so many other hikers around; we are in a bubble! We camped at 1,276.9; 16.9 miles today.

AT Day #90

We arrived at the thriving metropolis of Wind Gap this morning at 8:45 (the post office was .7 miles from the trail, so we walked in). There were birthday packages from Sugar Mama (I told her we had three kids with birthdays in July, and she sent lots of treats and party favors), my high school friend Andria, and the Boysens. We were delighted with all the fun stuff and goodies; we didn't even need to buy a resupply!

It took a long time to pack up, and we didn't get back on trail until 11 a.m. When we walked into the trailhead parking lot, we were handed Gatorade by Marley's dad. It was awesome! There were more "sufferfest" rocks (as I like to call them), and our feet were killing us. But we had read on the Far Out comments that there would be trail magic until 3 p.m. at PA Route 191. We hobbled in right at 3 p.m. (okay, I was the only one hobbling), and they were still serving food because they were waiting for us! Stretcher had told them about us, so they decided to not shut down their trail magic until we got there. It was unbelievable! Jeff and JC feed us hamburgers, hot dogs, pasta with meat sauce, watermelon, candy, chips, and cold drinks. Also, they had a generator so hikers could charge devices and operate a foot and calf massage machine (that was the best!). We thanked them profusely, then hiked seven miles into Delaware Water Gap. There was a restaurant grill smell as we entered town and jazz music floating down the street—magical. We camped at the Church of the Mountain Hiker Center at mile 1,296.9; 20 miles today.

AT Day #91

Zero day! I walked .4 to the only hotel in town that lets hikers use their washer and dryer, and it was $8 per load. Adam, Kaia, and Madi hitched to Walmart with a former thru-hiker (who told them she would just wait in her car while they shopped and give them a ride back too!). There were two bottles of Sawyer permethrin in the hiker box, just enough to spray all our hiking clothes and Muir! The trail provides! It was a relaxing day of visiting with hiker friends at the Church of the Mountain Hiker Center, getting chores done, and eating a lot!

AT Day #92

We crossed the Pennsylvania/New Jersey state line! I failed to let the kids know how badly I wanted a picture at this point, so just Adam and I got a photo. I caught up with the kids later, sitting on a guard rail. We got some great views of New Jersey this morning from Raccoon Ridge. There were lots of day hikers and thru-hikers (we meet new ones every day) on the trail today. A highlight was climbing to the 100-year-old Catfish Fire Tower and getting an informational tour by firefighter Bob. He spotted smoke while we were up there, and it was exciting to see him radio in the coordinates (but then the smoke quickly went away). We were surprised to get hit by a rainstorm at Crater Lake (we forgot to check the weather forecast during our zero day) and quickly found a spot to set up tents. We camped at mile 1,316.8; 19.9 miles today.

AT Day #93

We were so very fortunate to walk into trail magic this morning at about 11 a.m. Moose is an extremely generous trail angel who sets up the biggest spread of trail magic that we have ever seen! He said he has been doing this for years, and he serves up this trail magic from 9 a.m. to 2 p.m. for the entire month of July! He got the trail name Moose when he was hiking the AT in Maine and he came up on a moose that charged him. He had the foresight to throw his jacket (which happened to be draped over his arm) over the moose's eyes to blind it. After that, the moose stopped, shook off the jacket, and went back to eating. Moose had to patiently wait for about 30 minutes for the moose to move on so he could retrieve his jacket. He was full of great stories, having been a backpacking leader for the Girl Scouts for many years. I wish we would have gotten a picture with him!

After that caloric and social boost, we hiked up to the Culver Fire Tower. We got to visit with three nice firefighters with awesome New Jersey accents. We made it to the Rutherford shelter, .4 off trail with awful mosquitoes, but with a bear box and spring water. We camped at 1,336.9; 20.1 miles today.

AT Day #94

Four times on this trail, we've encountered what I ignorantly call an "alarm bird." This bird has a song with the volume of a megaphone that it only seems to sing after 9:30 p.m. and before 5 a.m. It is so loud! Five out of our six family members seem to sleep through this alarm without issue. After listening to the alarm for 30 minutes, I realize that is sounds like "whip-poor-will." Oh no, what if my number one enemy bird is actually a whippoorwill? (I looked it up later, and it is indeed!) I thought I loved whippoorwills because their call is featured in one of my favorite movies, *The Three Amigos*. Well, now I hate them.

The rain started very gently at 5:30 a.m. (our forecast called for it to start at 2 a.m. and dump an inch in 24 hours). I woke up the kids at 6, and the rain picked up intensity until about 7:15. We huddled in the shelter, calculating miles and food to see if we could pull off an on-trail zero day. We decided against it.

We stopped in the High Point State Park Headquarters for water, restrooms, and snacks. The climb up to the New Jersey high point and veteran memorial was totally worth it! The 220-foot-tall obelisk was built in 1930 as a war memorial and observation tower. We were socked in with clouds, barely able to see the top, but that made it more ominous.

Our next stop was Unionville, New York (we are hiking along the New Jersey/New York border for a while) for pizza and a general store, which had wonderful porches that protected us from the rain. We camped near Pochuck Mountain Shelter, grateful for the bear box, at mile 1,353.9; 17 miles today.

AT Day #95

Temperatures are supposed to reach over 93 degrees today, so we tried to hit the trail early (but failed; we didn't get everyone through their turn at the Pochuck Mountain privy until 8 a.m.). It is amazing to me that the leaves are already changing color and starting to fall! The forest in this section is beautiful!

We hit the Pochuck boardwalk and suspension bridge at about 10 a.m. Our trail angel, Moose, said he helped build them 21 years ago!

We were lured into the Heaven Hill Farm and picked up a few delicious bakery items at 50% off. Adam got a ride into Vernon from Running Water; she hiked the AT in 1998! Six pairs of Topo shoes were waiting for us at the Vernon post office. What a relief! The kids used a Sharpie to add some decals to their new kicks.

We hit the "stairway to heaven" climb at the hottest part of the day. Luckily for us, it is mostly in the shade and wasn't too hard of a climb (there were some big step stone staircases in some sections, and the trail was a 12% grade for a mile). About a mile from the top, on the north side, we rested by a stream and swimming hole. The water felt so good!

At the Warwick Turnpike, we got an easy hitch from an avid hiker named Glen. He took the girls in the first trip, then went back for the boys! It was so great! We picked up food at ShopRite, then walked next door to the much-anticipated Warwick Drive-in. The owner is so kind to let hikers set up camp here for free and watch movies on three different big screens! We went off trail at 1,365.9; 12 miles today.

AT Day #96

The state of New York issued a "heat advisory" for the next five days, with temperatures in the high 90s. We decided to do fewer miles and call it a resupply day. A very kind trail angel, Misty, left her number with Moose and asked hikers to give her a call if they needed a ride. I texted her, and we worked it out that she'd drive us (in two carloads) 10 miles up the trail, and we'd hike southbound for the day.

We were on the trail by 9:30 a.m., and the heat was already oppressive. It was a hard section, rocky and exposed, and we're so grateful we only had a half day of hiking. There is rebar drilled into the rock in some sections for ladder and handholds. We were worried about how Muir would do with these obstacles, but he had no issues. A highlight was Prospect Rock, where we had the faintest view of the NYC skyline. We crossed the New Jersey/New York state line too! Then we caught a ride with Big Country and enjoyed another night at the drive-in (with four times as many hikers!)

Adam has a great idea for a Triple Crown T-shirt with a "if you know, you know" theme. He was thinking of the three most iconic places on each trail and they all turned out to be trail angels. The shirt will have the Warwick Drive-in, Luna's Looking Glass Hostel, and Saufley's Electric (because at Hiker Heaven on the PCT the loaner shirts often have that logo on them, from Jeff's business). I say he needs to throw in a Hawaiian shirt, too, to represent Casa de Luna! Mile 1,375.; 10.4 miles today.

AT Day #97

We put off most of the resupply until this morning (so we could buy cold stuff). Right as we were packing up, Two Bars walked up to us and asked if we wanted a ride back to the trail. She is from New Jersey and has her car with her right now; she's slack packing with her tramily. It was so great to visit with her and be back on the trail earlier than I expected.

We had a quick lunch break at 11:30, then pushed on two more miles so we could siesta at Little Dam Lake. We were there until after 5 p.m., and it felt like it was getting hotter all afternoon! The rock scrambles were intense; we're so glad we weren't going over those obstacles in the heat of the day! Poor Tristan said his right knee was hurting, so maybe he hyperextended it while rock hopping? Mile 1,390; 15.5 miles today.

AT Day #98

Our morning started with a visit to the Lake Tiorati "comfort station." From there, we pushed as fast as we could to the pool at Bear Mountain State Park. We do our best to stay in the shade or the water as often as possible! The pool was very crowded, but it was a great spot to cool down and chill. We left around 5 p.m. and walked the half mile bridge over the Hudson River—very cool!

It was dark by the time we got to the famous Appalachian Market (a Shell gas station), and we were blown away by how delicious the cheeseburgers and subs were! We loaded up our leftovers (for breakfast tomorrow) and wandered in the dark to the Graymoor, a monastery that has allowed hikers to camp at their baseball field since the 1970s! Mile 1,413.9; 23.9 miles today.

AT Day #99

Water is a problem in this section: there are long stretches without it, and when we do fill up from a tap, it usually tastes terrible! However, we took a break in the shade at Dennytown Road and enjoyed the cold and delicious water from a faucet there.

While we were relaxing, a kind local named Richard rode up on his bike to chat with us. He has a great New York accent and funny stories to tell. He rode off on his bike, and we almost packed up to go, but then decided it was close enough to lunch that we might as well stay in the shade and eat. So we did. To our surprise, Richard showed up in his truck a few minutes later with a bunch of snacks for us! It was great timing, too, because Tristan was bemoaning that he didn't have enough food!

After another great chat, Richard drove off, and we hiked on to Canopus Lake. Again, there were so many people! We found a spot in the shade, went for a quick swim, and were delighted with the generosity of strangers sharing food with us.

Our last obstacle of the night was climbing to the top of Shenandoah Mountain (a nice, gradual climb), where someone painted an American flag as a 9/11 memorial. It was downhill from there, and we set up in the "overflow" of Ralph's Peak Hikers Shelter. Mile 1,432.7; 18.8 miles today.

AT Day #100

Yesterday we met a hiker named Valley Blue who said she is finishing the AT today (she has section hiked over the past 22 years)!

I'm so glad we ran into her again after a stop at the deli so we could hear more of her story! We pushed hard today to get into Pawling so we could do laundry and eat pizza. We camped in Pauling at the Edward R. Murrow Park (the city allows AT hikers to camp here, use the indoor restrooms and outdoor showers for free) at mile 1,452.6; 20 miles today.

AT Day #101

We decided to celebrate the kids' birthdays by hopping on a train in Pauling and heading to New York City! A highlight was being able to see our friends, the Smiths, and having a delicious homemade dinner with them!

AT Days #102–103

We got to celebrate both Madi and Tristan's birthdays in NYC. It was a quick, whirlwind of a trip, but so much fun! On the way out of the city, we casually walked to Grand Central Station, chatted with locals and bought souvenirs, only to realize the train we wanted was pulling away just as we got to the platform. No problem. By the time we found some food for lunch, the next train was ready for us.

We got to Pawling at 1:30 p.m. and started working on our resupply. A store near the train station let us take as many free samples of dog food as we wanted, so we grabbed enough for Muir for three days! We picked up a birthday cake from a local bakery and surprised Madi with it while she was on the phone with her sister who is on a mission in England. Then Adam and I started walking to the grocery store, passing by historical sites with informational signs (this area was George Washington's headquarters while protecting the Hudson Valley area). We were picked up by a guy who had hiked the AT last year. He drove us the rest of the way to the store, waited while we got our groceries, and bought everyone ice cream sandwiches! Wow! He dropped us at the pizza place where the kids were waiting, and we grabbed our last two New York pizzas of the hike (we can officially say we've eaten too much pizza in this state). They were so good, though!

Tonight we watched a beautiful sunset, and we had a great view from our free campsite (mile 1,452.6).

AT Day #104

We hiked out of town, and 10 miles later, we entered Connecticut! Did you know they have moths that look like mini hummingbirds? My picture didn't turn out so good, but I looked them up later, and it blew my mind.

We took a refreshing swim in the Tenmile River. Our friends, Aldo and Gumby, passed by while we were getting our shoes back on. Poor Gumby thinks she got giardia and walked into town a few days ago to see a doctor and get antibiotics. We camped at mile 1,468.2; 15.6 miles today.

AT Day #105

We started out the day with a quick trip into Kent, Connecticut (established in 1720!), to hit the post office and grocery store. This town kindly provides restrooms, quarter-operated showers, and water bottle fill stations for hikers. My grandma mailed a birthday care package with treats for everyone, so we were delighted to open that! We were so lucky to find trail magic right at lunchtime from Firefly and her friend. Afterwards, we joined a few other hikers and swam in the Housatonic River to cool off for a bit. At dinner time, we found an awesome church where we could rest in the shade. We camped at mile 1,483.9; 15.7 miles today.

AT Day #106

Falls Village, also known as Canaan, was delightfully hiker friendly. We charged devices at the library, mailed postcards at the post office, and ate at the delicious deli. We hit 1,500 miles today and passed a rock formation named "Giant's Thumb." We camped at 1,505.8; 21.9 miles today.

AT Day #107

Our morning started out with some fun climbs up and over Lion's Head and Bear Mountain. Then, before we knew it, we were in Massachusetts! What a beautiful state! We camped at 1,521.7; 15.9 miles today.

AT Day #108

Our mileage has been less than we hoped for this week. We are struggling with some trail injuries (and mentally struggling to get back into trail life after our visit to the Big Apple). It was a huge pick-me-up when we got a hitch into Great Barrington in two different carloads immediately after arriving at the road. One car was driven by a ridge runner, and he was dropping off Mother Goose and her three daughters (we had met them briefly in Pawling; they're an awesome family). Adam, Kaia, Madi, and Muir hopped in with the ridge runner, and the rest of us got a ride with a section hiker named Steady Stream (who keeps a "steady stream" of trail magic going in this area).

After a quick trip to the grocery store, we were having trouble getting picked up for the 1.8-mile hitch back to trail. Adam spotted our friend Galaxy, who was in a car with her mom. They stopped and took us back to the trail in two trips. It was so great! Then a few miles later, we ran into some of Steady Stream's deluxe trail magic. I got a mixed green salad with goat cheese and was so happy! We passed a few more historic sites, and I quickly snapped pictures of the informational signs to read to the kids later. We camped at 1,535.3; 13.6 miles today.

AT Day #109

The three-girl tent has a broken pole, so the girls cowboy camped last night. There was a visit from a noisy fox at about 2 a.m. that woke most of us up. It was a creepy sound for sure.

We got hit with an afternoon downpour, the likes of which we haven't seen since Georgia. Luckily we were mostly packed up after filtering water. It got dramatically dark, the wind picked up, then buckets of rain. We hustled as fast as we could to the Upper Goose Pond Cabin. It was crazy crowded too. We met Mother Goose and her girls again. She said they recently read the Trek article written about us and apologized for calling Duckie (Madi) the wrong name. We laughed and assured her that "Duffy" was a misprint, and she indeed goes by Duckie. We also met Locket, NaviGoat, and Honey Badger, a mama hiking SOBO with her two teenage sons. The kids swam in the pond, and the sunset was amazing! We camped at 1,552.8; 17.5 miles today.

AT Day #110

We hit the trail at 7 a.m. after a nice night at Upper Goose Pond camp area. The caretakers were gone on a family emergency, so there were no blueberry pancakes in the morning (as promised in the FarOut comments). We camped at 1,570.4; 17.6 miles today.

AT Day #111

We've met a few families on the trail this year. The past couple of days, we've been hiking near Mother Goose and her three daughters. They are posting to "Trekking Along" on YouTube. They're so fun! I'm so impressed with the hikers that can take the time to upload videos while on the trail. I feel like it is all I can do to keep everyone alive and write these few notes!

Today was an awesome "nero" in Dalton. We hiked three miles into town from the Kay Wood Shelter and set up in the gazebo next to the rec center. We got so many chores done! The rec center let us shower, asking only for a $1 donation for a towel. The laundromat was only a mile away, so I got all the laundry in my pack and walked there. Adam hitched in the opposite direction to the Walmart to get our resupply. Then we tried to "seam seal" our leaking air mattress and let it dry for six hours! It was a great time to rest and visit with other hikers. Eventually we made it to Father Tom's camp, which was so nice! We camped at 1,582.2; 12.2 miles today.

AT Day #112

We rolled out of Cheshire, walking past a model of the 1,235 lbs of cheese presented to President Jefferson in 1804. We climbed to the top of Massachusetts's highest peak, Mt. Greylock. Fortunately, it wasn't too bad of a climb. While admiring the monument there, a former hiker and his parents told us they had trail magic set up in the parking lot. We hurried over there and had a great time visiting with Seven Toes and his folks from Rhode Island (and we enjoyed eating the fresh fruit and treats they brought too!). We camped at 1,598.4; 16.2 miles today.

AT Day #113

We hit mile 1,600 this morning and entered Vermont! At lunch time, we were so fortunate to stumble upon Bacon Wrap and his Outtatheway Cafe! He fed us his last blueberry pancake (a really big one the six of us could share), then started cooking up hot dogs. He puts mixed green lettuce and chipotle mayo on his hot dogs—brilliant! A few colorful maple leaves are starting to fall, and it is so exciting to be entering cooler weather. We camped at 1,615.2; 16.8 miles today.

AT Day #114

The first obstacle of the day was the climb to the top of Glastenbury Mountain. We passed through Split Rock and made it to the Goddard Shelter just as a storm was hitting. It is a beautiful, newer shelter, and we had lunch there with a hiker from Cincinnati named Hot Spot.

Kaia took a fall this morning and scraped her knee pretty good. Then she noticed a picture from this day last year, and she has the same wound, which is funny. Climbing to the top of the Glasenbury lookout tower was fun, and the views were incredible. We passed by some lovely beaver ponds on our way to the Story Brook Shelter (we had it all to ourselves, which was so surprising because we've seen so many hikers on trail today!). We camped at 1,634.1; 18.9 miles today.

AT Day #115

Vermont is nicknamed "Ver-mud" for good reason. It is hard to capture it with a picture, but there is a lot of mud out here. It must be extra awful during wet seasons. There are a lot of boardwalks too, and they can be very slippery. One of us falls at least three times a day! We made it into the fancy town of Manchester Center with no food in our food bags (which is the first time!). Adam and I decided to stretch our three-day supply into five days because we had gotten so much trail magic. I don't think the kids will let us try that again.

We bought a lot of food at the Price Chopper, then went across the street to the VFW to camp for free. The people who run it are such kind people! There was a laundromat .2 miles away, so we did laundry (right as a big rainstorm hit). But the forecast that had once called for 24 hours of rain changed to just a few scattered showers. It was an extra hot and muggy night, though! Adam said, "I feel like one of those hotdogs on the rollers at 7-11. Just turning all night and sticking to the sleeping mat with sweat." From Virginia to Vermont, we've been wondering if it was possible to melt to death! We camped at 1,655.2; 21.1 miles today.

AT Day #116

Very kind locals got us from Manchester Center back to the trail this morning, but we didn't start hiking until after lunch. We passed Bromley Tower Ski Resort and took a quick siesta at the top. There was an informational sign up there that read, "In 1959 Fred Pabst had a chairlift built to the top of Bromley Mountain in Hapgood State Forest, to both serve skiers in winter and bring tourists to the summit in the summer. A wooden tower was built between 1960 and 1962, to provide a 360 degree view, with mountains in 4 states visible." We camped at 1,663.2; 8.1 miles today.

AT Day #117

It was a muddy slog through the Big Branch Wilderness, Green Mountain National Forest, today. There were some slippery logs to walk on, a nice suspension bridge, and plenty of poison ivy. Some kind soul labeled the poison ivy with a note in a zip lock bag, staked into the ground. It read, "Poison Ivy behind the sign; not a good place to put a tent or lounge with a cold drink." We camped at 1,684.9; 21.7 miles today.

AT Day #118

We passed the 1,700-mile marker, with a plaque on a tree telling us we have 500 more miles to Mt. Katahdin. We were able to catch a bus into Killington, Vermont and stay at the Yellow Deli hostel. The food was delicious and the people there were so very kind. They divided us up, boys on one floor and girls on the next. We had access to nice showers, laundry, and walking distance to the grocery store. We left the trail at 1,705.3; 20.4 miles today.

AT Day #119

It was an incredibly beautiful Vermont day! We missed the first bus of the morning because we were enjoying our breakfast at the Yellow Deli. There were at least 10 other hikers on the bus with us and we headed back to the trail. Wildflowers were in abundance; we passed lakes and waterfalls and we loved every step. Our elevation gain was 3,948.2 feet and loss was 3,752 feet. We camped at 1,720; 14.7 miles today.

AT Day #120

If you are ever hiking the AT in this section and wondering if you should walk .2 miles off the trail to the On the Edge Farm, do it! We ate the most delicious berry pie and muffins. Later we stopped by Teagos Deli for more food and ended the day at trail angel Lynda's place (she has a Porta-Potti on her property and lets hikers camp on her lawn). She is so kind and her family has been taking care of AT hikers for 30+ years! Elevation gain/loss was killer today: ascent 5,222.1 and descent 6,864.5 feet. We camped at 1,742.4; 22.4 miles today.

AT Day #121

This morning, trail angel Linda fed us some breakfast muffins. Then we hiked up the road to catch a hitch and ended up visiting with her neighbor, Jim Woods (he stopped us to chat when he saw we were hitchhiking). We explained we were trying to hitch to a historical site, the Joseph Smith Birthplace Memorial. He told us that he would happily drive us all up there in his truck. Adam sat in the front and got to hear Jim's cool stories; the rest of us rode in the back and enjoyed the wind in our faces. At the end of the day, a missionary from our church drove us back to Linda's. Our friends, Crispi and Longbird (whom we met on the CDT), drove up to bring us trail magic pizza and visit! It was so great to see them.

AT Day #122

Today we crossed the Vermont/New Hampshire border! We passed through Hanover. My Aunt Jane, Cousin Ryan, and his son, Oliver, drove for several hours to meet up with us to be our trail angels! They fed us, played at the park, and stored some of our gear that we don't need for the rest of the journey. It was wonderful to visit with them and get some much-needed logistics ironed out.

Then we were back on trail (with too many other hikers) looking for a spot to camp. Finally, we found a semi-flat spot (too close to the bustling civilization of Dartmouth College for my comfort) and just made do. We camped at mile 1,753; 10.6 miles today.

AT Day #123

We are fascinated by the maple sap collection systems we find in the forest. It makes me daydream about having waffles for miles. We saw a giant wasp nest way up in the trees, and we're so very grateful no one was stung today! There are so many bright orange salamanders on the trail; we are keeping ourselves entertained by counting them as we walk. Today we saw more than 30. Tonight, there was a big group of hikers camped at Lyme-Dorchester Road parking area, including our circus! We camped at mile 1771.6; 18.6 miles today.

AT Day #124

We started the day with a big climb to Smarts Firetower. We were very grateful for the water cache at Goose Pond Road, where we were hit by an unexpected rainstorm. We're starting to see leaves changing to yellow and red. We slept on the Greenhouse Restaurant lawn with about 15 other thru-hiker tents. We camped at 1,790.5; 18.9 miles today.

AT Day #125

Mt. Mist was the first climb of the day. We made it to the Hikers Welcome Hostel for a long lunch break. We bought six of their frozen pizzas and were delighted to cook them up in the microwave and eat them hot! Then we pushed to the rainy and windy summit of Mt. Moosilauke at 4,802 feet. The descent was slippery and steep! We camped at 1,804.6; 14.1 miles today.

AT Day #126

We got some sunshine today! We climbed Mt. Wolf and South and North Kinsman Peaks. We skipped the Kinsman Pond AMC camp and found a dispersed site. We camped at 1,817.3; 12.7 miles today.

AT Day #127

Our first stop was Lonesome Lake, which was beautiful! We really lucked out with getting hitches in/around/out of Lincoln and North Woodstock. We got food at the Price Chopper, did laundry, and took showers for $1 each at an RV park. We found dispersed camping and prepped for tomorrow's big climb. We camped at 1,821.4; 4.1 miles today.

AT Day #128

Today was Franconia Ridge day: we summited Mt. Lincoln (5,089 feet), Mt. Lafayette (5,260 feet), and Mt. Garfield (4,500 feet). I cannot possibly describe how beautiful it is out here! We camped at 1,833.3;

12.4 miles today. (We did 91.7 miles this week, which is 21.3 miles shy of our goal. Wow! The White Mountains are kicking our butts!)

AT Day #129

Today we hiked past Galehead Hut. We summited South Twin Mountain (4,902 feet) and Zealand Mountain (4,260). We stopped by the awesome Zealand Falls Hut. Later, we tried for 20 minutes to get a hitch into North Conway and Bartlett with no luck. It started to rain, so we quickly found dispersed campsites in the forest. After going through our food bags, we decided to skip town and just push forward with what we have. We camped at mile 1,849; 15.7 miles today.

AT Day #130

Today was a big climb day! We made it up and over Mt. Webster, Mt. Jackson, and Mt. Pierce. A storm rolled in as we got close to Lake of the Clouds Hut at mile 1,860. Because we arrived right at 4 p.m., four of us could do the "work for stay" option. The kids volunteered when they heard they could eat all the leftovers they wanted after the paying guests finished their meal. Kaia cleaned a giant gas stove, Tristan wiped tables, and Madi and Ruby swept the floors. They didn't get to eat until 8:30 p.m., but there were a lot of leftovers, fortunately. Adam and I paid $20 to sleep in the "dungeon" but then asked if we could crash on the dining room floor with the rest of the "work for stay" group (which was just our kids). We explained that our double-wide mat doesn't fit in the dungeon's bunk beds, and that helped our case too. The crew allowed it. 11 miles today.

AT Day #131

The climb to the summit of Mt. Washington was easy-peasy because we had done most of the work yesterday. It started raining as we reached the top. A kind employee of the visitor's center let us in the building (even though we arrived at 8 a.m. and they don't open until 9). We dried out in the hiker pack room and explored the museum. The storm was too much for us, so we walked the road to the trail, then hiked two miles to Pinkham Notch Visitors Center. Many different hitches got us to the post office and Walmart. A great guy named Gary got us all back to the visitor center in his mini-transit. We stealth camped at mile 1,874.9; 14.9 miles today.

AT Day #132

Our first challenge of the day: Wildcat Mountain (4,422 feet). Some say it is the hardest climb in the Whites. I would agree with that. Fortunately for us, the weather was clear. I would hate to be climbing that when the rocks were slippery with ice or rain. We had lunch at Carter Notch Hut, and the kids enjoyed playing games at their indoor tables. Next up were Carter Dome (4,832 feet) and Middle Carter Mountain (4,610 feet). Adam found an amazing camping site for three tents (set up very close together). We camped at 1,886.1; 11.2 miles today.

AT Day #133

We started the day with a climb up Mt. Moriah, which is the last 4,000-foot peak for us in the White Mountains. We hitched into Gorham at mile 1,896; 9.9 miles today. Our hitch dropped us off at the Dollar General. Within a few minutes, the rain was coming down in torrents, with wind blowing it under the awning where we were taking cover. After a few minutes of this, Adam booked us a hotel. It was so nice to get cleaned up, do some gear repair, and relax. We got creative with dinner since we had a microwave and easy access to the Dollar General (turns out even though the fish sticks box says, "microwave not recommended," that can be ignored).

AT Day #134

Our trail friends, Dave and Leisel (trail names Intro and Gillmore), drove three hours one way to visit with us this morning! They brought donuts and hung out with us in the hotel until we had to check out. They shuttled us back to the trail in two trips and hiked with us (teaching us a lot about the mushrooms in this area we have been curious about). We have crossed paths with this couple on the PCT, the CDT, and now the AT. They are our Triple Crown buddies, and we just love them! After parting, we hiked up to Cascade Mountain and Wocket Ledge, with views of the Presidential Range and the southern Mahoosuc Range. We camped near Dream Lake at mile 1,905.6; 9.6 miles today.

AT Day #135

Today we summited Mt. Success, where there are the remains of an airplane crash from the 1950s (miraculously, no one was killed in the accident). We crossed the New Hampshire/Maine border! Then we climbed three peaks, all named Goose Eye (East, West, and North). We camped at 1,917.4; 11.8 miles today. (We did 84.1 miles this week; 28.9 miles short of our goal.)

AT Day #136

Today we went through Mahoosuc Notch and Arm. We also went by Old Speck. We camped at 1,927.1; 9.7 miles today (but we were hiking from 7 a.m. to 6 p.m.). We had been warned that this section is very difficult. Again, we were extra grateful we had clear weather. Not surprisingly, the kids loved the obstacle course-like challenge, and it might be one of our favorite days on trail.

AT Day #137

Adam and I got a hitch into Bethel at 7:30 a.m. from a kind general contractor named Chris. We resupplied at the local grocery, charged devices at the hardware store, and got two offers for rides while we were stuffing food into our packs. There are some very kind people around here! When we made it back to the kids, we learned that they enjoyed sleeping in and got trail magic for lunch! We took our time packing up and didn't start the climb up Baldpate until 4. We're so grateful it wasn't raining per the forecast. That climb was already slippery enough.

We were hoping to set up in the Frye Notch Lean-to, but it was full when we arrived. Instead, we found some sloped tent spots nearby and set up in the dark (without a proper dinner break. I might have shed a tear or two about that). We camped at 1,932.9; 5.8 miles today.

AT Day #138

We had a nice, gradual climb up Wyman Mountain, and the forecasted rain never hit us. It was a lucky day! I'm mentally struggling to stay in the game out here; I'm so ready to be done with these big ups and downs. But the day after tomorrow, we are supposed to have some fast-moving trail—so there is that to look forward to. The "ice cream man" (trail name Onesimus) was parked at a road crossing and lifted our spirits with some ice cream sandwiches. Nearby, someone had left a cooler filled with goodies for hikers. Trail magic times two, that'll lift any one's mood! We camped at 1,947.5; 14.6 miles today.

AT Day #139

Onesimus gave us bananas first thing this morning! A former thru-hiker named Will was also there making egg sandwiches with bacon, so we happily waited around. We didn't leave camp until 8:35 a.m. About two miles north of the Old Blue Mountain summit, we saw Clair! She also hiked the PCT in 2019 and was one of the few hikers that didn't flip to avoid the snow in the Sierras. Since we've seen her last, she's had several awesome jobs, including a year in Antarctica. It was fun to visit briefly with her and wish her the best on her SOBO journey. We camped at mile 1,959.9; 12.4 miles today.

AT Day #140

We are really loving Maine! There are flat campsites, beautiful ponds and lakes, fall leaves, kind locals, and lots of NOBOs, SOBOs, and flip-floppers to visit with. We camped in Rangeley at mile 1,973.9; 14 miles today.

AT Day #141

We got our resupply at the IGA market, and Muir got to meet another trail dog there (he goes by Beef Jerky; Muir seemed jealous that he had a tail and a trail name!). Our first stop was some cool caves that the kids had fun exploring.

We made it to the summit of Saddleback Mountain, and we were so very grateful to have a view! The lakes we could see from the top included Mooselookmeguntic Lake (I'm not making this up), Rangeley Lake, Richardson Lake, and Cupsuptic Lake. We camped at 1,982; 8.1 miles today.

AT Day #142

Today was a stormy day, so we decided against going for the 4,000-foot peaks; we took the low road instead. Our friend Gumby (who started the AT the same day as we did—we've kept pace with her almost the entire trail) got off trail just before the Whites. Her dad was very sick, and her mom asked her to come be with them until he passed. I got this text from her today and share it here with her permission: "Hi! I'm heading back to the mountains. (I just flew into Boston, and I'm waiting for a bus to Gorham, New Hampshire.) I'm skipping a bunch, but I will be able to catch up with Aldo and Bed and Breakfast tomorrow. We'll all finish together (but I won't be a "thru-hiker"). I was able to be with my dad when he passed away. I helped my mom take care of stuff, and she wanted me to be able to get back to the trail. Dad had pictures of me at milestones all over his office. I'm bringing some of his ashes with me, so we can still celebrate together in Maine. I bet y'all are really close to finishing!" Sweet Gumby, what a heartbreaking event to happen while on trail. We had hoped to finish on the same day, but we are so happy she could return to trail and hike with her tramily.

At dusk, a very kind woman stopped to give us a hitch into a campground. She even made two trips to fit us all! I gave her a Kids Out Wild sticker, and she gave us a small jug of maple syrup from her farm! It was so great! We stayed at Mountain View Campground and rented a four-bunk cabin for $30! It didn't have water or electricity (or even a door, just a screen), but it kept us dry on a rainy night! The bunks were big enough that Adam and I shared one, Kaia and Madi shared another, and Tristan and Ruby each got their own (Muir happily slept under Ruby's bunk). We got a great night's sleep! We went off the trail near 2,006.1; miles unknown. (Miles this week: 88.7, which is 24.3 miles short of our goal.)

AT Day #143

Adam and I got a hitch into Stratton first thing this morning. (It was in a Tesla! We didn't have to even put out our thumbs, they just asked us if we needed a ride.) We got a four-day resupply and eggs, sausage, and pancake mix for breakfast (to put our maple syrup on). The campground has an awesome community house with a stove, oven, and microwave, a big table, couches, WiFi, coin-operated showers, restrooms, and lots of games. We had a feast, and it took longer to clean up and pack up than I expected, per usual.

A nice, retired veteran pulled up in his big Crown Victoria and asked if we needed a ride to the trail (at exactly the moment we were getting ready to start hitching). He had two high-energy large chocolate labs in his car, so only the four girls got in (he warned us that the dogs would go crazy, and they certainly did!). Adam, Muir, and Tristan got an easy hitch a few minutes later. It was pouring rain at the trailhead, but the chief of police was there passing out trail magic! This is such a hiker friendly community! It rained heavily almost all day. We camped near 2,021.4; 15.3 miles today.

AT Day #144

We passed by West and East Carry Ponds, which have an awesome informational sign telling the story about Colonel Benedict Arnold in this area. It was a great day for spotting many varieties of Maine mushrooms. We camped at Pierce Pond at mile 2,039.1; 17.7 miles today.

AT Day #145

Loons woke us up this morning. We rushed to get to the Kennebec River for our 9 a.m. canoe ferry. That was fun! The big climb of the day was Pleasant Pond Mountain. Tristan says that after years of not being able to smell his own body odor, he can now, and he doesn't like it. Haha! We camped at 2,055.1; 16 miles today.

AT Day #146

We crossed Baker Stream this morning on rocks, no fording necessary. We climbed to the summit of Bald Mountain (our app says it is "bald" because of a fire there in the early 1900s), stopping to visit a cool cave on the way up. We had a very pleasant lunch at the Bald Mountain Pond Lean-to (they don't call them "shelters" in Maine), which even had a picnic table!

We did have to ford Marble Brook and the West Branch Piscataquis River. Poor Madi took a bad fall while fording through the deep mud and hurt her knee. It is scratched and bruised, but she's so tough and insists she can keep going. We hope to be finished with the AT in a week! We camped at 2,070.8 at the Horseshoe Canyon Lean-to; 15.7 miles today.

AT Day #147

We left camp early and pushed hard all morning to make it to the road to town before noon. When we arrived at the parking lot, two section hikers offered us a ride into Greenville in two separate cars. We resupplied at the Indian Hills Shop and Save, then tried to track down laundry and showers. We talked Kaia and Madi into walking half a mile to inquire at a place that didn't pick up their phone when I called. That didn't work out, but a truck did stop to ask if they were AT hikers. Turns out, this kind man named Mark and his wife, Sheryl, hiked the AT in 2016, and he was eager to offer us some help! He loaded all of us in his truck and drove us to his awesome cabin (just a block away from the laundromat and two blocks from the lovely Moosehead Lake). They let us use their shower and towels and let us set up our tents in their yard. We got our laundry done and got two yummy pizzas for dinner. What an awesome last resupply celebration! We got off trail at mile 2,079.8; 9 miles today.

AT Day #148

Mark and Sheryl offered to drive us back to the trail at 7 a.m. I grabbed a quick breakfast at the gas station for everyone at 6:30 a.m. It was so great to visit with Sheryl on the 10-mile drive (they took us in two vehicles: their truck and a car they borrowed from a friend). They're an awesome couple, and we're so very grateful for their help!

The 100-Mile Wilderness is beautiful! We had a few very tricky water fords, and fortunately, there was only one where we had to remove shoes. It gets dark at 7:15 to 7:30 p.m., and we wanted to push further to the Long Pond Stream Lean-to, but we ran out of daylight and set up tents in three flat spots about .7 miles shy of our goal. We camped at 2,094.2; 14.4 miles today.

AT Day #149

We had an early wake-up call at 5 a.m.! It was a big day today with lots of elevation and needing to hike more than 20 miles (or we'll run out of food). The climb up Barren Mountain was fun; it surprised us to cross paths with day hikers. At the summit, we met a local hiker who said there is a road nearby with access to this area. There was also cell coverage, so we spent a lot of time checking emails and such. (Adam is trying to find the best deal on a vehicle to buy to get us home.)

The day turned out to be quite hot (probably in the 80s). Muir appreciated all the stream crossings. We had to remove shoes and ford two streams/rivers. At the West Branch Pleasant River, a ridge runner was there with helpful info on Baxter State Park (and she also took our trash!).

We passed through "The Hermitage," a stand of hundred-foot-high old-growth white pines. A FarOut comment said, "This is one of the last second growth stands in the Northeast, originally preserved by the British for ship masts. The trees are around 200 years old." It was very cool! We camped near 2,115.7; 21.5 miles today.

AT Day #150

We were up at 5 a.m. and on the trail in record time, before 6:15. By 9 a.m., we were enjoying the view from White Cap Mountain, the highest peak in the 100-Mile Wilderness. We passed some lovely ponds like Mountain View Pond and Crawford Pond. After summiting Little Boardman Mountain (2,009 feet), it was all downhill or level. We were hoping to make it further today, but we didn't want to hike in the dark after dinner. Adam and Tristan swam in the swimming hole at the base of Cooper Brook Falls. We camped in our tents near Cooper Brook Falls Lean-to at mile 2,134.6; 19 miles today.

AT Day #151

There was lots of rain today, so our views were limited. I asked the kids how they felt about almost being done with the trail:

Ruby: "Tomorrow we can say, 'Tomorrow is our last day on the trail.'"

Tristan: "Tomorrow is the eve of our victory."

Kaia: "I'm getting the end-of-trail blues. I'm going to miss it out here."

Madi: [In relation to Kaia's statement] "You must be playing; you can't be serious."

It's exciting to be so close to being done!

AT Day #152

It poured rain on us almost all night! 5 a.m. alarms went off, and fortunately, we packed up quickly in just a light drizzle. From the top of the Rainbow Ledges climb, Adam was able to call Baxter State Park and reserve a campsite at Katahdin Stream (someone had canceled because of the weather—lucky us!). We arrived at the Abol Bridge store at noon and picked up an over-priced one-day resupply and some hot dogs and buns for lunch.

Erin and Rosalyn were our awesome neighbors at the campground. Adam went over to chat with them, and before we knew it, they were giving Muir some extra cans of sardines, handing out a giant bag of tortilla chips, and making us a big pot of delicious soup (hot soup!). Oh, how we've loved the kind, generous people we've met on the trail!

AT Day #153

Our day started out with the highest of hopes. We were going to summit Mt. Katahdin, take a picture at the iconic Appalachian Trail Northern Terminus sign, and be done! But that didn't happen. We packed up by 6 a.m., left our packs in a lean-to that Baxter provides to hikers, and took a few essentials in daypacks we borrowed.

We knocked out the first three miles at an impressive pace, fueled by excitement and adrenaline. Then we started seeing hikers coming down the mountain—including a few thru-hikers—saying the wind was gusting over 50 mph above treeline, and the temperatures had dropped to about 20 degrees. We had to see for ourselves, so we kept going. Sure enough, when we got to the first rocky viewpoint, with no trees to protect us, the wind took our breath away and knocked a few of us off balance. Adam called for the girls in front to climb back down; we had to go back.

We chatted with other hikers on the way down, trying to formulate a plan. We got our gear, returned the daypacks, and got a hitch down the mountain in two groups. The kids and Muir rode in the back of a nice lady's truck, and Adam and I followed behind with David and Pete, two hiking buddies in their late 60s or early 70s. It was a fun conversation, and they took our picture so their other friends would believe their story (about meeting a family nearly done with the Triple Crown). We hitched into Bangor and started formulating a new plan. There are many things that must fall into place for us to get to the summit of Katahdin, and we're praying that we can!

AT Days #154–155

Logistics that fell into place the last two days: Adam found a vehicle online that he felt would safely get us from Maine to Washington state, and he hitched to Portland, bought the car, and came back for the rest of us. Then we were able to book a reservation at a campground in Baxter (someone had canceled their spot because of bad weather, woohoo!) and summit Mt. Katahdin. As we reached the monument, we pulled the celebration package from our packs: Sugar Mama had sent us sunglasses that look like crowns, bubbles, and fizzy Trader Joe's drinks for all of us (and even a bone for Muir!). It felt like reaching the summit was made possible by all of the trail angels who aided us along the way, all the prayers from our friends and family that we would stay safe, and all the encouragement from other hikers we met.

Post-trail thoughts from Ruby: "The AT was my least favorite trail; I'm not going to beat around the bush. This began when the heat started, crushing us with the 90- to 100-degree heat. The consonant ups and downs didn't benefit my opinion of the trail. I had heard that it was either going to be intensely hot or always raining. All the hikers that we met that were previously on the AT either hated it or loved it. Though I didn't like the AT, it doesn't mean it wasn't a beautiful and amazing trail; there were some incredible views and great people. I'm glad that I hiked the Application Trail—even though I didn't want to. The people I met and the experience I had will stick with me for the rest of my life, marking the end of the Triple Crown experience for me."

We hope by sharing our story we will inspire individuals and families to go on big adventures. If that is not your jam, we hope that you will take an opportunity to be a trail angel and help others on their journey. A big thank you to any and all who have helped those who saunter towards their goals!

Acknowledgments

I have a list in my "Rite in the Rain" notebook that I carry with me on hikes of over 150 people who helped us during our four years of sauntering. We didn't know we would need so much help, and we could have never made it as far as we did without trail angels (some mortal, some not). Thank you to all who housed us, fed us, gave us rides, pointed us in the right direction, and offered encouragement!

We have been so very blessed to have loving and supportive family members on both sides of the family tree who have helped us reach our goals. Our friends went above and beyond to support our crazy ideas and propel us forward. Thank you to those who hiked with us, especially Le Anne (who I'd say played a huge part in inspiring Adam to love backpacking as a teenager and helped our hikes be successful), Ellery (for being our "thru-driver"), Madi (who had never slept in a tent but jumped right in and made us laugh every day on the AT), the Allens, Rachelle, Makayla, and Angela for making the effort to join us.

My sister-in-law, Susanna, and my mom, Shelli, spent countless hours helping me edit this manuscript. I'm so grateful for their skills and dedication.

I want to thank and acknowledge my four incredible children who went along with their parent's wild ideas and taught me so much along the way. You are all full of grit and infinite potential.

You are my treasures, marvelous wonders, and I'm so happy to be your mama. Finally, thank you to my husband, Adam, for making the dream a reality and loving me and our children so passionately. I love you because I love you, and I always will.

Find Us

Website: www.KidsOutWild.com

Instagram and Facebook: @KidsOutWild

YouTube: www.youtube.com/@kidsoutwild9215

Email: kidsoutwild@gmail.com

Patreon: www.Patreon.com/KidsOutWild222

Books We Recommend

The Book of Mormon (download for free from the app store)

Irving Stone, *Men to Match My Mountains*

Bill Bryson, *A Walk in the Woods*

Colin Fletcher, *The Thousand Mile Summer*

Brendan Leonard, *The Benefits Of Discomfort*

Paulo Coelho, *The Alchemist*

Heather Anderson, *Thirst: 2600 Miles to Home*

Robert Jordan and Brandon Sanderson, *The Wheel of Time* (any and all of Brandon Sanderson's books)

Michael Easter, *The Comfort Crisis: Embrace Discomfort To Reclaim Your Wild, Happy, Healthy Self* (a lot of swearing in this one, listener beware)

Colin Fletcher, *The Man Who Walked Through Time*

Anthony Doerr, *All the Light We Cannot See*

Delia Owens, *Where the Crawdads Sing*

Paul Theroux, *The Happy Isles of Oceana: Paddling the Pacific*

Ben Crawford, *2,000 Miles Together: The Story of the Largest Family to Hike the Appalachian Trail*

John J. Ratey, *Spark: The Revolutionary New Science of Exercise and the Brain*

Ben Montgomery, *Grandma Gatewood's Walk*

Barney Scout Mann, *Journeys North: The Pacific Crest Trail*

Richard Louv, *Our Wild Calling* and *Last Child in the Woods*

J. K. Rowling, Harry Potter Series

Stephenie Meyer, Twilight Series (especially great on the PNT near Forks, WA)

Ayn Rand, *Atlas Shrugged*

Aron Ralston, *Between a Rock and a Hard Place*

Marc Reisner, *Cadillac Desert*

David Kaiser, *How Hippies Saved Physics*

Terry Hayes, *I Am Pilgrim*

Any Malcolm Gladwell book

John Henrik Clark, *Malcolm X*

Keven Fedarko, *The Emerald Mile*

Charles Duhigg, *The Power of Habit*

Daniel James Brown, *The Boys in the Boat*

George Samuel Clason, *The Richest Man in Babylon*

Jonathan Haidt, *The Righteous Mind*

Adam Smith, *The Wealth of Nations*

Laura Hillenbrand, *Unbroken*

Henry David Thoreau, *Walden*

Juliana Chauncey, *Hiking From Home*

David Smart, *The Trail Provides*

Heather Anderson, *Mud, Rocks, Blazes*

Made in the USA
Monee, IL
23 September 2023